Building Enterprise Systems with ODP

An Introduction to Open Distributed Processing

Chapman & Hall/CRC Innovations in Software Engineering and Software Development

Series Editor
Richard LeBlanc
Chair, Department of Computer Science and Software Engineering, Seattle University

AIMS AND SCOPE

This series covers all aspects of software engineering and software development. Books in the series will be innovative reference books, research monographs, and textbooks at the undergraduate and graduate level. Coverage will include traditional subject matter, cutting-edge research, and current industry practice, such as agile software development methods and service-oriented architectures. We also welcome proposals for books that capture the latest results on the domains and conditions in which practices are most effective.

PUBLISHED TITLES

Software Development: An Open Source Approach
Allen Tucker, Ralph Morelli, and Chamindra de Silva

Building Enterprise Systems with ODP: An Introduction to Open Distributed Processing
Peter F. Linington, Zoran Milosevic, Akira Tanaka, and Antonio Vallecillo

CHAPMAN & HALL/CRC INNOVATIONS IN
SOFTWARE ENGINEERING AND SOFTWARE DEVELOPMENT

Building Enterprise Systems with ODP

An Introduction to Open Distributed Processing

Peter F. Linington
Zoran Milosevic
Akira Tanaka
Antonio Vallecillo

CRC Press
Taylor & Francis Group
Boca Raton   London   New York

CRC Press is an imprint of the
Taylor & Francis Group an **informa** business

A CHAPMAN & HALL BOOK

CRC Press
Taylor & Francis Group
6000 Broken Sound Parkway NW, Suite 300
Boca Raton, FL 33487-2742

Version Date: 20110727

International Standard Book Number: 978-1-4398-6625-2 (Hardback)

Visit the Taylor & Francis Web site at
http://www.taylorandfrancis.com

and the CRC Press Web site at
http://www.crcpress.com

Contents

List of Figures

About the Authors

Peter F. Linington is Emeritus Professor of Computer Communication at the University Kent in the United Kingdom. He has been involved in the standardization of the ODP Reference Model and its various supporting standards since the activity started. He has co-chaired WODPEC, the main workshop in this area, since its inception. His recent research interests cover architectural description, use of policies and model-based techniques. Further information can be found at `http://www.cs.kent.ac.uk/people/staff/pfl/`.

Zoran Milosevic is a Principal of Deontik Pty Ltd., a small consulting and software company specializing in the planning, development and deployment of enterprise systems. He was involved in the standardization of the ODP Enterprise Language, and with several OMG standards, while working for the Distributed Systems Technology Centre (DSTC), based in Brisbane. He was the founder of IEEE's Enterprise Distributed Object Computing (EDOC) conference. Further information can be found at `http://deontik.com/About/Zoran.html`.

Akira Tanaka is a founder of view5 LLC, a small consulting company in Japan, specializing in applying viewpoints and model-based approaches to software development. He has been involved in RM-ODP standardization from its early days. While with the Hitachi Ltd. Software Division, he led the ODP committee of INTAP in Japan, and participated frequently in EDOC's WODPEC. He was also active in OMG, including as a contributor to the UML Profile for EAI specification and SoaML RFP. Further information can be found at `http://www.view5.co.jp/`.

Antonio Vallecillo is Professor of Languages and Information Systems at the University of Málaga, Spain. His research interests include open distributed processing, model-based engineering, componentware and software quality. He was co-editor of *ISO/IEC 19793 (UML4ODP)* and of the revised versions of RM-ODP Parts 2 and 3 *(ISO/IEC 10746-2/3)*. Further information can be found at `http://www.lcc.uma.es/~av`.

Foreword

Working as the rapporteur for Part 3 of the ISO/ITU-T Basic Reference Model for Open Distributed Processing (RM-ODP) was one of the most stimulating periods in my professional career and I am grateful to the authors for asking me to write a foreword to their excellent book describing the model and its application to the design and specification of practical distributed systems. The role of a foreword is to set the scene for the reader and, to that end, I offer a personal perspective on the origins of RM-ODP.

RM-ODP was in many ways a breakthrough in its approach to standardization, arising from a decade of fast-paced innovation in telecommunications and computing technology. Prior to RM-ODP, international standards for networking had been focused on the needs of mainframe computer operating systems for file transfer, remote job control and remote terminal access over relatively slow network links provisioned by regulated telecommunications providers. The ISO Open Systems Interconnection family of standards and its associated seven-layer reference model were developed to meet these needs. For point-to-point services such as file transfer, modelling communication as a protocol state machine moving messages back and forth between two service state machines, one at each end of the communications path, was sufficient. However, as OSI evolved to include multi-party distributed applications, limitations of the OSI model became clear. There was the need for a new framework that could better represent system-oriented concepts such as network management, network security and directory services. The missing capabilities from the OSI reference model were the ability to describe system structure and to model interactions richer than just basic data interchange.

During the 1980s and 1990s, there were huge changes to the landscape of computing driven by the advent of the microprocessor. Minicomputers brought computing out of the data centre and were rapidly followed by single-user workstations and in due course the now ubiquitous personal computer. In parallel, there was an equally revolutionary change sweeping through computer networking, driven by the growth of Local Area Network (LAN) technologies. LANs permitted the low-cost interconnection of computers by high speed links, leading to the appearance of *client-server* architectures in which a powerful server computer provides print, file and database services to a group of smaller user workstations and personal computers. Alongside client-server architectures there was also a parallel evolution of network and distributed operating systems, which followed a decentralized architecture. The client-server model came to dominate as the personal computer became more popular, but the peer-to-peer model remained an important technology for building powerful servers from clusters of machines, a strand of development which has continued through to modern parallel high-performance supercomputers for scientific processing and from there to the scalable highly parallel architectures of modern data centres for online services and *cloud computing*.

The co-evolution of operating systems and LANs spawned an explosion in new network protocols and services. The greater bandwidth and reliability of LANs compared to earlier wide area telecommunications overlaid on the telephone network removed many of the constraints that had driven the design of the OSI standards. The relevance of OSI was further diluted by the growing adoption of the Internet protocols IP and TCP as UNIX emerged as the dominant workstation operating system of the time. At the same time, the implementation of TCP/IP for the personal computer displaced proprietary client-server protocols, making TCP/IP the *de facto* standard.

With the growth of LANs and client-server computing, the emphasis for standards moved from the protocols as networking functions like file transfer to more generalized access to operating system services and libraries for building distributed applications. For example, *Remote Procedure Call (RPC)* protocols allowed functions on remote machines to be invoked through programming language procedure calls, albeit with more complex failure modes. It was a small step from RPC to *Network Objects*, which generalized the model to method invocation on remote objects and introduced the concept of a *Remote Object Reference* as a pointer to an object that could be given to other computers to enable them to invoke the methods of the object. With these facilities, it became common to talk of a network object as something that provided a *service* defined in terms of the set of method calls provided by the object.

A number of RPC and network object systems were constructed building on these ideas, and standards began to emerge both for the programming interface and the protocols for interworking. First to appear was the Open Software Foundation's Distributed Computing Environment (OSF/DCE) based on RPC and then subsequently the Object Management Group's Common Object Request Broker Architecture (CORBA) and associated *CORBA services*. Both were examples of what came to be commonly described as *middleware* — a layer of distributed computing infrastructure that sat between the basic machine operating system and the (distributed) application.

As these technologies were applied to practical distributed applications, it became clear that while RPC and network objects were useful basic system components, they didn't address the need to build dependable systems and so further developments in middleware provided more advanced facilities such as atomic transactions, support for service replication, service migration and so forth. Generally, these took one of two forms: *explicit*, in which the capabilities were exposed to the application programmer or *transparent*, in which the capability was hidden behind the RPC or network object model. The

explicit model was more complicated to program, but offered greater control
and the ability to exploit application-specific knowledge to improve system
performance, whereas the transparent model, as its name suggests, required
no special intervention on the part of the programmer.

All these technology developments defined the context in which RM-ODP
was developed, with the ambition to define a reference model that would
provide a descriptive framework for creating standards for interoperability
between systems, to allow for the construction of such systems from components glued together by *middleware* and for (distributed) applications to be
portable between different vendors' technologies.

During this period, I had personally been involved in several of the technological developments, first as an academic researcher in the Computer Laboratory at the University of Cambridge, England helping build the Cambridge Distributed System [86] and then subsequently as the Chief Architect of
ANSA, a project funded by a consortium of computer and telecommunications
suppliers. ANSA started as part of the UK government Alvey Programme,
and subsequently became part of a European Union funded project called *Integrated Systems Architecture*. Starting slightly earlier than OSF and OMG,
the vision for ANSA had been to develop a practical architectural framework
and supporting components that could encompass the new distributed computing concepts demonstrated in research prototypes at that time. Alongside
the architecture, the ANSA project also developed a reference implementation, called ANSAware, which was used by many of the project partners to
build, evaluate and deploy practical distributed systems.[1]

Concepts from ANSA found their way into OSF/DCE, OMG/CORBA
and ISO/RM-ODP, and there was close cooperation between the three organizations and the teams involved in each activity, with some overlap in membership. While OSF and OMG focused on producing standards for specific
distributed computing functions, the RM-ODP gravitated towards providing
a higher-level reference model into which such technical standards could be
placed and with which the means of interoperation between systems using
these standards (or others) could be discussed.

Possibly the most important idea to come to RM-ODP from ANSA was
the concept of *viewpoints* (which in ANSA were called *projections*). These
arose initially from a desire to separate discussion of the engineering structure
of a distributed system as a composition of computers, communication links,
operating systems and middleware components from the abstract distributed
computational model seen by the programmer in terms of network objects,
interfaces, concurrent threads and so forth. We also recognized that the ANSA
computational model could be instantiated over several different engineering
models, depending on what kind of transparency was required. This led to
the concept of having separate *languages* for describing systems from each
viewpoint and the need to be able to show consistency between models of the

[1]An archive of ANSA project documents can be found at http://www.ansa.co.uk

same system expressed in each such language. To do this, ANSA borrowed from Sowa's work on conceptual structures [93] by treating the architecture as an existential graph in the form originally proposed by the logician C. S. Pierce. The graph showed relationships between concepts in the architecture and the term *projection* was taken for its mathematical interpretation as a slice through the graph that included every architectural concept in the graph, at some level of abstraction. This gave us the means to explain *correspondences* between viewpoints, and the adoption of a logic-based approach opened the door for other colleagues with an interest in formal methods to apply rigorous mathematical specification techniques to the development of RM-ODP.

In adopting ideas from object-oriented programming as the basis for the ANSA computational model, we struggled with concepts such as *inheritance*, *class* versus *type*, *object* versus *interface* and so forth, not helped by great debate about the relative importance and relationship between these ideas in the programming language community. In the end, we settled on objects as a unit of modularity and encapsulation as the key property in distributed systems and relegated *class* and *inheritance* to be software engineering concepts relating to how specifications are organized. We further took the view that an object could exhibit multiple interfaces, with different interfaces possibly encapsulating different partitions of the object state and giving different kinds of service to different types of client. We talked about *selective transparency* as the abstraction of engineering viewpoint capabilities, controlled by engineering (that is, system management) interfaces in the computational view. The computational viewpoint turned out to be a very powerful system modelling tool but gave problems to colleagues who wanted to implement ANSA directly in object-oriented programming languages, forcing them either to restrict the ANSA model or to use programming language objects to represent both ANSA interfaces and ANSA objects.

The two initial viewpoints were not sufficient for the needs of ANSA or RM-ODP. Taking ideas from colleagues working on OSI protocol conformance testing, we introduced a *technology viewpoint* to give us the means to state which standards applied to specific interfaces in a system and how to go about testing for conformance at those points. To talk about topics such as system management and security we found the need for a language to describe the purpose for which a system was intended, the system's boundaries and the roles undertaken by people using the system. This led us to introduce an *enterprise viewpoint*. Additionally, we wanted to be able to look at a system in high-level terms as an information processing system, without committing to a specific computational structure, leading us to add an *information viewpoint* that allowed for specifications in terms of a conceptual schema for the information handled by a system and an information flow model for the processes by which that information is processed.

The enterprise viewpoint gives terms for describing organizational structures, policies for security, dependability, quality of service and other so-called *non-functional* requirements and the roles of human actors in the system. The organizational concepts centred on the notion of *federation* representing the notion that many systems arise from the interconnection of previously autonomous systems (for example, as in *enterprise application integration*). In a federation neither system is subordinate to the other; rather, there must be an agreement of what is interconnected, what interactions can occur at those interconnections, and the meanings that are given to the interactions. In this last respect, ANSA work based on Searle's [90] development of Austin's *speech act theory* [48] provided some of the foundations. It gave RM-ODP the concepts of *performative actions* (ones that change the state of affairs in the system, such as making an online purchase) versus purely *informative actions* to exchange data (for example, looking up prices in an online catalogue). By expressing system behaviour in terms of its effect on the external environment, the enterprise viewpoint provides tools needed to express system policies and the desired outcomes and impact of system behaviour. Expressing correspondences between the enterprise viewpoint of a system and the other viewpoints is then essentially an exercise in showing how the technical system meets the external requirement — in other words, showing its fitness for purpose.

An associated concept that came with federation was the engineering viewpoint concept of *interception* to capture the idea of system components that allow bridges to be built between systems based on different infrastructures. Through the related concept of selective transparency, there was a similar decoupling between the computational (or programmatic) interfaces of the system — and the selection of engineering mechanisms that provided the necessary infrastructure to deliver the non-functional requirements set out in enterprise viewpoint policies. This was a contentious approach, standing against the philosophy at the time of seeking a universal set of standards to which all vendors and users would adhere. Recognizing that a model that could talk about interoperability between diverse systems run by separate authorities would be more general, the RM-ODP community embraced the ANSA federation and interception concepts and by that means ensured the model would remain relevant beyond the lifetime of many of the technologies that inspired it.

There were areas where ANSA was deficient and others in the RM-ODP community developed new ideas (several of which were pulled back into ANSA and ANSAware). Perhaps the most significant were concepts added to allow the modelling of other than RPC-based interaction. This need came from representatives of the telecommunications industry who wanted RM-ODP to be able to accommodate the signalling systems used to control switched networks and the need to carry synchronous streams of voice or video traffic as well as asynchronous data. To fill the gap J-B Stefani, at the time with France Telecom, introduced the concept of *signals* as synchronous atomic communication events from the Esterel [50] programming language into the RM-ODP computational viewpoint. This opened a broad vein of further development of rich multimedia systems based on RM-ODP and spawned a further industry consortium, TINA-C, which explored the application of RM-ODP ideas to the design of *intelligent telecommunications networks* to support new kinds of telecommunications services being offered by the increasingly deregulated and privatized telecommunications industry.

Looking back now, some 20 years later, the obvious question is what impact RM-ODP had on subsequent developments. Certainly it provided ISO with a necessary tool-box for further work on distributed computing standards, although, with some exceptions, the momentum moved away from ISO to the industry consortia, with new ones springing up alongside OSF and OMG as distributed computing moved to new technologies such as *web services*. RM-ODP had a strong influence on the Object Management Group's CORBA and CORBA service standards, which then went on to strongly influence the distributed computing provisions of the Java programming language and virtual machine and, in turn, from there through to web services. Certainly the ODP work helped educate many in the computer and telecommunications industries, whether as supplier or customer, on how to exploit distributed computing during rapid evolution of networks from early LANs to today's global Internet.

What of the future? RM-ODP remains of significant value — the concepts are general and powerful enough to describe current systems. Moreover, as we come to grow ever more dependent on computers to run the modern world and need to manage the complexity of these systems and the rapid evolution of the technologies they use, the ability to model and specify them accurately and completely remains a key challenge. Looking further ahead, in the Microsoft Research laboratory where I work, some colleagues are using concepts from distributed computing to construct computational models of DNA replication, splitting, and recombination along with the systems biology of human cells driven by a vision of being able to program *theranostic* molecules to diagnose and treat genetically based conditions. Perhaps one day we will see humans modelled in the computational and engineering viewpoints of RM-ODP as well as the enterprise viewpoint where they mostly live today!

In terms of RM-ODP itself, the enterprise viewpoint has remained an active area of development through to the current day linked to work in formal methods for system design and specification used in approaches such as *Model-Driven Architecture* where the collaboration between the RM-ODP community and the OMG remains vigorous and productive.

I commend the authors for continuing with the RM-ODP agenda from the early days when we worked together and I welcome the opportunity to acknowledge the contributions of all those who have participated in RM-ODP. In this book the authors have done an excellent job in relating the concepts to modern systems and needs, retaining the rigour of the model found in the ISO documents but with a refreshing and informative style to make them more approachable.

Andrew Herbert
Cambridge

Preface

The Reference Model for Open Distributed Processing (the RM-ODP) is an international standard created by the standardization bodies ISO and ITU-T. It gives a solid basis for describing and building widely distributed systems and applications in a systematic way. Emphasis is placed on the need to build such systems with evolution in mind by identifying the concerns of major stakeholders and then expressing the design as a series of linked viewpoints representing these concerns. Each stakeholder can then develop an appropriate view of the system with a minimum of interference from the others.

Although ODP has been available as a standard for more than 10 years, standards are not easy bedtime reading. The ideas presented have an enthusiastic following, but, outside of it, many practitioners are still unaware of them. This book aims to provide a gentler pathway to the essential ideas that make up ODP and to show how they can be applied when designing and building real systems. It offers an accessible introduction to the design principles for software engineers and enterprise architects. In addition, it explains the benefits of using viewpoints to produce simpler and more flexible designs. It is not limited to any single tool or design method, but concentrates on the key choices that make an architectural design robust, flexible and long lived. The book also shows the power of enterprise architecture for the design and organization of complex distributed IT systems.

The book has been prompted by the recent revision of the standard, during which ISO has incorporated experience from the application of ODP to many different domains and has taken account of new technologies and fashions. We cover the most up to the minute developments in the ODP standards, including the recent updates to the ODP reference model and the ODP enterprise language. The book provides fresh insights into the design of enterprise systems. Another reason for producing this book is to mark the publication of the ISO/IEC 19793 standard (known as UML4ODP), which uses the Unified Modelling Language (UML) notation to provide a familiar and accessible way of expressing ODP designs; it does this by defining a standardized UML profile. The book also provides guidelines for using the UML notation for structuring and writing system specifications and for fitting such specifications into the Model-Driven Engineering toolchain. This gives users of the ODP ideas a simpler way of expressing them with existing design and modelling tools.

Finally, there is an ongoing interest in using ODP when addressing new standardization approaches and interoperability frameworks such as those in e-government, e-health, and the energy and transportation industries. The book shows how the RM-ODP ideas can be applied to modern movements such as service engineering, cloud computing and the creation of the open enterprise.

This is the first book to introduce the ODP material in language that is common to software engineers and software architects. It offers a short, concise and focused presentation of the essentials of RM-ODP and shows where it fits within today's software processes. The book describes all the major concepts and mechanisms of the ODP framework, explains how to use them in a practical way for the specification of large open distributed systems, and presents the basic notation used for creating the specifications. It follows the standards faithfully, but provides extra information on the thinking behind them, and on how they should be interpreted. The reader can get acquainted with the best design concepts and practices, which are essential to anyone who designs large software applications professionally.

The Roadmap

The book is targeted at a number of different audiences. It has been written to be attractive both to the technical experts working on system architecture and to a much broader audience working on realizing such systems.

The book is divided into four parts, each having a different focus and each exploring progressively more detail of the different concepts and their use. There are also two appendices. The four parts provide

- An extended executive summary introducing the basic structuring ideas of ODP, particularly the central idea of there being a set of viewpoints.

- A more detailed explanation of the five ODP viewpoints and of the correspondences between them. Reading this part gives an idea of the style and use of the main elements of the ODP architecture.

- An explanation of the way these concepts are used to solve a number of the common problems met in the development and evolution of distributed systems. This part will help the reader to understand how use of the structure results in more flexible and adaptable systems.

- A discussion of some of the subtler ideas underlying this kind of system modelling and the new requirements they place on the supporting tools. This part answers some of the immediate questions people often want to ask about why the framework was defined in the way it is.

The first appendix brings together all the example model fragments used in the book to provide a single overview of a simple ODP-based design. Space limitations mean that even this needs to be selective, and a fuller version is available from the authors' website (see `http://theodpbook.lcc.uma.es/`).

The second appendix presents some questions and scenarios that can be used to support teaching and training using this book. In addition to providing information for practicing professionals, we expect the book to provide a resource for graduate students and researchers who want to understand the main problems and principles involved in the design of large software systems; the book can also be used in Masters or Doctorate courses for teaching the concepts and design principles of ODP and for preparing students to research new problems in this area.

The whole structure is unified by the use of a single running example describing the IT support needed by a medium-sized company as it grows and develops. One of the problems in understanding a system's architecture is in seeing just how it helps the day-to-day activities of the system builders. Abstract structures in their purest form can seem dry and remote, so we have tried to relate them to the problems developers face by including a series of short vignettes illustrating why the various aspects of the architecture are needed. These fragments support, but do not form an essential part of, the main exposition. The individual chapters generally start with one of these fragments to give an informal introduction to the problem to be solved.

The book is targeted at three groups of readers. It is primarily intended for enterprise architects and software engineers who want to understand the concepts, mechanisms and problems involved in the design of complex enterprise systems and to use this knowledge in establishing a tool-based approach to documenting, evolving and testing systems. Readers will become more aware of the issues and options available for designing within a strong architectural framework. They can apply the ideas in general terms, or study the full detail further in the standards or in one of the reference books based on them.

A second target audience includes IT project managers and CIOs, who will be able to understand the possibilities of the RM-ODP framework and a viewpoint-based design approach, and the potential benefits that the adoption of this approach can bring to their companies and organizations. There are a growing number of large, multi-organizational information systems projects, for example in the aerospace and healthcare areas, and the designers involved are seeking urgently for a systematic architectural approach. ODP provides such an approach.

A third group, CEOs and business architects, can get an overall idea of this design approach and be able to evaluate the advantages of the use of a mature set of ISO and the ITU-T standards within their organizations, and also for interoperating with the IT systems of their customers, providers, financial services, and so on. The use of international standards is now essential to achieve (and to guarantee) the level of interoperability required in these large and complex IT systems with hundreds of customers, providers and developers, which need to exchange data and services with other IT systems in a seamless way.

Historical Background

The requirements for ODP and its reference model can be traced back a long way, from the earlier work on Open Systems Interconnection. It became clear to experts working on application protocols that the prevalent focus on peer-to-peer communications was not enough and that distributed systems design needed to take a more holistic approach, starting from the structure of the organizations involved. It was necessary to begin with a thorough understanding of the enterprise before proposing any technical solutions.

At the same time, there was considerable work in progress on the idea of middleware supporting a uniform distribution platform, leading, for example, to the ANSA architecture [72] and to early Object Management Group (OMG) specifications. The work on ODP started by harvesting the current research ideas available at that time and then used them to construct a vendor-neutral architecture. This principle of maintaining a broadly applicable framework by using the best current thinking has continued to be the basis for work on ODP.

Currently RM-ODP is being maintained and developed by an ISO/IEC Working Group (JTC1/SC7/WG19: *Techniques for the Specification of IT Systems*). This group works in close cooperation with ITU-T on the joint publication of a series of standards, and also maintains strong collaborative links with other international bodies, such as the OMG. These links help to provide the intelligence for continuously updating and improving the framework as new technologies and paradigms emerge, and for maintaining the consistency of a broad range of specifications and standards.

Conventions Used

Much of the explanation of architectural elements is about the way different concepts are represented and what artefacts might result from their application. It is easy to lose track of which use falls into which category, so we introduce some graphical conventions to help sort things out. Throughout the book, we will use the following typographical conventions:

- A **_bold italic_** font highlights a word that is an ODP concept.

- A sans serif font indicates that an element is from a UML model.

- A `typewriter` font flags an item as being a concrete instance.

Trademarks and Copyright

UML®, CORBA®, XMI®, MOF™, MDA®, OMG®, Object Management Group™, and Unified Modelling Language™ are either registered trademarks or trademarks of Object Management Group™, Inc. in the United States and other countries.

Java™ and Java EE™ are trademarks of Oracle or its affiliates in the United States and other countries.

Unix® is a registered trademark in the United States and other countries, exclusively licensed through the X/Open Company, Ltd.

Figures 1.5, 7.2 and 7.3 are reproduced from ISO/IEC 19793:2008 with permission of the American National Standards Institute (ANSI) on behalf of the International Organization for Standardization (ISO). No part of this material may be copied or reproduced in any form, electronic retrieval system or otherwise or made available on the Internet, a public network, by satellite or otherwise without the prior written consent of the ANSI. Copies of this standard may be purchased from ANSI, 25 West 43rd Street, New York, NY 10036, (212) 642-4900, `http://webstore.ansi.org`.

Acknowledgements

The ODP standards are the result of the efforts of a great many experts working within the standards process over many years. There is not room here to give credit to all of these people, but we should like, in particular, to acknowledge the contribution of the ISO conveners and document editors in leading the effort, particularly Joost J. van Griethuysen, Eng Chew, Bryan Wood, Jean Bérubé, Fausto Caneschi, Jean-Bernard Stefani, Andrew Herbert, Richard Sinnott, Mirion Bearman, Pramila Daryani, Peter Furniss, Lea Kutvonen, Laurent LeBoucher, Joaquin Miller, Kerry Raymond, Gerd Schürmann, and Sandy Tyndale-Biscoe. Arve Meisingset played a pivotal role in coordinating our link with the ITU-T, and Tom Rutt provided vital liaisons links with the OMG.

A number of people have read drafts of this book and provided us with very useful suggestions; in particular, our thanks go to Andy Bond, Fred Cummins, Andrew Herbert, Jishnu Mukerji, Bruno Traverson and Bryan Wood.

The authors would also like to thank No Magic, Inc. for making their UML tools available to facilitate the production of this book, and José Raúl

Romero and Juan Ignacio Jaen for building and maintaining the ODP plug-in for MagicDraw, and for maintaining the RM-ODP website.

Finally, we would like to thank all those involved at CRC Press, particularly Randi Cohen, Amber Donley and Karen Simon, for their expert help and advice throughout the publication process.

Peter F. Linington
Zoran Milosevic
Akira Tanaka
Antonio Vallecillo

Part I

The Framework

About Part I

This first part explains the objectives of ODP and gives an initial introduction to the common concepts on which the framework is based. In particular, it describes the idea of viewpoints and how this idea is used to structure system specifications. It also introduces the taxonomy for supporting functions, which is used to establish a common vocabulary and, using human-computer interfacing as an example, indicates how planning for distribution interacts with other facets of system design.

Finally, notations are discussed, and a particular standardized profile for a UML-based notation is introduced. This notation will be used in the rest of the book.

Throughout the book, the problems being solved are put into context by a series of dramatized vignettes showing the everyday activities within the PhoneMob organization, a fictional company whose activities provide our running example. These are not, in general, essential to the technical points being made in each chapter, but you should certainly read the first episode, since it introduces the broad structure of the example to be used in the rest of the book.

Chapter 1

What Is ODP About?

Marcus Steinberg was a self-made man, and he had built his business on his ability to select a strong team. As he walked into the executive meeting room, he wished that events had not moved quite so quickly, but he would be a fool not to take advantage of the current state of the economy. He had snapped up the PhoneMob, a promising startup with a cash flow problem and a serious need to automate its working methods. Their business, providing a complete facilities management package to mobile phone owners, was close enough in concept to his current camera rescue empire for there to be some real opportunities for synergy, but PhoneMob would need sorting out first. Still, this acquisition would give him the platform he needed to make a real impact as the recovery kicked in.

Marcus knew the IT team he was about to address was technically solid, but he had begun to think that they needed a new approach. Recent projects seemed to have taken longer than expected, with too many last-minute snags and small misunderstandings. He liked a well-oiled machine, and their current performance grated. He had decided to call in some favours and had, as a result, been introduced to Alex Wren, a consulting enterprise architect whose new approach was, he had been told, finding favour in all the right places.

"Good, you're all here." He looked round the room and noticed his people had grouped themselves, as usual, into the primarily technical and the primarily business oriented. He also noticed the empty seats on either side of Wren; there was a job to be done there in getting Wren accepted. "You all know we have a big job on our hands in bringing the PhoneMob up to date, and I want to make this happen fast and efficiently. We need the relaunched organization to make a mark as a modern outfit, without losing its existing customers."

"I know you already have a lot on your plate, and it would be unfair to saddle any of you with the responsibility for coordinating this," — he wished this was his real reason — "so I have asked Alex Wren here to join us and help pull things together." He could see from their faces that some of the business team would happily have done without this help. Eleanor Hewish, his volatile but ambitious CIO was staring directly at him, while the fastidious compliance officer, Ivor Davies, was looking critically at Wren, who still seemed relaxed and confident. The technical side seemed less threatened. Claire Moss, the lead system analyst, was still studying her papers, while Trevor Clark, the configuration manager and Trudy McNeal of procurement were giving him their polite but guarded attention. Nigel Oliver, the infrastructure manager was sketching some sort of diagram on his pad, although Marcus couldn't make out whether it related to this meeting or to something else on Nigel's mind.

He turned towards the other member of the meeting, who was from outside his core team. "I'm assuming you already know Edward Faversham, from the PhoneMob; you must all have had some dealings with him during the negotiations. He is here to give us his experience of their current services and processes, and his view of the requirements for the merged system." Faversham shifted nervously and looked round the table, acknowledging the nods of recognition. "So, let's get down to business. Edward, perhaps you can give us a quick run-through of the main business units to get us started?"

Faversham flicked the remote control to display a picture of a dishevelled businessman jumping up and down on his mobile phone. "As you know," he said, "our mission is to take the hassle out of owning a mobile. We get the phone fixed if it breaks, and we provide a replacement if we can't get it going again straight away. We have outlets all over Europe, so we can help while you are travelling and return the repaired phone to you at your home base." He clicked, and the view changed to a map spattered with dots, although, Marcus thought, not that many, yet.

"To be honest," Edward said, "our main problem at present is that these sites are not that well integrated, but so far we have grown from a base where each local office franchise did its own thing, and had its own PC-style support, and we can't grow any more without a proper infrastructure."

He clicked again, revealing a complicated block diagram on the screen, and pointed to a set of paths highlighted in red. "This," he said, "is the work scheduling and logistics. That's where there is the main scope for automation. This other area over here covers the liaison with the handset suppliers, and at present is mostly person-to-person negotiation; and this is the corporate relationship management, which is one of the areas we need to put on a much firmer basis. Down here are the charging and account management processes. No, it's the logistics that we should concentrate on here, at least initially." He paused and considered his chart, as if seeing it for the first time. "I guess the main difference from what you are used to is the complexity of the data management involved."

Eleanor interrupted. "What's the problem?" she asked sharply. "It looks simple enough." "Oh no," he said, "far from it. Think about the investment a user has in the content of his mobile phone. The SIM is bound to the number, and can be swapped, but the contact lists and the message and call history are needed to keep things moving, and all that data is potentially sensitive."

This brought Nigel in. "So your service engineers have access to sensitive customer data? Isn't that a security problem?"

"Well, at present we don't provide the flexibility customers want, but data privacy certainly will be an issue in what you are planning now. Let's look at the most common use case," Edward said. "A corporation takes out a contract with us to support its salespeople. One of its representatives is in Stuttgart, and his phone keypad fails. He visits our Stuttgart office, and we put his phone into a test harness to bypass the keypad and download the state into a courtesy unit; we swap the SIM into this new unit, and the salesman can go on his way. Before he leaves we estimate the time to repair, and he tells us that by then he will be in Berlin. We commit to deliver the repaired phone to his Berlin hotel."

"What about if there is some extra delay?" Eleanor asked. "Suppose there was a deeper problem requiring a return to the manufacturer that didn't show up until you had done the keyboard replacement?" "Well, then we send an SMS giving a revised estimate. He can then reply to the SMS, or access our website, to confirm the new time." Claire leaned forwards. "But he might have returned home by then." "Yes, but he can change the delivery address if necessary. He can also do that if his own plans change." Claire was not satisfied. "What happens if the phone is already in transit to Berlin when he makes the change?" "Well, our logistics support has to cope with that. We do a confirmation check before the phone leaves the local depot, and the couriers are instructed to ensure the customer has not yet checked out before they complete the delivery."

"The loan phone is returned using a prepaid wallet; the user's information was copied to the repaired phone before it is dispatched. After all this, the corporate account is billed for the work." Nigel frowned. "What about the state in the loan phone?" "Well," Edward spread his hands. "If the user needs complete synchronization, he can come in to the local office to make the exchange; that also means we can do the SIM swap for him. But we find people are generally happy to make separate records if they know they are using a loan phone. We can e-mail the state back to them after return of the phone if they want."

Marcus looked around the group. "Well, any comments on what we have heard so far?" Nigel looked up. "It seems to me that there is a huge piece of design work to do here," he said. "We need to look at a number of different infrastructure use cases, and it will take my team some time to understand the application structure, plus the security aspects, and the user interface issues, just for starters." "Hang on," interrupted Eleanor, "we need a design the business side can understand; we have got to keep it simple for them, or we can't have a meaningful discussion about the processes they need." Ivor frowned. "But we need to check over precisely that detail to pick up inconsistencies that would give us compliance problems later." Trudy nodded. "And we need to think from the start about whether our corporate standards and procedures will be suitable. We need to have all the detail there," she said. "But look here," said Claire, "we can't add all that into the application design, or we will lose sight of the application architecture. It will be a mess. And we don't need the application and infrastructure teams to duplicate each other's work."

Marcus banged the table. "Hold on now. You are all talking at once. Alex, you haven't spoken yet. What's your take on what you have just heard?"

Alex stood up and walked over to the flipchart. "I think you have all made good points." He said. "This is a very large design, and there are conflicting requirements, needing different focuses and levels of detail. The best way to handle it is to divide and conquer; you should identify the key stakeholders, and then describe the problem from their points of view. If you can identify the right stakeholders, the different views can be largely independent, and so they can be worked on in parallel. The framework I want you to work with is called ODP, and it stresses five such viewpoints." He sketched a diagram on the chart with five arrows converging on the design problem. "These correspond roughly to organizational responsibilities in a situation such as yours, namely business processes, systems analysis, data integrity, infrastructure and intellectual or physical resources. If you each start with your own focus and the level of detail you need, we can then link the different views together to describe the complete problem."

"What I would like each of you to do is prepare an outline of the requirements as you see them, and then we can see how they fit together and move on from there."

"OK then," Marcus said, "let's do it, and meet again on the 28th to see how well it works. That's all for now; I've got to talk to the finance people again." He stood up and stalked out of the room, leaving the discussion going on; it was still going on hours later.

1.1   The ODP Reference Model

The aim of the Reference Model for Open Distributed Processing (the RM-ODP) is to provide a framework for specifying and building large or complex systems; we call the systems being produced **ODP systems**. These systems may be classical IT systems, information systems, embedded systems, business systems, or anything else in which we are interested.

If a system is at least moderately complicated, it is useful to extract the description of its structure and external properties from the details of its components or subsystems. If this abstract view concentrates on the distillation of general principals, it is called an **architecture**. When presented in a way that is useful for the derivation of a whole family of future systems, it is called a framework. Hence, when describing a business system supporting a broad range of applications, it is common to talk of an enterprise architecture or an enterprise framework. However, of late, these terms have been over-used and now lack focus. In these terms, the RM-ODP is an architectural framework for the design of any distributed system, particularly those whose complexity poses a challenge.

The Reference Model was published in the mid 1990s, following almost 10 years of work in the International Standards Organization to harvest the best architectural work up to that time. The results were published as common text by both ISO and the ITU-T (the telecommunications standards forum). The RM-ODP was published in four parts [2–5]. These four parts provide an introduction, a set of rigorous basic concepts, the architectural framework, and a link to supporting formal techniques. The users of this framework are expected to be system designers, but it is also intended to help people who build tools to support such design activity, or who produce standards to capture best practice and reusable mechanisms in this area.

The RM-ODP defines a framework, but not a methodology. It gives the designer a way of thinking about the system, and structuring its specification, but does not constrain the order in which the design steps should be carried out. There are many popular design processes, and the framework can be used with practically any of them.

Since ODP system designs are typically large collaborative efforts, it is likely that the actual process will be iterative, filling in detail in different parts of the specification as ideas evolve and requirements are better understood. However, the sequence in which this is done will depend on circumstances. In a green field, design may follow a classical top-down, waterfall-style pattern. In a legacy migration exercise, it will start by capturing existing constraints. In an agile or rapid prototyping environment, design will stress modularization and fine-grained iteration. The ideas for structuring specifications presented here can be applied within any of these methodologies. They remain valid if the design approach changes, and provide a common framework and vocabulary for collaboration between designers using different processes.

Many competing architectural frameworks have recently been proposed, and some of the better-known ones are reviewed in section 16.5. However, ODP offers a set of distinguishing features that make it particularly relevant for the specification of open distributed systems for enterprise and information handling applications. First, it has the authority and stability that goes with its status as an international standard. You can use it with the confidence that it is controlled by proven international processes, and will not be unilaterally changed by some individual group or private organization. Second, it is based on a rigorously defined set of formal concepts, and so has a precision that positions it in close alignment with the current software engineering and model-driven trends within the industry. Third, it is based on well-developed enterprise modelling languages and a distributed system architecture, which jointly position ODP as a perfect framework for modelling large, cross-organizational and cross-jurisdictional systems that communicate over the Internet. Finally, it has a well-integrated and fully developed treatment of conformance and compliance that makes it a practical tool, feeding naturally from design to development. All these factors contribute to ODP's position as the most effective architectural vehicle for understanding and achieving system interoperability.

1.2   Viewpoints

1.2.1   The Idea of Viewpoints

The RM-ODP is perhaps best known for its use of viewpoints. The idea behind them is to break down a complex specification into a set of coupled but separate pieces. This is a very old idea, used, for instance, to simplify engineering drawings (as shown in figure 1.1) and in the building plans produced by architects.

The writers of the reference model were keenly aware of the need to serve different stakeholders, and introduced the idea of there being a set of linked

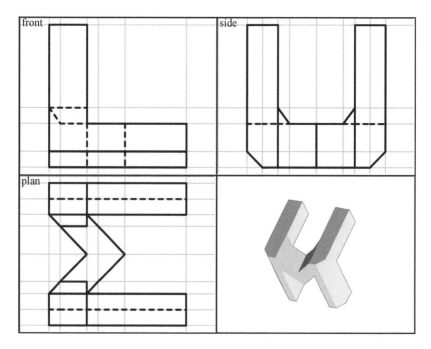

FIGURE 1.1: A traditional use of viewpoints in a mechanical drawing with first-angle orthographic projection.

viewpoints to maintain flexibility and avoid the difficulties associated with constructing and maintaining a single large system description.[1]

The idea is that, because the viewpoints in the set are interlinked (as explained in section 1.2.4) they are equivalent to a notional single large model. This equivalent model is not presented to any one user, since it would be too complex to be useful. However, tools may construct part or all of such a model where they need to manipulate information from more than one viewpoint.

Indeed, the idea of having a well-integrated set of tools, or toolchain, is fundamental to the success of the viewpoint approach. Without such a toolchain, it would be necessary for programmers to consult every viewpoint to discover all the constraints on the code they are to write, largely nullifying the advantages of the approach.

The viewpoints are coupled to form a complete system specification, but it is not necessary to use the same techniques when expressing each member of the set. Each stakeholder will be familiar with languages and notations well tuned to handling their particular interests, and so the techniques used will often be different. Of course, the more similar the techniques, the simpler it is to correlate the various views, so there is a trade-off between ease of solution to the specific constituent problems and ease of integration.

One of the aims in selecting a set of viewpoints is for them to be as loosely coupled as possible. A benefit of using viewpoints is that they allow parallel activity in different teams, and so allow some parts of the specification to reach a level of stability and maturity before others. It takes skill to pick a good set of viewpoints; if two viewpoints are linked in too many ways, independent activity will be difficult, and if they do not reflect common groupings of activity in the industry, they will not belong to clearly identifiable stakeholders.

Thus we can see that, for example, separate descriptions of system state and behaviour would be poor candidates for viewpoints; they are linked by a fundamental duality and so closely intertwined. On the other hand, service use and service provision are good candidates because, for a well-chosen service, they each deal with independent detail; as long as the right service is provided, the details of how it is provided and how it is used do not interact and can be handled by different teams. The two sets of concerns are nearly orthogonal.

1.2.2 A Specific Set of Viewpoints

The idea of separating concerns by using a set of viewpoints can be applied to many design activities. However, components are more likely to be reused if the same set of viewpoints is accepted by many different teams. The largest possible degree of commonality is needed to support the creation of an

---

[1]The idea of providing a set of viewpoints has arisen in a number of different design and software engineering areas, and an attempt has recently been made to capture the general idea in IEEE 1471, *Recommended Practice for Architecture Description of Software-Intensive Systems* [75], which has recently been refined within ISO as the standard ISO 42010 [24].

international standard, where a single approach is needed to cover a large and
long-lived community of users. The ODP reference model therefore defines
five specific viewpoints (see figure 1.2), intended to appeal to five clear groups
of users of a whole family of standards.

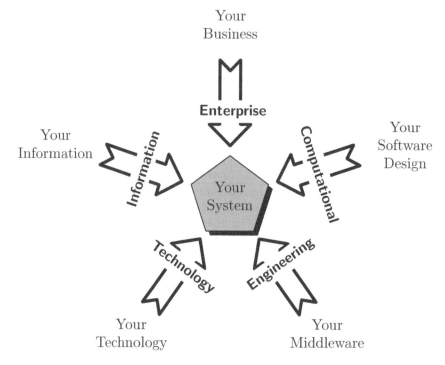

FIGURE 1.2: The five ODP viewpoints.

These five viewpoints are each the subject of a subsequent chapter, but
they are introduced briefly here, concentrating on the broad objectives and
areas of concern they cover.

The *enterprise viewpoint* focuses on the organizational situation in
which the design activity is to take place. It concentrates on the objectives,
business rules and policies that need to be supported by the system being
designed. The stakeholders to be satisfied are therefore the owners of the
business processes being supported and the managers responsible for the setting of operational policies. The emphasis is on business and social units and
their interdependencies.

Note that the use of the word *enterprise* here is intended to cover any activity of interest; an enterprise can be whatever the specifiers have been tasked
to describe. It can be a single product and its users, or a commercial organization, or a larger social structure involving many corporate or governmental
entities. It captures whatever field of application we are currently focusing
upon in this particular design activity.

The *information viewpoint* concentrates on the modelling of the shared information manipulated within the enterprise of interest. The creation of an information specification has broadly the same objectives that creation of a data dictionary had for previous generations. By providing a common model that can be referenced from throughout a complete piece of design, we can ensure that the same interpretation of information is applied at all points. As a result, we can avoid the divergence of use and incomplete collection of information that would result from separate members of the design team each making their own decisions about interpretation.

As an ideal, we would like there to be a single universal information model, but this is clearly not practical. The aim here, therefore, is to achieve a shared model for the particular design activity, but we shall see later that even this may not be achievable when we are considering federation of systems or legacy integration. The best we can achieve is a single model used within the scope of a particular design authority. However, this is already sufficiently challenging, while giving potential for huge quality improvements.

The *computational viewpoint* is concerned with the development of the high-level design of the processes and applications supporting the enterprise activities. It uses the familiar tools for object-oriented software design, expressing its models in terms of objects with strong encapsulation boundaries, interacting at typed interfaces by performing a sequence of operations (or passing continuous streams of information). The computational specification makes reference to the information viewpoint for the definitions of data objects and their behavioural constraints.

The computational design is abstract in that its objects are not placed at specific locations and allocated particular resources to run on; this is done elsewhere. The same design can be implemented in many different ways by placing its objects on different platforms.

The *engineering viewpoint* tackles the problem of diversity in infrastructure provision; it gives the prescriptions for supporting the necessary abstract computational interactions in a range of different situations. It thereby offers a way to avoid lock-in to specific platforms or infrastructure mechanisms. A particular interaction may involve communication between subsystems, or between objects co-located in a single application server, and different engineering solutions will be used depending on which is currently the case. The engineering specification is akin to the specification of how middleware is provided; there are different solutions for use in different operating environments, but the aim is to provide a consistent set of communication services and other supporting services that the application designer can rely on in all cases.

The engineering viewpoint in ODP is also concerned with the provision to the computational designer of a set of guarantees, called *transparencies*. Providing a transparency involves taking responsibility for a distribution problem, so that the computational design does not need to worry about it.

Many of the mechanisms needed are nowadays available in the form of standard middleware or web services components, simplifying the engineering specification, since it can reference the existing solutions and merely state how they are combined to meet the infrastructure needs of the system.

The ***technology viewpoint*** is concerned with managing real-world constraints, such as restrictions on the hardware available to implement the system within budget, or the existing application platforms on which the applications must run. The designer never really has the luxury of starting with a green field, and this viewpoint brings together information about the existing environment, current procurement policies and configuration issues. It is concerned with selection of ubiquitous standards to be used in the system, and the allocation and configuration of real resources. It represents the hardware and software components of the implemented system, and the communication technology that provides links between these components. Bringing all these factors together, it expresses how the specifications for an ODP system are to be implemented.

This viewpoint also has an important role in the management of testing conformance to the overall specification because it specifies the information required from implementers to support this testing.

1.2.3   Viewpoint Languages

We can think of any mechanism for conveying ideas as being a language, be it written, drawn or spoken. The communication can be between people, between machines, or understood by both.

Thus, we can speak of the set of concepts, conventions and constraints expressed in a particular viewpoint as forming a ***viewpoint language***. The rules of interpretation for such a language can, in a particular instance, be seen as representing a viewpoint virtual machine. We can think of the supporting tools as parsing the language's grammar and checking its semantic rules, or as implementing the equivalent virtual machine; these are just two sides of the same coin.

From an architectural point of view, we need not be concerned with the physical representation of this language as marks on paper or encoded in messages. An abstract language can be represented by a number of different concrete notations, suited to use in different situations. Many tools, for example, can work with either a graphical or a textual notation, and store designs in a third, machine-oriented format, such as a dialect of XML. These are all different notations expressing the same abstract language.

Thus for each of the five viewpoints being considered here, we have a corresponding viewpoint language. We talk about the viewpoint when we wish to stress the perception of the stakeholder concerned, and about the language when we want to emphasize the way the ideas are communicated, but the two aspects are intimately coupled; one cannot express the ideas without using the language.

Because the different viewpoints stress different aspects of the design, and do so using different techniques, the stakeholders will each be most comfortable working with their own style of language and notation. For example, someone writing a business policy may be happier expressing goals in a declarative way, saying, perhaps, that a target level of production should always be achieved, while someone documenting a process may naturally think in imperative terms, expressing what has to be done as a sequence of instructions.

As another example, a business process may involve extended activities with real-time deadlines and have measures of the fraction of work completed, while a computational task may concentrate on sequences of events that are considered indivisible (or *atomic*), with deadlines expressed by equivalent events, with no model of continuous time at all. Working with sequence, but without continuous time like this simplifies analysis, but makes the expression of continuous properties of the system, such as quality of service, more difficult.

1.2.4   Viewpoint Correspondences

Although we achieve a powerful simplification by dividing a system specification into the views seen by different stakeholders, the specification must continue to be a coherent description of a single target system. If we had no links between the viewpoints, this would not happen; what was intended to be a single design would just fall apart into five bits. It is therefore vital that the viewpoints be linked, and this is done by establishing a set of correspondences between them, as visualized in figure 1.3.

In current software tools that present different user views, this linkage is often derived from the names of objects. If the same name appears in two diagrams, they are assumed to represent two aspects of the same thing.

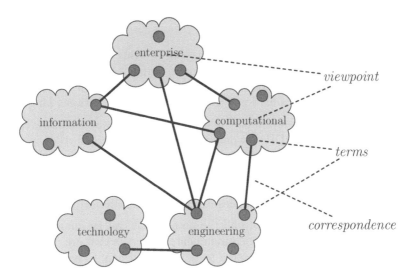

FIGURE 1.3: How correspondences link terms in different viewpoints.

However, if the viewpoints are to be developed by loosely coordinated teams, it is not safe to assume they share a single namespace; it is just too expensive to ensure that name assignments are unique. It is also often the case that the correspondences are not simply one-to-one; the relationships will generally be more complex.

This can be seen by considering the correspondences between the computational and engineering viewpoints (a situation similar to that between the user and provider of middleware). The computational viewpoint takes a very simple view of interactions, abstracting away from the platform-specific details of particular interactions; the engineering viewpoint, on the other hand, abstracts away from most of the detail of the computational design, distinguishing just a few categories of interacting objects, not worrying about why the interactions take place. Thus, the correspondences between computational object types and basic engineering object types representing them are typically not one-to-one. The correspondences often involve some level of abstraction or filtering in one direction or the other.

1.3   Fundamental Concepts

Part 2 of the ODP Reference Model sets out a family of basic concepts, explaining precisely what is meant when we say that ODP is based on an object model. This is particularly important when dealing with the coordination of a number of tools that all share the general idea of an object and an interface at a ball and stick level, but often diverge in subtle ways when the fine detail is examined.

Precision is essential when we are trying to bring together multiple viewpoint languages, together with the languages implicit in the available tools, to create a consistent framework. This integration depends on knowing exactly what the basic concepts used are, and where they vary between languages.

The fundamental concepts are defined in a general way, and they can then be used in any of the ODP viewpoints. Often, a concept is further specialized in a particular viewpoint, but always in a way that is entirely consistent with the basic definition. For example, the concept of an interface is defined in full generality as one of the fundamental concepts, but viewpoints specialize it, so that we have engineering interfaces, computational interfaces and so on.

This book does not go into all the detail; that can be found in the standards. However, there are some fundamental concepts that are used in all the viewpoint languages; these deserve to be discussed here. They are presented in outline in this section, and more detail can often be found when they are used later in the book.

1.3.1 Object Model

ODP system specifications are expressed in terms of **objects**. Objects are representations of the entities we want to model, including physical elements (mobile phones), human beings (John, the repair centre clerk) or more abstract entities (a pending repair order). An object contains information and offers services. In other words, an object is characterized by its **state** or, dually, by its **behaviour**. Depending on the viewpoint and the style of the notation used, the primary emphasis may be placed either on behaviour or on state.

The use of the object paradigm provides **abstraction** and **encapsulation**, two important properties for the specification and design of complex systems. Abstraction allows highlighting of those aspects of the system relevant from a given perspective, while hiding those of no relevance. Encapsulation is the property by which the information contained in an object is accessible only through interactions at the interfaces supported by the object. Because objects are encapsulated, there are no hidden side effects outside the object arising from the interactions. It also implies that the internal details of an object are hidden from other objects, which is crucial in ensuring the interchangeability of alternative implementations, and in providing the basis for dealing with heterogeneity, interoperability and portability.

Behaviour is expressed as a collection of **actions**. Actions can be anything that may happen, and can be classified into **interactions** (which involve participation from the object's environment) and **internal actions** (which take place without such participation). An example of an internal action is the one that models the sudden breakdown of a mobile phone. Interactions are used to model, for instance, a customer's request to the PhoneMob clerk to have his handset repaired, or the act of transferring the data from one phone memory card to another. Each of the objects involved in an interaction plays a particular **action role** characterized by the information it contributes or accepts and by whether or not it originated the action.

A **system** is composed of a configuration of interacting objects. Objects interact at **interfaces**, which are subsets of their possible interactions with other objects, together with the set of constraints on when they may occur. An **event** is the fact that an action has taken place. When an event occurs, the information about the action that has happened becomes part of the state of the system and may thus subsequently be communicated in other interactions. Such a communication is called an event notification.

The specification of an interaction concentrates on the objects participating in it. However, in some circumstances, we may want to focus on exactly where the interaction takes place and how it might be observed. This is done by introducing the concept of an **interaction point**, which is concerned with where, in time and space, the interaction happens. We shall see later, in chapter 8, how this concept leads to the more specific ideas of **reference point** and **conformance point** when we are concerned with ensuring that some interactions are observable during testing.

Finally, a ***service*** is a behaviour, triggered by an interaction between provider and consumer objects, that adds value for its users by creating, modifying or consuming information.

1.3.2   Types, Classes and Templates

As in most object-oriented modelling and programming languages, ODP objects, actions and interfaces are generally specified in terms of their ***types***. In ODP, a type is a predicate that characterizes a set of elements, and serves to identify and describe them. For instance, type Customer describes the common characteristics of the company's customers that are relevant to the system. Similarly, type RepairOrder captures the information that any repair order in the system should have. Predicates can be expressed in many different notations, from textual languages to graphical modelling notations (a UML class is a typical notation for representing types, describing both the state and the behaviour of the corresponding objects in terms of attributes and operations).

Types help to classify entities into categories, which form collections of objects that satisfy a given type. Such collections are called ***classes***. Note, however, that the UML concept of class differs from the ODP concept of class. A UML class is a *description* of a set of objects, while an ODP class is the set of objects itself. Therefore, the UML concept of class is closer to the ODP concept of type. There is no UML concept that is similar to the ODP concept of class.

In addition to types and classes, ODP also uses the concept of ***template***, which refers to the specification of an element, including sufficient detail to allow an instantiation to take place. For example, object-oriented programming language concrete classes are templates. Types can only be involved in testing whether instances satisfy them or not; templates can be used to create instances. Templates may also include parameters, which will need to be bound to specific values at instantiation time.

1.3.3   Composition

Composition and its inverse, ***decomposition***, are key concepts in ODP. We have already mentioned that systems are composed of interacting objects. The composition of two or more objects is itself another object (called the composite object). The characteristics of the new object are determined by the objects being combined and by the way they are combined (the composition operator used).

Behaviours can also be composed, yielding a new behaviour. This can apply either to behaviour fragments or to the behaviour of complete objects. Thus, the behaviour of a composite object is the corresponding composition of the behaviour of the component objects, possibly hiding some interactions to make them internal actions.

Action compositions can be specified to form processes. A *process* is a collection of steps taking place in a prescribed manner and leading to an *objective*. A *step* is an abstraction of an action, used in a process, that leaves unspecified the objects that participate in that action. Steps are introduced in the definition because not all the action details need be specified in the composition. The objective is present because the goal of a process should always be made explicit in its specification. In ODP, the objective of an element expresses its practical advantage or intended effect. It is expressed as preferences about future states.

1.3.4 Grouping Objects Together

ODP distinguishes different ways of organizing sets of objects. In the simplest case, objects can be organized into *groups*, which are sets of objects with a particular *relationship* that characterizes either some structural interdependence between them, or an expected common behaviour. Examples are the group of all the information objects, or the group of engineering objects that are related to a given computational object.

Domains are often used in describing these groupings; a domain is a set of objects related by a characterizing relationship to a controlling object. Every domain has its associated controlling object, which is not generally itself a member of the domain. One example of this is a naming domain, in which a set of names are associated with objects by the controlling object. Another is a management domain in which a set of printer objects is managed by a controller.

Objects can also be organized into *configurations*, which are collections of objects linked by their interactions at particular interfaces. Examples are the configuration of objects that together provide a given service, or the configuration of engineering objects that implements a channel.

These concepts can be specialized in specific viewpoints. For example, in the enterprise language, a *community* is a configuration of enterprise objects formed to meet a particular *objective*, as specified in a given *contract*. In our PhoneMob example, one community is the configuration of objects that together provide the basic repair services to customers. Another community is the logistics organization formed by a set of objects with the objective of providing delivery services to users in a secure and timely manner. A third example is the banking community, which is a configuration of enterprise objects that together provide a set of banking services (payments, money transfer and so on) to its customers.

Finally, a *federation* is a community of domains formed to meet a shared objective. It models many commercial situations, such as the setting up of partnerships and joint ventures; examples are the federation of a set of airlines that agree to work together to provide transportation services to their customers by means of code-shared flights, or a federation of banks that share their ATMs so that customers can use any of them interchangeably. In our example, the PhoneMob company and a large insurance firm can federate to provide a wider range of services to their individual customers. Each member of a federation agrees by participating in the federation to be bound by the contract and policies of the community (which may include obligations to contribute resources or to constrain behaviour) so as to pursue the shared objective. At the same time, a federation preserves the autonomy and independence of the original participants.

1.3.5   Contracts

As a general concept, a **contract** defines the rules governing the collective behaviour of a set of objects. It specifies obligations, permissions and prohibitions that apply to these objects when they act as a group. These could express, for example, quality of service constraints, indications of duration or periods of validity, behaviour that invalidates the contract, or liveness and safety conditions.[2]

The contract concept can be used in any viewpoint. In the enterprise viewpoint, we have community contracts (see chapter 2) reflecting a business context for interactions. For example, the community contract representing a repair organization expresses obligations on its service centres, their staff and customers, as well as conditions about efficiency, security, response times and confidentiality to be met when delivering the repair services.

There are several uses of the concept of a contract in the computational viewpoint. One example is its use to describe a service contract, which defines the obligations that an object makes when providing an interface with which arbitrary other objects will interact. Another is the binding contract which captures the properties agreed upon when a particular binding is established (this may be either a primitive or a compound binding; see chapter 4).

Finally, any computational object interacts within an environment representing its place in a configuration, and an **environment contract** states non-functional properties of the interactions in which an object participates, such as response time, throughput or resource consumption. These computational environment contracts reflect constraints on the corresponding objects and interactions in the engineering viewpoint.

1.3.6   Policy Concepts

Policies provide a powerful mechanism for declaring business rules, and also for specifying and implementing the structural and behavioural variability required in any open distributed system. Policies serve to identify the pieces of behaviour that can be changed during the lifetime of the system, as well as

---

[2]Liveness is the property of a system that says it will eventually do what it is supposed to do, and safety is the property that says it will never do something it is supposed not to do.

the constraints on these behaviours. In other words, a policy can be seen as a constraint on a system specification foreseen at design time, whose details can be modified to manage the system to meet particular (and changing) circumstances. More details are given in chapter 10.

Policies are defined in terms of *rules*. A rule is a constraint on a system specification. Rules are normally expressed as obligations, permissions, authorizations or prohibitions. For instance, one rule may say that any phone user associated with a customer can place an order to have a mobile phone repaired (*permission*), while another rule may dictate that the repair centre must repair the handset or provide a substitute phone within 48 hours (*obligation*); a further rule may state that VIP customers are entitled to get substitute phones immediately (*authorization*); a fourth rule may say that, for security reasons, a SIM memory must not be returned to any customer other than the one who placed the original repair order (*prohibition*).

1.4 Useful Building Blocks

One of the aims of the reference model is to promote the use of common terminology for describing distributed architectures, particularly with regard to the functional elements needed to support and manage distributed applications. Many vendors have their own names for these functions, making it more difficult to draw parallels between different solutions, and to find vendor-neutral terms to describe interworking mechanisms.

The reference model therefore provides a catalogue of architectural functions needed to support distribution. This vocabulary can be used in any of the viewpoints, but it concentrates on giving full coverage of the engineering viewpoint and many of the functions identified are normally contained within the system's infrastructure. However, some may be available as services for use in the computational specification, and others may be exploited in a more abstract form, for example when modelling repositories in the enterprise specification.

The catalogue covers four main areas. The first is the *management* of different groupings of engineering objects, providing control of resourcing, protection and activation. Then it categorizes *synchronization* mechanisms, followed by various *repository* functions, together with different specialized features to aid resource discovery and interworking. Finally, it identifies important building blocks for the provision of a range of distributed *security* functions.

Use of this taxonomy helps different teams to understand the functions offered by existing components and so aids reuse. The functions can be used as keywords to index catalogues of components or collections of higher-level technical design patterns, aiding design. This provides a common vocabulary for explaining a system's architecture to potential users or external assessors or conformance testers. It also allows the expression of platform-independent designs in a commonly understood way without reference to specific technological choices, making it easier for teams using a model-driven engineering approach to exchange ideas on requirements and solutions.

1.5   Service Orientation

In recent years, much play has been made of the use of service orientation as a design principle. From an architectural point of view, however, there is no significant difference between service-oriented architectures (SOA) and the architectural framework defined in ODP; current service-oriented schemes can be seen as a subset of the more general ODP approach.

The main tenets of SOA are that functions should be packaged into loosely coupled units that provide clearly defined services, and that applications should be constructed by composition of services that can be discovered dynamically based on some form of publication or brokerage mechanism. More recent SOA activities add to this a distinction between services offered from different design perspectives, yielding different flavours of service, such as business services, technical services and so on.

ODP defines service as a fundamental concept, representing the added value offered as a result of interaction at some interface. Since the ODP object model is based on strong encapsulation, this means that there is a close alignment with the SOA view of service. The discovery and dynamic use aspects are covered by the ODP binding model and the definition of common functions such as the trader. The different types of services are captured by the ODP viewpoints, with business services being expressed in the enterprise viewpoint and the technical services being expressed primarily in the computational viewpoint. However, in the ODP enterprise viewpoint, as we shall see in the next chapter, there is a greater emphasis on declarative expression and flexible structures, so the definition of a business service is only one of the available design tools. Correspondences defined between the different aspects of a service in different viewpoints are also needed to provide a consistent specification of the service as a whole.

So what differentiates a service-oriented architecture? The main differences are not architectural, but are more concerned with raising the engineering expectations about openness and resilience, largely as a result of years of implementation experience with web-based systems and of striving for the widespread adoption of open resource identifiers like Uniform Resource Identifiers (URIs).

1.6 Human Computer Interaction

An essential aspect of the design of any information system is the specification of the interfaces the system offers to the people that will interact with it, something that is normally called human-computer interaction. In this design field, the user interface (or UI for short) is where interactions between humans and machines occur.

A typical enterprise design will be concerned with many kinds of activity. Some of these will involve people, some will involve automated solutions, and some will involve human-computer interaction. However, these categories are not fixed; there will be a progressive migration towards automated solutions, without there necessarily being major structural changes in the design.

While, in a sufficiently abstract description, the functions performed can remain the same when such changes are made, the disciplines involved in expressing their detail are quite different; middleware providers and user interface designers use different tools and techniques. However, both disciplines make heavy use of tools. In the middleware world, tools automate generation of stubs from interface definitions and handle the incorporation of mechanisms to ensure reliability and fault tolerance. Tools applied to the user interface design, on the other hand, can produce software components to act as user proxies within the system and manage user dialogues in terms of interaction with, for example, a sequence of web forms and other pages. These tools can also be used to apply a uniform look and feel across the organization.

In the descriptions that follow, we will focus primarily on system structure, but we will indicate how the approach also enables the management of human-computer interaction, using either the same information that captures the system structure or specific information added to support this aspect of the design.

Thus, the enterprise description can be used to identify interactions between human and system-supported activities, while the information viewpoint can define data types that can be used either in system-to-system interactions or in user interfaces and the computational viewpoint can contain details of the dialogue needed to support human-computer interaction.

Introducing the support of user interfaces into the design will, in general, result in the inclusion of distinct objects into the computational design to represent each user and the proxies for these users within the supporting system. Doing so adds precision to the specification of the user interactions expected and, as we shall see in chapter 8, provides a basis for testing the correctness of conformance to the user interactions specified.

The support for user interaction is thus incorporated within the viewpoint framework, but we shall return to this topic to bring out the consequences for the individual viewpoint languages as they are discussed in following chapters.

1.7   The Right Tools for the Job

1.7.1   Reusing UML via UML4ODP

Although, as we indicated earlier, the ODP viewpoint languages are defined in an abstract way without commitment to a particular concrete notation, we do need to select such a notation before we can write a real, useful model. It does not matter particularly what notation we choose, as long as our toolchain can handle it and integrate it with others already in use, but it will help the designers to get started if the notation is already familiar.

UML [30] is currently the most popular modelling language in the industry, and most designers have some familiarity with it. Its expressive power can be increased by using the associated object constraint language (OCL) [36]. So why not use it here? The problem with UML as it stands is that it does not support the separation of concerns we want, or the structuring concepts ODP introduces to support it. UML has functional views, expressed in its diagram types, but they are closely coupled, and there is a single hierarchical namespace underpinning them. This makes the separation we want difficult to achieve.

What about model-driven engineering, then? Many MDE prototypes use UML for expressing their source and target models, don't they? Yes, they do, but that's the point. They work by translating between quite separate models, each with its own internal consistency and its own namespaces. The transformations provide the level of decoupling that is needed (see chapter 15).

With the development of these technologies, and of an increasing number of domain-specific dialects of UML, the originators of ODP returned to UML and decided that, because it was now widely accepted, it could be used in many cases to provide a familiar notation for the individual ODP viewpoint specifications. In consequence, they produced a new standard, *ISO 19793: Use of UML for ODP system specifications*, or UML4ODP for short [22]. This standard provides a profile that maps the ODP concepts to the UML notation,[3] so that they can be manipulated with conventional UML tools. A suitable plug-in to a UML tool allows consistency checking across multiple viewpoints.

Of course, ODP can be supported by other notations, tailored to other user communities, such as business process designers, as long as a similar level of tool integration can be achieved. However, in this book we will keep things simple and concentrate largely on the UML4ODP notation.

---

[3]The UML4ODP standard is based on UML 2.1.1 [30].

1.7.2 UML4ODP in a Nutshell

The UML4ODP standard defines both a UML-based notation for the expression of the ODP system specifications and an approach for structuring them using that notation, thus providing the basis for model development methods. This makes the UML4ODP notation useful not only to ODP modellers who want to use UML to describe their ODP systems, but also to UML modellers who have to deal with the specification of nontrivial systems and need some approach to structure their large UML system specifications.

UML4ODP uses standard UML concepts and relies on the standard extension mechanisms provided by UML for defining new languages and, in particular, on UML profiles. More precisely, UML4ODP defines seven related UML profiles: one for each ODP viewpoint, one for describing correspondences and one for modelling conformance in ODP system specifications (see chapter 8). All the model diagrams shown in this book are drawn using these profiles.

Thus, an ODP system specification expressed in UML4ODP consists of a single UML model stereotyped «ODP_SystemSpec» that contains a set of models, one for each viewpoint specification, each stereotyped «<X>_Spec», where <X> is the viewpoint concerned (see figure 1.4). Each viewpoint specification uses the appropriate UML profile for that language.

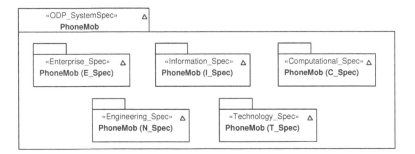

FIGURE 1.4: The viewpoints contributing to an ODP system specification, expressed using UML4ODP.

In the profiles, stereotypes are used to represent the ODP concepts as specializations of the appropriate UML metaclasses. For example, figure 1.5 shows the UML profile for the information viewpoint language, as specified in the UML4ODP standard. It defines eight stereotypes and the UML metaclasses they extend. Some of the stereotypes have associated icons (shown in the right upper corner of the stereotype box). Icons are very useful because they provide an intuitive notation to the users of the ODP specifications. This becomes particularly important in some viewpoints, such as the enterprise viewpoint. The designer must decide how much of this information to show in any particular diagram. In this book, for example, we generally show the icons, and include stereotype names where doing so helps understanding,

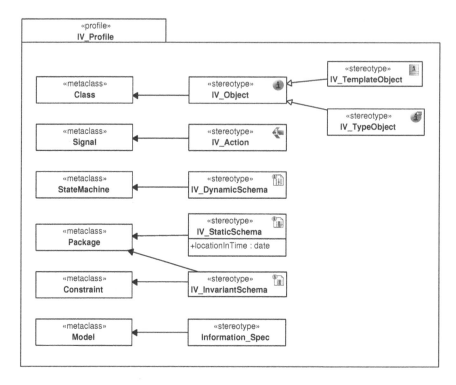

FIGURE 1.5: The UML profile for the information viewpoint.

Taken from the UML4ODP standard; for copyright, see Preface.

but omit them where the meaning is already clear, so as to avoid cluttering up some of the more complicated diagrams.

Tag definitions are also used to specify stereotype properties. For example, the tag definition locationInTime of stereotype IV_StaticSchema allows the specification of the exact location in time of the static schema being modelled. Figure 3.4 in chapter 3 shows an example of how this tag definition is used in the specification of a concrete static schema.

1.7.3 The Integrated Toolkit

Most software development now uses some form of integrated development environment (IDE), which takes care of much of the routine housekeeping concerned with building and archiving complex project structures. Eclipse [65], for example, is a particularly popular environment because of its extensibility. The same principle applies to other areas, such as business planning, and the trend is towards greater integration of the tools used, forming them into a single integrated toolchain.

One area where there has recently been a step forward in this respect is the development of *model-driven engineering* solutions, in which transformational techniques are applied to a quite abstract design, filling in detail to generate code suited to a particular environment. This process is generally not completely automatable, but reports based on test cases show that up to 85% automatic generation can be achieved in a typical database application [56]. OMG maintains an interesting library of such case studies [38].

This kind of integration is essential for the effective exploitation of a multi-viewpoint framework. Information needs to be taken from each viewpoint and combined to create a running system. As the design evolves, there need to be simple ways of checking that its parts have at least a basic level of consistency (just as compilation of a multi-package program gives some check on its structural coherence). All this requires the tools used in the different viewpoints to interwork so that checks can be made to see that the rules in the different viewpoints do not lead to contradictions.

Model-driven tools offer not only a much smoother pathway from design to implementation, but also a much more efficient basis for the management and evolution of large systems.

Marcus was sitting in on the design review to support Alex. Although the consultant was now known to the team and largely accepted, there had been teething troubles and a few bruised egos, so that support was still needed. Marcus had to admit he didn't follow a lot of the detail, but he could see that the main features of the new PhoneMob system were coming together.

It always intrigued him to see how the different groups imposed their own style on their models. He could recognize the organic style of the data modellers, with the branches and leaves growing and unfolding across the page, and could distinguish it from the Norman crypt style of the platform people, with whole solid blocks of function stacked up into stocky columns leading up to a broad vault of interconnections. The applications designers favoured tight modular balloons, kissing to exchange their messages. And the business analysts, with their narrow striped shirts, favoured road maps with the main routes and the special byways picked out with graphical symbols for all the world like service stations and tourist attractions.

But, putting aside these speculations, he knew it was not all going smoothly. There were rough edges and there were disputes. Even Marcus could see from the presentations that some things were being repeated by the different groups, but each in their own way. This needed to be sorted out.

"Look," said Alex, "there is excellent work here, but you need to move towards seeing what you are doing as part of a bigger whole, and exploit it to simplify your lives." He turned to Claire. "Here, in the initial client registration, you have a big set of classes dealing with identity, account and contact details. And here, in the billing step, you have a different presentation of roughly the same stuff." She looked hurt. "Yes, but this is a first cut; I would expect to refactor those into a common set of classes when the structure is clear." "But remember Ivor's presentation. He has exactly the same information in his customer object already. You can just reference it." "But he has too much information, and his names don't correspond to the way we look at the process." Alex smiled. "Remember what I said earlier about correspondences. You can refer to the classes in your design as being in an abstract package. Then, if you have a correspondence with the information view that renames and selects items as appropriate, the tools can construct the correct concrete classes in your view for you, based on that linkage. You don't need to do it all from scratch again."

Ivor scowled. "But then, if I change that part of my design, I might break the computational view." "Certainly, it's possible," said Alex, "but when you ask for a global check before committing, you would get a warning. However, that should be rare, and if it happens, it probably means there is a shared issue you should be discussing anyway. Without that linkage, you would still be thinking about that common part of the design in different ways, but no one would know."

Nigel waved his pencil in the air. "But that means that when the business analysts have a bright idea and decide to add a video feature to customer notifications, it ripples all the way down to the infrastructure, and the nightly builds will break! That would be ridiculous." "Of course," said Alex. "That would be silly. But what happens at the moment?" "Eleanor raises it in the weekly meeting, Claire looks at the application implications and sends me a memo, and I cost the deployment change with Trevor and Trudy. That's generally the end of the matter." Everybody laughed, except Marcus. "And we don't improve our market position," he growled.

"But hang on," said Alex, "you still have the version management to protect you from any real damage. The business guys try the change, do a check, and get a red flag. They can then start the consultation process; maybe Eleanor starts a thread to discuss it, and everyone can contribute. You can all see the branch with the new change in it and trace the flags it has generated in your own view to see the consequences, so the resolution should be much quicker and the results more reliable. In the end, you all win. And we can do the same sort of thing with most of the other overlaps we have found this afternoon."

Part II

The Viewpoints

About Part II

This part introduces the five ODP viewpoints one after another. In its final chapter, it then explains how the family of viewpoints is bound together into a coherent whole by establishing a set of correspondences between terms in the different viewpoints.

Although a book imposes a linear structure, and its sequence could be read as a journey from requirements to implementation, this structure is not intended to suggest any particular design methodology. The development of the viewpoints is best seen as consisting of a set of concurrent but interacting design processes.

Each chapter explains the concepts most central to the viewpoint concerned, and then illustrates their use by working through elements from the running example. Finally, there is some guidance on how the viewpoint specification might be structured and the way in which it relates to the other viewpoints.

Chapter 2

Enterprise Viewpoint

"I still don't quite see why we are going into so much detail on this," said Eleanor. She was meeting with Alex to work on an enterprise model for the PhoneMob, and they had started off with a fairly stressful cross-examination by Alex about its likely structure after the reorganization.

Alex looked up sharply. "Have all your projects come in on time in the last couple of years?" he asked, "or have there been any that slipped?" "Well, we are getting pretty good at predicting the development time needed. There have been a few occasions when Marcus has given us a hard time, but it's generally not really been our fault; the requirements have changed in midstream." "What was the worst slippage?" "Well, I guess last June, when we got the first release of the new system for handling e-mail acceptance of repair quotes into prerelease test before someone pointed out that a manager approval step was missing; it had never been captured in the requirements review." "Didn't your people know it was done that way?" "No; it had been in a manual part of the process, so we knew nothing about it, and didn't know to ask the right questions. We had to rework a significant part of the workflow design because just sticking the extra step in would have violated the response requirements. We missed the release target by over a month."

Alex leaned back. "And the customer design review didn't catch it?" "No, worst luck. In the old process, that step was the point where responsibility for the work moved from front office to workshop, and both thought it was being handled by requirements from the other." It was clear this whole incident was one Eleanor was still angry about, although she could understand how it had happened.

Alex smiled ruefully. "It can easily happen," he said. "Working on a small piece of the activity in isolation just isn't enough." His voice was sad and a little wistful, and he smiled sympathetically at Eleanor. "If the company had maintained a proper enterprise description of how its organizational units related to each other, and a proper view of its business processes, including all the manual parts, then you could have seen there were things not being covered. You might even have got a red flag from your design tools if some obligations were not being fulfilled. Of course, the whole idea is not just about preventing disasters — having a clear view of the organization helps improve quality generally."

"OK," said Eleanor, "I'm beginning to see how it might help, but how do you express the interplay of responsibilities between different parts of the business?" "Well, we need to focus on how business units interact. We can do that by treating them as participants in a community. This involves each participant playing a role that defines its expected behaviour and its interactions with the rest of the participants. Some assignment policies could then specify how the different participants in the organization could fulfil the roles, and who becomes responsible for what."

"That sounds like sociology to me." "No," said Alex, smiling a little, "but it's better to talk in these terms than to overload names that are already in use within the organization; doing that just causes confusion."

He turned back to the whiteboard and started to sketch out a structure.

2.1 Designing with Communities

The enterprise viewpoint defines the organizational, business and social context in which an ODP system is designed and deployed. It is primarily through using the enterprise language that the business stakeholders and the design team develop the shared understanding they need if the system is to be fit for purpose. The enterprise viewpoint should be able to help answer a set of questions about the ODP system, such as: "What is the purpose of the ODP system?" "What are the business requirements for the system?" or "Who are the key stakeholders and how do they interact with the system?"

Business processes are more flexible and less cleanly delineated than software processes, so a more flexible structuring principle than traditional modularity is needed. The right thing for a business system to do in some particular circumstances is determined by a number of overlapping sets of rules, rather than by a single algorithm; some constraints will come directly from the business process, but others will come from organizational norms, like security policies, or from agreements with trading partners, or even from legal constraints. We need to merge these various kinds of constraints. This is achieved by basing the enterprise specification on an interrelated set of **communities**.

A community defines how some set of participants should behave in order to achieve a particular **objective**. To make the rules reusable, they are expressed in terms of interactions between **roles** in the community, decoupling their definition from the details of the resources available and the responsibilities in effect at a particular instant. This is like using roles when writing the script of a play, where the author states what each character should say, but the actor actually playing a particular role is not determined until a particular performance takes place. Note that, although in this chapter we just speak of roles without always saying that they are community roles, the idea of a role

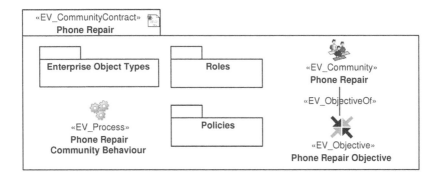

FIGURE 2.1: Anatomy of a community specification.

is general, and is used in structuring other kinds of collaboration; for example, we can also speak of roles in an interaction.

Figure 2.1 illustrates the main elements involved in specifying a community; more detail of the relationship between these key concepts is given after this initial introduction. Here, and throughout the book, the PhoneMob specification is used as a running example; further supporting detail from this specification can be found in appendix A.

First, we have the **behaviour** of the community, which is normally defined as a composition of processes addressing separate business concerns. This composition itself results in a process, and is represented in figure 2.1 as a UML activity stereotyped «EV_Process». The process is parameterized by the community's roles. In addition, the community will generally also have a number of policies, which allow aspects of its behaviour to be modified to react to changing circumstances. These policies perform an important function in allowing the community's behaviour to be modified dynamically to satisfy changing requirements. The way policies allow controlled flexibility so that the objectives can still be guaranteed as situations change is discussed in detail in chapter 10. Finally, there are declarations of a number of supporting **enterprise objects** owned by the community and used to represent its internal state and resources.

The community is described by a **community contract**. Making this description (which is effectively a community type) explicit in the specification helps the design to capture dynamic processes, such as negotiation of the rules under which the community operates; it gives a reflexive representation of the behaviour and of the roles in it, the policies and the local objects. The contract also includes a declaration of the **objective** of the community.

The high-level description typically states the **scope** and **field of application** for the enterprise specification in question. The scope is expressed in terms of the behaviour the system is to exhibit. For example, the PhoneMob ODP system may have a scope that expresses its key functions such as keeping track of all repair orders, customers, users and user locations. The field of application of the PhoneMob enterprise specification might state properties of a franchised business to which the enterprise specification applies, for example indicating that this is not, and will never be, a safety critical business system.

2.2   Identifying Roles

A community is, in essence, a collaboration; the objects fulfilling its roles agree that their objective is to achieve a stated business purpose. In simple cases, the parties performing roles in the contract, and the behaviour expressed in it, can remain the same throughout its lifetime. Alternatively, the contract may define behaviour that modifies the community membership, or changes details of its behaviour. One way of modifying behaviour dynamically is to define mutable policies (see chapter 10) for the community. Note that the community concept can be used to model the structure of a particular organization, or a collaboration between different organizations stated in terms of business contracts, service level agreements (SLAs) or as a federation between different legislative domains (see chapter 11).

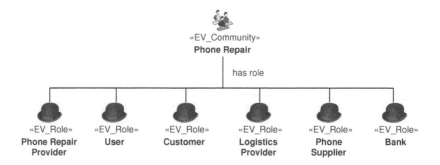

FIGURE 2.2: The business and its partners.

Figure 2.2 shows the roles involved in the top-level view of the PhoneMob business.[1] This first representation deals primarily with the positioning of the business in its environment. There is a role for the business as a whole (called the Phone Repair Provider) and roles for the main external players with whom the business deals — its customers, suppliers, banks and the PhoneMob's subcontractors, such as the logistics suppliers. When using UML4ODP, these roles

---

[1] In this book, we have chosen to use the hat as an icon for role, rather than the theatrical mask suggested in the UML4ODP standard; we feel this icon and the metaphor of "wearing a hat" are more immediately recognizable.

are represented by the stereotype «EV_Role», which are referred to in the behaviour definition of their owning community (stereotyped «EV_Community»).

In more detail, the roles are:

- The Phone Repair Provider role, which represents the PhoneMob organization as a whole. In this case we are defining a singleton entity, but in other circumstances we might be defining an organizational unit that could be instantiated many times.

- The User role, representing the actual user of the phone.

- The Customer role, representing the party that has a contractual relationship with the PhoneMob, and is responsible for paying the bills. We shall see later how separating customer and user roles lets the community definition cover a wider range of customer organizations. In some cases, both these roles may be filled by the same person.

- The Logistics Provider role, which models the use of a subcontractor to transfer the broken or repaired phones between other role players, such as users or suppliers.

- The Bank role, representing a financial institution providing billing and payment services for the customer.

- The Phone Supplier role, representing the party responsible for performing return-to-manufacturer repairs.

2.3   Organizational Structure

Later, we will look at expressing the business processes as activities within this high-level view, but, for the moment, we will concentrate on the organizational structure. Having established the environment, we now want to expose the structure of the organization, which is done by refining the community to yield a concrete service provider community. This is done by replacing the single service provider role with a number of smaller units. In this case, we can do so in two stages; first, we identify the business units involved, and then we make distinctions within them. The business units involved are based on both function and location:

- A headquarters (HQ) role, representing the central activities of the company, such as accounting and customer and supplier relationships. Policies set by this role constrain the individual branches when offering services to their users.

- A number of Branch roles, representing offices located around the world, each of which deals directly with users and their broken phones, diagnosing them and either carrying out simple repairs directly or arranging for their return to the supplier if things are more serious.

The second distinction we want to make is between the automated and manual systems within the organization. We need to make this distinction because we need to position the automated systems and user interfaces, which will be the main focus of other viewpoints, within the business activities. In our simple example, we divide each of the business units into a staff role and a system role. Note that this refinement step is applied just to the PhoneMob itself; the business partners are seen as black boxes here, since we do not wish to make any assumptions about their internal structure. These two refinement steps lead to the set of roles shown in figure 2.3.

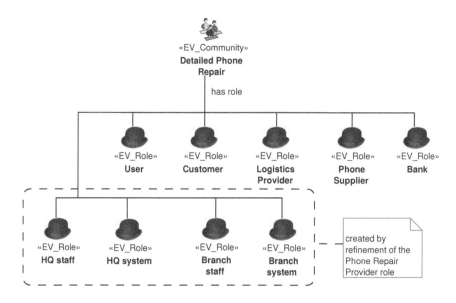

FIGURE 2.3: The roles of the Detailed Phone Repair community.

The design is already getting quite complicated, so we divide the system into a number of distinct activities, seen as smaller subcommunities. Each of these subcommunities must operate in a way that is consistent with the contract of the complete community and this will be expressed by associating each of them with a specific simplified contract. The key activities are repair, customer liaison, performance review and negotiation of contracts with the subcontractors dealing with logistics and supply. Each can be described by a simplified view of the complete community, containing just the roles engaged in the particular activity. For example, the repair process does not need to be concerned with the negotiation of customer contracts, and local branch repair centres delegate financial concerns, like contact with a customer's bank, to be handled centrally in headquarters. As a result, the community directly involved in the repair process at a local centre, which we call the Branch Repair Provision community, can be reduced to having the set of roles shown in figure 2.4.

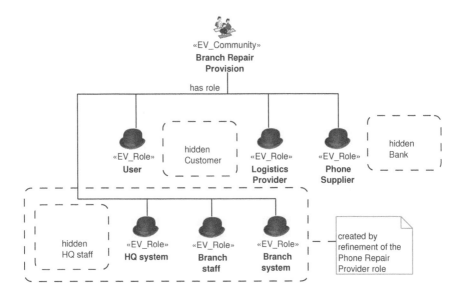

FIGURE 2.4: The roles of the Branch Repair Provision community.

The whole sequence of developing the local repair process roles thus starts with the abstract role set for the Phone Repair community, introduced in figure 2.2. This is transformed to give the Detailed Phone Repair community, in figure 2.3, by replacing the single repair service provider with the interaction of headquarters and local branch roles and by differentiating between staff and system participants. In a second step, just the roles concerned with the local repair process in the branch are selected, yielding the Branch Repair Provision community, with the role set shown in figure 2.4.

2.4   Roles and Role Filling

Roles are the glue that holds the enterprise specification together. There is some similarity between the use of roles in a community and the software concept of formal parameters for a procedure. Both enable reuse by providing a local identity that can be referenced in the reusable part of the specification and which is then linked to an appropriate external item at the specific point of use. In this case, a role is referenced in the community behaviour and linked to the objects filling the role in each particular instance of its use. As a result, these objects are required to satisfy the behaviour of the community.

The objects filling a community's roles will, in general, each have their own lifecycle; they may already be engaged in other activities in the enterprise before they fill a particular role, and may go on with other activities after they have ceased to play that role. On the other hand, the responsibilities of a role may be transferred from one object to another, if the rules of the community allow. As long as an object satisfies the behavioural conditions stated in the role definition, it can be assigned to the role and thus participate in the community, contributing to the community objectives (and also helping to achieve its own goals). These conditions can be related to certain competency requirements for joining the community (for example, only an accredited logistics organization can fulfil the role of logistics provider), to security policies covering authentication and access control and to performance obligations such as might be found in the repair services SLA between the phone repair service and its customers. Formally, this corresponds to each role having an associated role type, and there being a requirement that the object filling the role should satisfy this type. Again, we can draw a parallel here with the rules governing type checking and implicit casting when using formal parameters in a programming language.

There is a question of modelling style that arises when deciding whether model elements are expressed in terms of instances or types. An enterprise modeller may often use a shorthand style, referring simply to the object type, talking about a Phone User object as filling the User role when they really mean that there exists some anonymous enterprise object whose type is Phone User and which fills the User role.

A community's behaviour is stated in terms of actions that the enterprise objects assigned to the roles are expected to exhibit — that is, constraints on when the actions may occur. The way this is expressed depends on the style adopted; some possible techniques are to use state machines, event sequencing or a process-oriented style.

A role is always defined with respect to its containing community, which owns the namespace for its roles. This means that roles in different communities can be distinct in spite of having the same name; for example, it is legitimate to define a Customer role in both the Phone Repair community and the Logistics Provision community. However, these will each have their own behaviour, which is derived in each case from the community in which they are defined.

At any point in time at most one enterprise object can fill a particular role in a community, but different objects can fill the same role at different times; for example, a specific logistics organization is assigned the Logistics Provision role, as a result of an underlying business contract with the PhoneMob, but different contracts can be established in different epochs, each with a distinct logistics organization. Note, however, that a community may define several roles of a specific role type, each with the same behavioural constraints, allowing for multiple objects to share responsibilities in a community. This can be specified by associating an appropriate cardinality constraint with the role, as is the case with the Branch staff role in the Detailed Phone Repair community.

In general, one object can play several roles in the same community. For example, in the PhoneMob scenario, an individual can play both the User role and the Customer role in the Phone Repair community, although, for organizational customers, these will usually be filled by separate objects (see the following section).

Finally, the community specification may include additional constraints on the filling of roles. The most familiar example of this is the requirement for dynamic separation of duties, in which there is a requirement that two or more roles must be filled by different objects; for example, where a financial transaction cannot be both proposed and approved by the same individual.

2.5   More than One Community

Any problem of significant complexity will generally require the use of flexible structuring techniques, and this is particularly true of enterprise specifications. If communities are to be kept sufficiently simple to be understood, they need to be combined, and this can be done in a number of ways.

The way communities are combined will be chosen to support the modelling of complex organizational structures, closely reflecting the real-world environments within which ODP systems are positioned. These structures can be expressed in terms of relationships between communities and of the policies that govern their establishment and change.

A community as a whole can be seen as an enterprise object, and so can itself fill a role in some higher-level community. Thus, in a top-down design approach we can start with a general view and then refine it by using subcommunities to fill the top-level roles. The object resulting from considering a community as a whole is called a ***community object***.

For example, we can capture the behaviour of a logistics provider, perhaps to express details of their collection and delivery procedures, by introducing a Logistics Provision community; the community object representing this can then fill the Logistics Provider role in the Phone Repair community (see figure 2.5). Note, however, that there are some additional constraints that need to be stated in making this linkage. Consider the Green Transport object, which is the community object that is going to be refined when defining the Logistics Provision community. This fills the Logistics Provider role in the Phone Repair community, and the way that some of its own roles are filled is already determined as a result. The Customer role in the Logistics Provi-

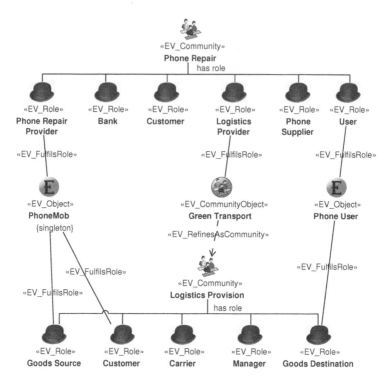

FIGURE 2.5: Using role filling to link two communities.

sion community is no longer just any object, but becomes the object filling the Phone Repair Provider role in the Phone Repair community, which is the PhoneMob itself. Since the customer is, in this case, having their own goods shipped, they also fill either the Goods Source or Goods Destination role, with the corresponding destination or source being filled by the Phone Supplier or User. In figure 2.5, the User role is the destination and the PhoneMob is the source. As long as these constraints are satisfied, we can use any logistics provider able to offer a community object whose type matches the role type in our higher-level community.

Another way in which two or more communities can interact is by having one or more roles from the different communities filled by a single shared object. Since the behaviour of this object is constrained by each of the roles it fills, there is then an indirect linkage of the various communities involved. This can be used to merge constraints arising from different organizational units. For example, the Phone Repair community in figure 2.2 distinguished two roles relating to their clients: a Customer role concerned with the agreement to use and pay for the service, and a User role concerned with using a phone and requesting specific repairs. A simple community called the CustomerOrg community is introduced to capture the linkage of these roles. This allows us to express how the organization's contract manager constrains who can request work to be done under the repair agreement.

If a single enterprise object, such as a salesman, fulfils the Employee role in the CustomerOrg community and, at the same time, fulfils the User role in the Phone Repair community, then the behaviours of the two communities are coupled. Similarly, a single infrastructure manager object might fill both the Contract Manager role in the CustomerOrg community and the Customer role in the Phone Repair community. This linkage might, for example, model the need for the user to be authorized by the contract manager in the customer organization, and to have this checked against the customer contract held by the Phone Repair Provider role (see figure 2.6).

In some cases, we want to couple two communities in such a way that two roles are always linked, whatever object fulfils them. This is often the case when building a hierarchy of communities. In our scenario, for example, there is a requirement that a particular HQ system enterprise object fulfils the HQ system role in the Detailed Phone Repair community and also the role with the same name in the simplified Branch Repair Provision community; this is achieved by placing a role-filling constraint on the role in the Branch Repair Provision community. We require the HQ system role there to be filled by

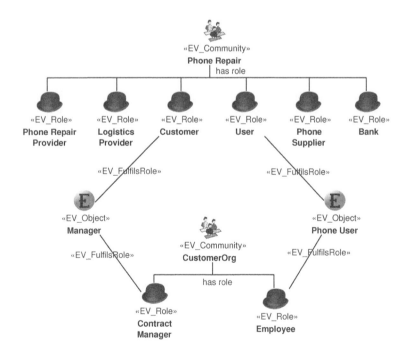

FIGURE 2.6: Linking the Phone Repair and CustomerOrg communities.

whatever object fills the HQ system role in the Detailed Phone Repair community where the Branch Repair Provision community object fulfils the Branch role. There will also be a refinement relation between the two role types.

Finally, a community can, as part of its behaviour, create another community, possibly, but not necessarily, to fulfil one of its own roles. This is similar to the familiar factory design pattern; for example, a headquarters community can create a new Branch Repair Provision community when expanding its territory.

2.6   Community Behaviour

So far, we have concentrated on the way objects are linked to community behaviour by using the concept of a role. We now turn to the way in which such behaviour is specified. But first, it should be noted that the behaviour is not just concerned with actions performed by players of roles. Roles are concerned with linking the behaviour into a broader picture, but, as we saw previously when introducing the elements of a community, the community may also introduce additional enterprise objects that are only of concern within its specification, and so have a scope local to it.

For example, a particular realization of a branch might have internal procedures involving some actor, such as a storekeeper, without this object actually being exposed in the broader specification as a role. The fact that there is a storekeeper is not visible to objects filling roles in the Phone Repair community, and is a purely local matter for the branch concerned. People sometimes ask whether such local objects should be seen as roles, but doing so complicates the external view of the community without bringing any real benefit, so they are better kept as having a local scope and can therefore be simple enterprise objects.

Roles or local enterprise objects can be involved in behaviour in a number of different ways. Firstly, the enterprise language allows distinctions to be made regarding the way enterprise objects participate in interactions. If an object participates in performing the action, it is termed an **actor** with respect to that action. For example, the object fulfilling the Branch staff role is an actor who initiates the Inspect Phone action. If an object is essential for the performance of an action, requiring allocation or possibly being used up, it is termed a **resource** with respect to that action. For example, the Loan Handset objects form a pool of resources; so do various spare parts. Further, if an enterprise object is mentioned in an interaction, but is not an active participant in it, then the object is termed an **artefact** with respect to that action; one example is the User Handset enterprise object. All these qualifications are with respect to particular actions; an artefact in one action may be an actor in another.

Secondly, the enterprise language accommodates the expression of business services. A *business service* is a particular description of behaviour that focuses on the functionality or capability provided by one party to the others who can then use the service to satisfy their own business needs, resulting in some added value to them. A business service can be provided by a single role in a community or it may involve several roles; for example, the phone repair service of the Phone Repair community is provided by the Phone Repair Provider role (encompassing HQ system and Branch staff roles of the Detailed Phone Repair community jointly), which both interact with the service users. This business service is the central part of the Phone Repair community and can be used by other members in the Phone Repair community, such as the Customer and the User.

Business services can be made public by a community; that is to say, they can be used not only by the objects filling other roles in the same community but may also be accessed by the behaviour of different communities. Note that a business service can be supported by one or more technical services, described in the computational viewpoint, and that these different uses of the concept of service are in line with the current SOA frameworks, such as the *OASIS Reference Architecture* [46].

A *process* is a specific form of behaviour expressed in terms of sequential or concurrent ordering between *steps*. Each business step may consume and produce information. A process will thus involve one or more community roles, which perform actions associated with business steps. Each process is aimed at satisfying an objective, and many processes can be defined in a community, each of which contributes to the overall objective of the community. This abstract definition of the process can be further refined to give more detailed process definitions represented in notations such as BPMN, or UML activity diagrams (as in UML4ODP).

Interactions are the basic elements of the community behaviour. Each interaction indicates which roles it involves, and what part they each play in it. For example, in a message exchange requesting a repair, the community roles of User and Branch staff may be involved, with the user acting as initiator and the branch as responder (where initiator and responder are interaction roles, not community roles). Multiple interactions can then be composed into sequences or concurrent activities, forming extended pieces of behaviour, building up first steps and then complete processes. Thus, simple interactions can be used to build up control flows, yielding a style of behaviour familiar from process modelling.

The complete behaviour of a community can generally be decomposed into a number of distinct processes. In the PhoneMob (see figure 2.7), we have, for example, the repair process, concerned with dealing with a faulty phone, and two separate administrative processes, one dealing with the negotiation of service levels with a logistics provider and the other providing assessment and reporting of key performance indicators. Finally, we have a management process concerned with the maintenance of the phone loan policy.

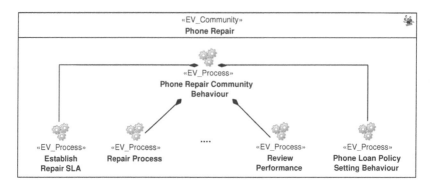

FIGURE 2.7: Community behaviour expressed as a set of processes.

2.6.1   A Community Process

Let us look further at one of the constituent processes in the community behaviour. Figure 2.8 shows the definition of the process concerned with the lifecycle of a single phone repair, in the case of a VIP user who is entitled to

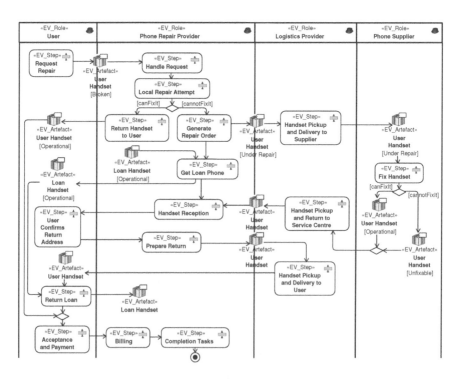

FIGURE 2.8: The Repair Process in the Phone Repair community.

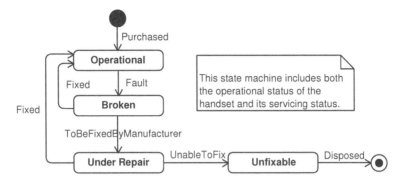

FIGURE 2.9: The handset state machine.

be issued a loan phone while her own is being dealt with. The roles involved are the user, phone repair provider, logistics provider and phone supplier. The Phone Repair community has other roles, but they are not directly involved in this process.

Several of the flows in this figure are marked as referencing a user handset as an artefact, shown as an «EV_Artefact»; the flow from the Request Repair step is one example. In this specification, we have chosen to use an artefact reference to highlight the fact that the flow is associated with the physical transfer of the handset concerned between roles. After the request repair step not only does the process flow transfer to the phone repair provider, but also responsibility for the broken handset is transferred. Note that the artefact is decorated with its assumed state [broken]; this state is drawn from the state machine defined for handsets (see figure 2.9). In places where the state is uncertain, such as on the return of the loan handset, this decoration is omitted.

The steps in this representation of the process are comparatively coarse grained. Thus, for example, the detail involved in saving the user's state and SIM is subsumed into the Handle Request step when the phone is first received, and the restoring of this state forms part of the Prepare Return step. These details are important in ensuring the user receives a high quality experience, but the choice of exactly what order the necessary actions are taken in is not of concern to the user or customer roles.

2.6.2   Refining the Process

The behaviour shown in figure 2.8 is generic; it applies to all repair activities in the organization and is expressed in terms of the roles shown in figure 2.2. It can be refined by each branch independently, in ways that suit their local situation. Figure 2.10 shows one such refinement, defining the

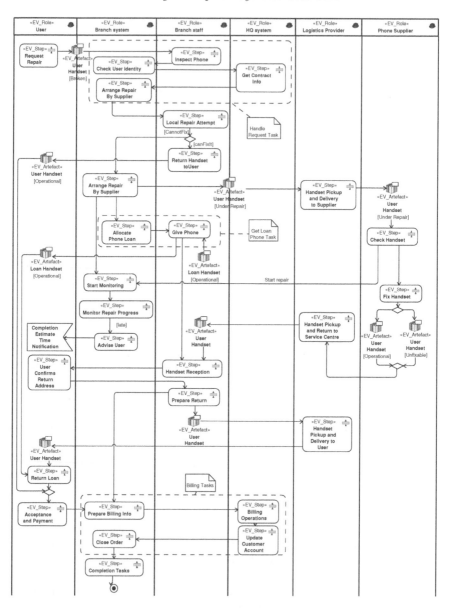

FIGURE 2.10: The repair process as seen from one of the branches.

Branch Repair Provision community. This community has a community object that offers one way of fulfilling the top-level branch role.

This process adds detail; it now distinguishes between the different internal roles of the PhoneMob organization, using the refined roles shown in figure 2.4. However, the process as seen by the external parties should be essentially unchanged. In fact, this is not the case, since some additional detail of the user interaction has been made visible, which involves providing the user with up to date progress information about the repair. This in turn requires that additional progress signals and a query facility need to be provided by the Phone Supplier role so that progress of return to manufacturer repairs can be monitored. These have been added at this stage to underline that, although ideally this part of the design would be a transparent process from the point of view of the external parties, in practice it will be an iteration, and in the real design we would expect tooling facilities to assist in propagating these additions back into the abstract view.

We mentioned previously that community behaviour could be managed by the definition of mutable policies (see chapter 10). Doing so narrows the gap between specification and implementation, since a policy needs to be updated at runtime, either by replacing some code fragment or adding indirection, so that the policy is accessed as a separate service. Often, the policy is written in a separate language, designed to make runtime interpretation straightforward. A policy may take a number of forms, being either a small fragment of behaviour, controlling a particular decision, or a constraint or invariant applied to a broader behavioural scope. In either case, the way the policy is to be changed forms part of the community behaviour.

2.7   Accountability and Related Concepts

The enterprise language includes a family of concepts for expressing responsibility, called accountability concepts. Their aim is to support the traceability of obligations in the overlapping and interacting communities that make up the enterprise. The basic idea here is that, despite a significant amount of automation and use of supporting agents, there are *parties* that have broader responsibilities derived from some social or legal framework. These may be natural persons, such as the Phone User, or organizations, such as the logistics provider Green Transport in figure 2.5. In either case, we need to be able to trace the way that their rights and responsibilities are linked to individual system actions and to their consequences.

To help do this, the enterprise language defines a number of kinds of action that have different consequences for the future behaviour of the system; distinguishing these different kinds of action provides a framework for analysing the way responsibilities evolve. First, a *commitment* is an action that results in the object performing it undertaking some obligation. Obligations can then be passed on by their current holder (the *principal*) performing a *delegation* in which obligation is passed to an *agent*. An object can also make facts known in its environment by performing a *declaration*. This may be the result of some analysis of available information to derive more general information by performing an ***evaluation***. Finally, an object may perform an action which is a ***prescription***, creating a rule that constrains the future behaviour of the community. Prescriptions provide a flexible and powerful mechanism for changing the system's business rules at runtime, enabling its dynamic adaptation to respond to business changes and new needs.

Expressing accountability for actions allows the party responsible for the changes in the rules to be identified, which is something that fits well with the deontic nature of enterprise policies, because the party must be authorized in order to perform the prescription. These concepts can be used to express various governance frameworks. We can see these mechanisms at work in the PhoneMob example when a new contract is established with an organization fulfilling the role of Customer. The contract may be enacted by clicking on a button in some web page, but it is binding on the PhoneMob because the organization has performed a ***delegation*** to the Chief Information Officer, who is the ***party*** taking responsibility for the information system that acts as her ***agent*** in accepting the web interaction that enacts the agreement.

2.8   Quality of Service and Other Constraints

So far, the treatment of behaviour has concentrated on the sequence of tasks to be performed — the so-called functional aspects of the processes. However, we also need to be able to place constraints on various aspects of the quality of performance, such as how quickly things are done, how low the failure probability should be, or how good the security properties should be. This typically involves decorating the basic behaviour, which is a set of permitted event sequences, with conditions on what variations in performance are allowed.

For example, there will be policies that arise from a service level agreement between the PhoneMob and a VIP customer, such as obligations on the PhoneMob to observe response times for repairs and, in the case of violations, to provide compensation, such as arranging for replacement of a troublesome user handset.

This is a complex issue because there are many dependencies between the parties, and any quality guarantee asked from one community member is contingent on proper behaviour by others. For example, a requirement that the logistics provider shall deliver a shipment within 12 hours is contingent on the receiving party being available to take delivery before the end of the period. In general, any obligation placed on an object depends on guarantees of support given by its environment.

The details of how such quality constraints are expressed depend on the property being considered, and would take us beyond the scope of this book, but this is an area where much research is currently underway, and new proposals are emerging [51, 68, 69].

2.9 Identifying the System's User Interfaces

The enterprise specification identifies the points at which users interact with the supporting system. For example, figure 2.10 shows a process definition that contains interactions between the role Branch system and the roles User, Branch staff, HQ system, Logistics Provider, and Phone Supplier. In this diagram, at least the interactions between the User or Branch staff (roles that are filled by human beings) and the Branch system (fulfilled by a computer system) occur at a visible user interface. We will concentrate on these because the other roles are not expressed in sufficient detail in this figure to determine whether the interactions are between humans and machine or machine and machine.

The nature of the interactions can be expressed in many different ways, but a common approach is one that divides the design activity into three separate but related aspects (or, in our terminology, viewpoints), which are concerned with content, navigation and presentation.

- *Content* focuses on the persistent information handled by the system. In hypermedia systems, the content viewpoint may include not only raw data about the entities managed by a traditional system (orders, customers or inventory items) but also more complex entities, such as images, video clips, audio tracks and animations.

- *Navigation* deals with how the content can be accessed; it covers which content items can be visited and how a user can move from one to another. Navigation thus establishes the possible paths that the user can take through the content maintained by the system.

- *Presentation* deals with the visualization of the content and of the various interactive elements that support the functionality of the system.

These views can be mapped into the RM-ODP viewpoints in quite a natural way. In the enterprise viewpoint, we are concerned primarily with an abstract view of navigation. The other aspects are dealt with in different viewpoints. The content elements are precisely those represented in the information viewpoint and the computational viewpoint will address how the broad navigational flows are realized. Presentation is described in the engineering viewpoint, where the presentation styles and templates are specified — at the end of the day these elements belong to the same category as the message

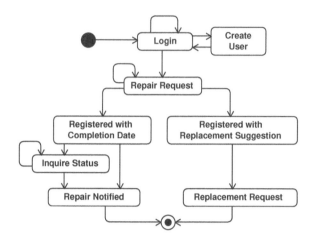

FIGURE 2.11: Navigation state machine.

data formats that need to be specified for the computer-to-computer interactions. Finally, the ODP technology viewpoint imposes some constraints on the presentation, including, for instance, usability and accessibility standards that need to be considered in the specifications.

In the enterprise viewpoint, we are concerned with the functionality available for obtaining and manipulating data, and the actions that the system will take as a result. Intuitively, navigation deals with the sequence in which enterprise objects and artefacts will be visited and modified.

A navigation specification can be obtained from the models of the enterprise specification by focusing on the interactions between the role pairs identified previously and extracting the state machine describing just these interactions (see figure 2.11). Such a diagram indicates the sequence in which information is requested and provided in the steps of the dialogue between the user and the machine. Each state will correspond to a group of pages or forms, displayed to the user or soliciting information from them. The transitions mark the stages in the progress of the dialogue.

2.10   Writing Enterprise Specifications

The ODP enterprise language does not prescribe any particular method for building the enterprise specification of a system, as the approach taken will depend very much on the system being specified, the business that it will support and the constraints that arise from the environment in which the system will operate. For this example, the following process has been followed:

1. Identify the communities with which the system is involved, their objectives and the roles involved in them.

2. Identify the enterprise objects within each community.

3. Define the behaviour required to fulfil the objectives of the communities. This may be in the form of processes, their constituent actions and the community roles or local enterprise objects performing them.

4. Define any constraints on the way roles can be filled by enterprise objects.

5. Identify the policies that govern the behaviour.

6. Identify any behaviours that may change the rules that govern the system, and the policies that govern such behaviours (changes in the structure, behaviour or policies of a community can occur only if the specification includes some behaviour that can cause those changes).

7. Identify the actions that involve accountability of the different parties, and the possible delegations.

8. Identify any behaviour that may change the structure or the membership of each community during its lifetime, and the policies that govern such behaviour.

Of course, the order of these activities need not necessarily be linear, and not all activities will be appropriate in all modelling situations.

Alex held open the swing door, with its engraved glass panel decorated with climbing plants — hops, he supposed — and Eleanor walked past him into the bar, her three-quarter length dark tan jacket speckled with rain. It had been a long session struggling with their enterprise model, and they were both in need of a break. They took their drinks to a corner table. The place was in traditional city style, divided into small bays by plush bench seats, upholstered using small brass tacks, and with backs rising to form shoulder height screens of machine-turned wooden columns finished in a heavy light-devouring varnish.

"Here's to modelling," she said, sipping her Shiraz, "although I still don't see how all this organizational stuff is really going to help us build the systems."

He sighed. "How long have you been in this business?" "About ten years, and before that five as an analyst." "Well then, were the systems you started on giving the same support we are aiming for today?" She thought briefly. "No, they were pretty basic separate applications; what we do now is much better integrated." "And you must agree that trend will continue." She nodded, the light glinting from the jewelled lizard that was frozen climbing the contour of her right ear. "That means time invested in capturing organizational detail today is an investment in making it easier to introduce tomorrow's systems," he said. "Besides which, it helps promote understanding between business types and systems designers — avoiding what the trendies would call the *cognitive dissonance*."

She looked thoughtful. "But where do you stop? You could just go on adding business rules and goals, and it would get harder and harder as you tackled the less tangible aspects like legal and social responsibilities." "You have to be pragmatic, of course, and look just a little bit further into the future than the minimum, but think where we may be going. What will you be doing in twenty-five years time?" "Enjoying a world cruise on a fat pension, I sincerely hope," she said. "But I see what you are getting at. And the emphasis on roles in communities rather than individuals is for the same reason?" "Yes," he said, "and on a quite short timescale, so that you end up with a set of reusable building blocks, and can respond to organizational change. This is helped, of course, by taking a model-driven approach, so that changes to business models can be applied to the running systems with a minimum of recoding."

There was a pause while she went up to the bar for more drinks. "Isn't there a problem here?" she asked as she opened a packet of crisps, neatly slitting the aluminized Mylar with one burgundy nail. "If we build everything from business models, aren't the technical designers like us heading for a more mundane job?" "I don't think so," he mused, selecting one of the few unbroken crisps, "the way I see it, the really accurate enterprise models are going to be the crown jewels of the organization; building and maintaining these models is not easy and their custodians will have a central role in the business, probably more so than at present."

"What about the architectural consultants, then?" she asked, with a challenging tilt of her head. "What does the future hold for them?" He grinned. "Personally, I've always fancied myself as a jewel thief," he said, taking a deep swallow of his warm, dark beer.

Chapter 3

Information Viewpoint

"Come in, Ivor," Marcus said. "You want to talk to us?" He was sitting not behind his clear, stylish light-ash desk, but by a long table under the window, which supported a huge flat screen and was covered in piles of reports, pert charts and trade magazines. Eleanor was already occupying one of the chrome and leather visitor's chairs. Ivor took the other and turned towards Marcus. He looked tense.

"I think we need to talk about how we organize things. This new approach is changing the balance and our way of working, and that has consequences. I've been Compliance Officer for three years, and I've been very happy to be responsible for seeing that we had the right type and quality of information to fulfil our statutory obligations. I came into the current project with that brief, but the information modelling that is going on here is much more central to the design activity. It just doesn't fit under compliance."

Marcus and Eleanor exchanged glances. "Yes, we can see that," Marcus said, leaning back in his chair. "The emphasis is changing and we must make the organization respond. What do you suggest we should do about it?" "Well, I think we should establish a new responsibility for creating and maintaining the necessary information models. It will need dual reporting, looking to both the CIO and the Compliance Office to ensure all the requirements are covered."

Eleanor looked at her folder of notes. "I agree we need a new responsibility," she said, "and that it needs the muscle to make our developers take the centrally defined types seriously. But the skills needed are about maintaining a repository that plays an active role in the development, not a monitoring role. We should pick one of our proven developers who is sympathetic to the approach and give them the brief of establishing the necessary processes. They would need at least two staff reporting to them initially."

Marcus stood up and walked over to his desk. "OK, so we are in agreement that a new structure is needed. I don't buy the dual reporting idea, though; that kind of structure has all sorts of problems. We will bring the new position in at planning group level, reporting to the CIO, like the other development and operation leads, but with an obligation to get model sign-off with your people, Ivor, before key design commitment steps." Ivor was tight-lipped, but not devastated; he had expected this ruling, but he knew in his heart that something along these lines was going to be needed. "Do you have someone in mind?"

Eleanor smiled. "I was thinking of Ira Vernon; he has the modelling experience and was Release Manager for the Janus Two project — he did a good job there." "What? The guy with the bootlace ties and that pretentious blue and silver clip? He's from Texas, isn't he? Seems rather detached."

"I think he is from Arizona, and very proud of his family; I know the bolo clip is Zuni; I'd like some of their fine turquoise stuff myself." Marcus cut in. "How he dresses is not the issue; would he make a commitment to the job?" "Yes, I believe he would. I think he can really see the benefits and wants to make it happen." "OK, he'll be reporting to you, so I trust your judgement. We'll meet with him and then you do an initial job description for the internal announcement and we'll work on procedures. Do you see any problems with implementation? You first, Ivor."

"Well, as always, the problem is in stopping people from taking well-intended shortcuts, and so duplicating definitions. We need to stress the importance of having a single source for data items in our code review process, and in staff induction." Eleanor nodded. "Yes, training is important, but so is responsiveness. One of the things Ira will have to do is ensure people don't see common models as a nice ideal but a practical bottleneck. There have to be rapid change processes for the information view."

"But we are also facing a culture change in the content of the models. People just aren't used to centralized behaviour constraints; they are always more prepared to use templates for data structures than for interaction sequences. We need to work on the tool vendors for better ways of refactoring behaviour; there may be some useful plug-ins out there that would help."

"OK," Marcus said, glancing out of the window at the gathering clouds, "you have an intern starting — why don't you set them on to doing a search. One final thing; are we sure that taking this direction will improve quality?"

Eleanor paused. "Well, you know Alex did a trawl through our trouble tickets when he was first getting involved. He reckoned almost 60% of our faults fixed were attributable to errors in code that duplicated something already done correctly elsewhere in the system. Mostly the smaller things, of course, but still a major hassle taken overall."

Marcus nodded. "Fine, let's do it. Eleanor, you'll let me have that draft job spec by this evening? Then I think we are done." He turned to his screen to check for messages; the meeting was over.

3.1 The Primacy of Information

The goal of the information viewpoint is to model the shared information that is manipulated by the system, in order to provide a common understanding to all parties. In this viewpoint the focus is on the information itself, without considering further platform-specific or implementation details, such as how the data is represented, implemented or distributed. The information viewpoint is also independent from the computational interfaces and functions that manipulate the data, or the nature of the technology used to store it. In this way, what we get is a common abstract model for the shared information in the system, which can be used to ensure its consistent interpretation by all stakeholders.

Thus, the objective of this viewpoint is similar to the aim in having data dictionaries for achieving interoperability between all interested parties, or the goal of ontologies for providing a common and unique interpretation of the shared information entities of a particular domain.

The information viewpoint should be able to answer a set of questions about the system, such as: "What are the data types of the information that the system will handle?" "What are the relationships between these types?" "How will the state of the data in the system evolve as the system operates?" "What are the allowable actions that the system will accept, and how will they affect the state of the data?" or "What are the constraints on the data and its processing?"

To respond to these questions, the information viewpoint uses the ***information language***, which provides a set of elements and constructs to model the information specification of a system.

3.2 The Elements of the Information Language

An information specification defines the information handled by the system and the rules governing the processing of such information. It does this by defining a configuration of information objects, the behaviour of these objects, the actions that can happen and a set of constraints that should always hold for this collection of elements. Let's describe each of these elements, one by one.

Information objects model the data handled by the ODP system about entities in the real world. Information objects, just like any other ODP objects, exhibit identity, state and behaviour, and interact with other information objects. Examples of information objects are the handset with serial number "SN33433/09", the user called "Joe Smith", or the repair order with number "2010-VIP-0003".

Every information object has a ***type***, which is a rule (strictly speaking, a ***predicate***) that characterizes the set of objects that share a common set of features and a given behaviour. Information object types can be considered to be similar to abstract data types in programming languages. Examples of information object types are Handset, User or RepairOrder.

Information actions model the information processing in the system. Every action of interest for modelling purposes is associated with at least one object. Actions also have types, which characterize the sets of actions that share particular properties. An example of an information action is the request by user "Joe Smith" for the repair of the user handset with serial number "SN33433/09" at the PhoneMob service centre in downtown Amsterdam. The corresponding action type is RepairRequest, whose parameters are a user handset, a user and a PhoneMob service centre. Note that this is an abstract action, independent of the more detailed functional specification to be dealt with in the next chapter.

Actions cause state changes in the objects that participate in them. For example, after a RepairRequest action the state of the information object User Handset is initialized to Broken — see figure 3.3. These state changes are described by means of dynamic schemata,[1] as discussed later.

Apart from these elements, the information language also defines three kinds of structure (called a ***schema***); this allows us to organize the information specification in terms of the behaviour of the information objects, described by a set of ***dynamic schemata***; the constraints that apply to the objects and their behaviours, described by a set of ***invariant schemata***; and a configuration of information objects at some moment in time, described by a set of ***static schemata***.

The different kinds of schema may apply to the whole system, or they may apply to particular domains within it.

A ***dynamic schema*** specifies how the information evolves as the system operates, describing the allowable state changes of one or more information objects. A dynamic schema can, for instance, describe what happens when a valid request for repairing a handset is added to the system (figure 3.3), or express the overall behaviour of User objects. A state change involving a set of objects can be regarded as an interaction between those objects.

In addition to describing state changes, a dynamic schema can also describe the creation and deletion of information objects. For example, a RepairRequest action results in the creation of a RepairOrder information object and, optionally, of a Loan object if the user is allowed to have a loan handset during the repair process and there is a free loan handset in the shop.

An ***invariant schema*** is a set of predicates constraining one or more information objects that must always be true, for all valid behaviours of the system. It can describe the types of the information objects, their relationships, and the constraints on those types and those relationships. The predicate constrains the possible states and state changes of the objects to which it applies. The behaviour specified in any dynamic schema is subject to the constraints of the invariant schemata. For instance, an invariant schema can constrain the values of a given information object, or the occurrence of an action, such as "Repair orders can only be placed by users whose companies

---

[1]In English, the plural of schema is *schemata*.

are known by the system." An example of such an invariant schema is shown in figure 3.1.

A *static schema* models assertions that must be true at a single moment in time. A common use of a static schema is to specify a given state of a set of information objects, in situations of particular interest to the modeller. For instance, it might describe the final state of a successful repair order.

3.3 Writing Information Specifications

This section describes how to use the concepts and structuring rules of the information language to write an ODP information specification. We need to describe the process of developing the specification, and the notation to use. RM-ODP does not impose any methodology to build the information specifications, but, to illustrate the ideas, we will follow a simple process by which we specify:

1. The types of the information objects and the types of the relationships between information objects.

2. The types of the information actions that can happen during the operation of the system.

3. A set of dynamic schemata that describe the behaviour of the objects when the actions occur.

4. A set of invariant schemata that describe the constraints on the system elements.

5. A set of static schemata which provide instantaneous views of the system or of any of its constituent objects.

There are many possible options for representing the information language concepts, depending on the experience and skills of the information modeller; Entity-Relationship Models (ERM), Object Role Models (ORM) or UML class diagrams can all be used. In this book, we will make use of the corresponding UML4ODP profile, which provides a set of UML elements to write information specifications in UML.

3.3.1 Information Object Types

In the first place, we need to specify the types of the information objects that model the data being handled by our ODP system. Information objects are generally specified in terms of their types, which in UML are expressed by classes stereotyped as «IV_Object».

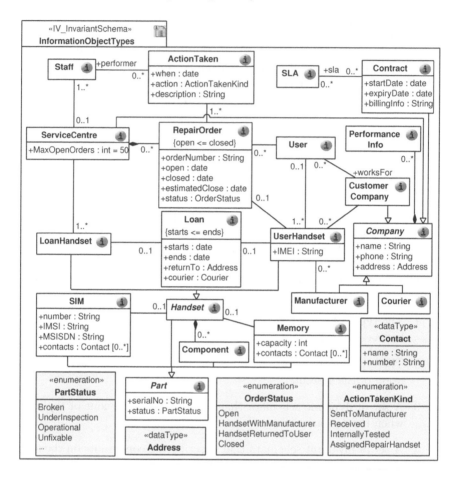

FIGURE 3.1: Invariant schema showing information object types.

Figure 3.1 shows the ODP information object types of the PhoneMob information specification. Note that the information specification captures the information handled by the system, and there is no need to represent the computerized system itself (in contrast to the enterprise viewpoint specification).

The class diagram in figure 3.1 also expresses the allowed relationships between the information object types. For example, it defines that an information object representing a service centre should be related to the information objects that represent its staff, to the set of loan handsets owned by the shop (either in stock, or given to VIP users while their phones get fixed), and to the set of repair orders for which the centre is responsible. In turn, the information objects that represent such orders are related to the information objects that represent the broken handsets, the users that took them to the shop, and the records logging the different actions that have been performed on the broken phone since the repair order was opened.

Furthermore, the model specifies constraints on the kinds of objects and the kinds of associations that can appear in a valid information object configuration for the system (in terms of the multiplicities of the association ends or specific constraints on some of the objects, for instance).

All of these elements are defined within a UML package that is stereotyped as an «IV_InvariantSchema», which represents an ODP information invariant schema.

3.3.2   Information Action Types

In the information viewpoint, actions are used mainly for describing events that cause state changes of information objects. Figure 3.2 shows some of the action types of the PhoneMob system.

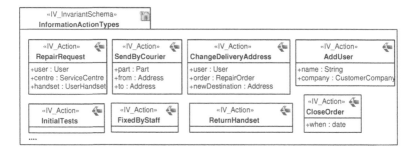

FIGURE 3.2: Invariant schema showing selected information action types.

In the UML representation, the information actions are expressed as action types within the invariant schema package. Information action types are expressed by UML signals stereotyped «IV_Action». Attributes of the signals represent the information conveyed by the ODP interactions expressed by such signals. Thus, the instances of the classes that represent the action occurrences will be expressed by signals, sent or received by the state machines of the corresponding information objects (see next section). Internal actions are expressed as internal transitions of the state machine for the information object concerned.

3.3.3   Dynamic Schemata

UML state machines can be used to describe the behaviour of information objects; state changes are triggered by signals that express information actions. Thus, the state machines express dynamic schemata. Note that a signal causes changes in all the state machines that define a transition for it, reflecting the fact that an ODP interaction may cause state changes in all the objects involved in it. In other words, an ODP interaction is a piece of shared behaviour.

Figure 3.3 illustrates the state machine of the Handset information object. This diagram shows not only the effect of the actions on the corresponding information objects, but also the states in which the actions are allowed, serving as pre- and post-conditions for those actions.

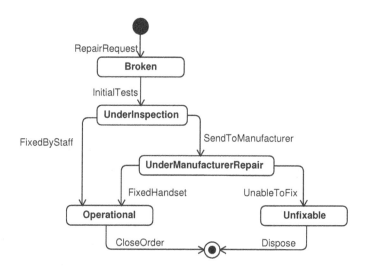

FIGURE 3.3: State machine for the Handset information object.

3.3.4   Invariant Schemata as Constraints

We have seen how invariant schemata can be used to specify the information object types and their relationships, but they can also be used to express other kinds of constraints on the information handled by the system.

For example, we may need to express the fact that no handset can be referenced simultaneously by more than one repair order, or that users should have unique names in the system. These kinds of invariant have already been incorporated into the UML class diagram that describes the information object types by choosing the multiplicity of the association ends, or adding some OCL constraints to the elements (see, for example, the constraints specified for classes User or RepairOrder in figure 3.1).

Other OCL constraints can be used to specify further restrictions on the model, or to express integrity constraints. For example, we could restrict the number of repair orders currently open in a centre, in accordance with a possible enterprise policy stating such a business rule, by simply adding an OCL constraint to the ServiceCentre information object type, as in the following fragment.

```
context ServiceCentre inv:
    self.repairOrder->select(status <> OrderStatus::closed)->
                        size() <= MaxOpenOrders
```

Further invariant schemata can be specified in this way, defining the integrity constraints and well-formed rules of the information model that specifies the shared data model handled by the system.

3.3.5 Static Schemata

Sometimes it is very useful to be able to describe instantaneous views of the information, for example at system initialization, or at any other specific moment in time that is relevant to any of the system stakeholders. This specification of the instantaneous state of the objects is precisely the one

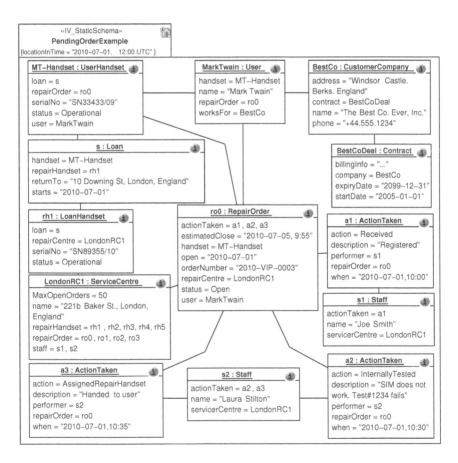

FIGURE 3.4: Current state of an example RepairOrder.

provided by static schemata, which in UML are expressed by means of object diagrams.

For instance, the UML package shown in figure 3.4 expresses a possible state of one repair order, in which the order has been registered, the telephone tested and found faulty, and a loan handset has been assigned and given to the user. No further actions have been done for that order so far — for example, the faulty handset has not yet been sent to the manufacturer for repair.

3.4   Structure of the Information Specification

All the elements that constitute the information specification of the system are gathered together within a single model, stereotyped «Information_Spec». This model contains the set of packages that express the invariant, static and dynamic schemata of the information specification, structuring them in different packages for organizational purposes. Figure 3.5 depicts the «Information_Spec» model for the PhoneMob system.

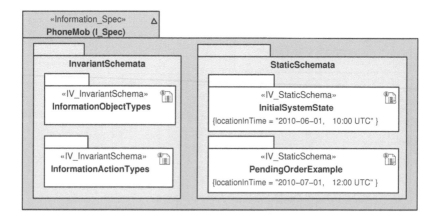

FIGURE 3.5: Structure of the PhoneMob information specification.

Note that in this figure there is no package for the specification of dynamic schemata. Given that they are modelled in UML as state machines associated with the corresponding object types, splitting their specification across different packages does not make much sense.

3.5   Relationship with Other Viewpoints

Although the different ODP viewpoints can be defined independently and there is no explicit order imposed by the RM-ODP for specifying them, a common practice is to start by developing the enterprise specification of the system, and then prepare the information and computational specifications. These specifications may place constraints on each other, and usually each viewpoint specification is revised and refined as the others are developed.

In the case of a notional incremental development process of the ODP viewpoint specifications, whereby the information specifications are developed taking into account the previously defined enterprise specifications, information objects may be discovered through examination of an enterprise specification. For example, each artefact referenced in any enterprise action in which an ODP system participates will correspond in some way with one or more information objects. Similarly, computational objects, interfaces and interactions can be derived from information objects and their associated information actions.

In general, not all the elements of the enterprise specification of a system need to correspond to elements of its information specification. For example, not all role types in the enterprise specification correspond to object types in the information view. Likewise, not all information objects or actions correspond to enterprise elements. One example is the decomposition of the handset into individual parts in the information viewpoint specification; these parts are abstracted away in the enterprise view. Similarly, the Logistics Provider enterprise community and all its constituent elements correspond to the single Courier information object type and the Branch enterprise community corresponds to the ServiceCentre information object type. In every case, the information viewpoint complies with the policies of the enterprise viewpoint and, likewise, all enterprise policies are consistent with the static, dynamic and invariant schemata of the information specification.

In chapter 7, we will describe how the relationships between the elements of two different viewpoint specifications are explicitly specified and described in terms of correspondences. For the moment, let us simply highlight the fact that both viewpoint specifications are views of the same system, and therefore what is specified in one viewpoint specification about an entity needs to be consistent with what is said about the same entity in any other viewpoint specification. Any two views should not make mutually contradictory statements; that is, they should be mutually consistent. The correspondences will be used to check that this is so.

Chapter 4

Computational Viewpoint

Claire looked across at Ira as he bent over his laptop, navigating through the information model to find the diagram dealing with phone properties. She had seen him around the office, of course, but this was the first time she had worked with him directly. He was tanned with fair hair and was dressed in a slightly formal ranch style with a strongly patterned shirt and had a self-confident, but rather reserved air. He certainly seemed to have picked up the ideas quickly enough, and his modelling background was strong, but he didn't seem so familiar with implementations.

"Here it is," he said, switching the diagram to the projector. "You can see that the definition here breaks down into owner and organizational properties on this side, and hardware structure and replaceable units over on the other side. We can derive the different specializations you have been talking about from this." "OK, but there are items in our design that are not here." "Sure, that's fine. There are bound to be elements describing the process details that would only be of local interest. I would expect your model to import a selective view of this, and then extend it to include new material." He traced one subtree of the diagram. "Here is the structure concerned with the SIM and its properties. Suppose we want to order a replacement for a faulty SIM. That requires a message containing the SIM's description, which means transferring an object of this SIM type, with fields to give the required capacity. You just have to pick an encoding for it."

"Not me," laughed Claire; "that's Nigel's problem, not mine. The models I'm building are platform independent, because we want them to be valid across a lot of different technologies. My group really shouldn't be concerned with the engineering detail." "Hang on, though," Ira said, "if we want to hide the engineering detail, why am I being asked to describe SIMs?" Claire smiled. "But your description is of the phone as a business object, which we need to repair, not as part of our infrastructure that supports the business. Unless you are a network operator, you should try to keep the two topics separate."

"And if I were a network operator?" asked Ira. "Well, then you would be using the network, which is your main product, to manage itself, and the same network components are both business objects and part of the supporting infrastructure. You would still try to compartmentalize these roles, though." Ira loosened the top of the coffee flask. "OK then, Claire, how do we know where to draw the boundaries?" "Well, that's one of the value judgements that an architect has to make, isn't it? What do we want to treat as a platform? Whatever we choose, below it multiple technical solutions can be selected to suit different situations. Over time there is a gradual upward movement, as we understand how to standardize and integrate more complex technologies." She held her cup out for a refill.

"All right then," he said, picking up an oatmeal biscuit, "what about the boundary between the information and computational models?" "Well, we know it's normal to import chunks of the information specification and extend them in the computational view, but computational objects are generally coarser grained, so there are information objects that become just properties in the computational view. Actually, I should have raised this just now when you were talking about the SIM object as a parameter; it's not actually a computational object." He frowned and looked straight at her over his cup. "But why? What's the basis for making the distinction?

Claire thought for a moment, then leaned back, running her fingers through her hair. "What's the smallest object in your models?" "Well, I guess it would be a specialization of one of the basic types; let's say an integer specialized as an employee's age." "OK, and would you expect to migrate the age object to a different system and interrogate it remotely?" "No, that would be much too inefficient." Claire smiled. "Well, that's the basis of the distinction. A computational object is a candidate for distribution. That doesn't mean it will actually be moved about on it's own, but that we would be prepared to consider doing so at the design stage." "That seems a bit vague to me," he said. "Yes, it's another architectural judgement call, and depends on what's reasonable use of the technology available, but it's generally pretty clear in practice. We tend to be a bit generous in making the decisions, because there are ways of constraining groups of objects so that they are managed together when the actual distribution decisions are taken in the engineering and technology models."

"Don't you sometimes feel a bit frustrated not to be making hard and fast decisions about that sort of thing?" "Goodness, no," she said, "I'm aiming for stable designs that don't have to be revised every time there is a new wave of technology to cope with. The applications are too complex to keep reinventing them all the time." She sat up and looked back to the screen. "What about the set of identifiers on the SIM. Do we need a common model of the roaming control data?"

4.1   Designing with Computational Objects

The goal of the computational viewpoint is to model the basic functionality of the application, the services it offers, and how these services are realized internally in terms of components and connectors; in other words, this viewpoint focuses on the system functionality and on the software architecture that realizes it. Other concerns, such as the distribution of software components to platform nodes or the technology used to implement the functionality, fall outside its scope.

In this way, the software architecture of the system becomes distribution and platform independent, and therefore it can be reused across different platforms, and can have a much longer lifespan than the technologies used to implement it. This separation of concerns also allows incorporation of those aspects at a later stage and in a modular fashion, as we shall see in chapter 5.

The computational language allows system architects to express their designs using a set of basic elements, which are common to most software architectures and languages. More precisely, a computational specification describes the functional decomposition of an ODP system as a configuration of **computational objects**, the **interactions** that occur between those objects at their **interfaces**, and the **environment contracts** for them. This chapter describes these elements in more detail.

4.2   Computational Objects

Computational objects model the basic functional elements of the system, offering services to other objects and using services from them, but without considering their distribution across networks and nodes. Thus, computational objects each encapsulate part of the system state and functionality, allowing a modular system design. One way to choose the computational objects for your specification is by identifying the basic pieces of work that are candidates for separate development and are thus the building blocks of your software architecture.

The set of interface types a computational object has specifies the services it provides and requires. Each service is in turn characterized by the behaviour involved in its use and by the syntax of its elements. The syntactic aspects are expressed in the **signatures** of the operations, streams or signals that it supports (see section 4.4 for a definition of these concepts). For example, figure 4.1 shows two UML components that represent two computational object types (UserOperations and CorporationDataMgmt); these interact because the UserOperations component requires a service that is provided by the CorporationDataMgmt component. Each object declares one ODP interface (iUser2Corporation and iCorporationMgmt, respectively). The signature of the operations that comprise the services are specified by a UML interface called IUserMgmt. The compatibility between the required and provided services is ensured because the signatures of the operations coincide (both services

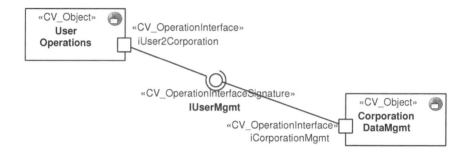

FIGURE 4.1: The concepts involved in connecting computational objects.

share the same signature specification, IUserMgmt), but with complementary causalities, reflecting their client and server roles.

UML (enhanced with the appropriate stereotypes defined by UML4ODP) provides a natural and faithful representation of the computational language concepts. Thus, UML components can be used directly to represent computational objects, their interfaces and the signature of their operations. UML components represent computational object types, UML ports are used to represent ODP interface types, and UML interfaces represent the signatures of computational signals and operations.

UML is not the only way to specify the interfaces of computational objects in a platform-independent way — that is, without committing to a particular programming language or implementation technology. For example, CORBA [31] is a specification from the OMG that, amongst other things, provides a platform-independent language to describe object interfaces. This language, called *CORBA IDL (Interface Definition Language)* was also adopted as standard ISO 14750 [12] as part of the RM-ODP family. It offers a textual notation for specifying object interfaces and operation signatures. Therefore, if you take an ODP computational specification, it is not that hard to create a mapping onto CORBA. ITU-T has another interface definition language, called eODL (*ITU-T Rec. Z.130, ITU object definition language* [26]), which provides some facilities additional to those in OMG's IDL. In the realm of service-oriented architectures, the interfaces used to represent web services are specified using WSDL [100]. This can be considered as a specialized version of an interface definition language for web-based services, which also allows expression of the ODP computational language concepts in a textual manner. It is therefore also relatively straightforward to create a mapping from a computational specification to a web service specification.

The ability to specify interfaces precisely is extremely valuable. In the first place, it allows users and other IT systems to exploit a specification that describes both the services provided by our computational objects and the way they should be invoked. These technical services can then be exposed as discussed in section 1.5. In the second place, service descriptions can be used for locating and discovering services in repositories or via the web. Service descriptions are already used in existing middleware service registry mechanisms, such as the JINI lookup service. To provide a shared terminology and common functionality across service search solutions, RM-ODP defines the ODP trading function. This function is further elaborated in an international standard for the description of service types and the discovery, within distributed and heterogeneous service repositories, of objects that provide particular services [9]. This standard was also used by the OMG as the basis for its object trading service [27].

Finally, if we consider interfaces as types we can make use of existing type theory to reason about service (or object) substitutability and compatibility. The former refers to the ability of one object to replace another in such a way that the change is transparent to external clients, while the latter defines the requirements for two or more objects to work properly together, if connected. These concepts can be considered as two sides of the object interoperability coin. This is critical for connecting independently developed parts and services in a predictable way and without undesirable errors, something that is essential in most SOA and cloud systems.

4.3 Bindings

Apart from the computational objects that encapsulate the system functionality, there is a need to represent the bindings between these objects. This is particularly useful for modelling connections that have nontrivial behaviours, such as ones that report exceptions to other parts of the system. Connecting two or more objects in a seamless way is not a trivial task, and therefore the RM-ODP is very careful about how a binding is specified and realized. In ODP, a **binding** is a context created by establishing a communication relationship between two or more objects, and a binding is created by a **binding action**. Normally, a computational object initiates its interaction with another computational object by performing a binding action that allows them to connect to each other and start exchanging services and data. However, in some cases, particularly where multimedia communications is involved, one object can initiate a binding between a number of other objects; this is known as third-party binding.

RM-ODP distinguishes two kinds of binding: primitive and compound. In a primitive binding, the connection between the objects is direct and does not require the use of any other object between them; this is the situation when we connect the required and provided services of two components by simply sharing the UML interface that defines the signature of their operations. This is shown, for instance, in figure 4.1, where the UML ball-and-socket notation is used to indicate the binding.

There are other situations in which a **compound binding** action results in the creation of an explicit **binding object**. A binding object is a particular kind of computational object that encapsulates the functionality required to connect two or more further computational objects. The object itself provides a control interface to allow these connecting mechanisms to be configured and managed. Binding objects represent the architectural connectors in the application's software architecture. They are needed, for example, in the case of multi-party interactions, or when the connection between the two components is not trivial. In this case, a binding computational object links the participants, acting as an architectural connector that provides the binding functionality. Binding between computational objects is only possible if, for each participant, their interfaces match with the defined interfaces of the binding object.

Binding objects are useful to encapsulate and reify the communication media that two computational objects use to interact, especially when such a medium exhibits a complex behaviour (as happens with any LAN or WAN connection between two objects) or when we want to model the connection as an independent entity (to allow QoS constraints to be attached to it, such as requirements for throughput or bounds on jitter, for instance). Alternatively, compound bindings can be used to represent more abstract groupings reflecting, for example, contracts or other forms of collaboration. Figure 4.2 shows how a binding object can be used to encapsulate a publish and subscribe event

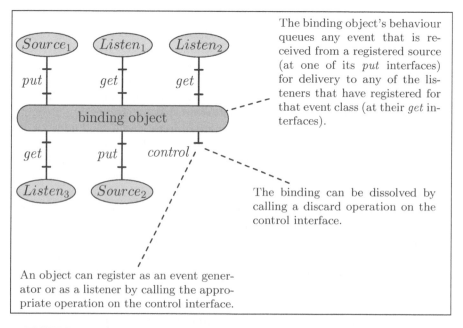

FIGURE 4.2: A compound binding object encapsulates an event channel.

channel, in which any number of computational objects can register either as sources or listeners for various kinds of event.

4.4   Interactions between Computational Objects

The interactions between objects are described using a number of standard interaction types: *operations*, *streams* and *signals*. These types of interaction are supported by the corresponding computational object interfaces: *operation*, *stream* and *signal interfaces*.

The most primitive interaction type is the *signal*, which is defined in a *signal interface*. A signal is an atomic shared action resulting in one-way, localized communication from an initiating object to a responding object. For example, a message that passes from a computational object to its local infrastructure can be modelled by a signal, as can a local exception. Sequences of signals can also be used to define the properties of more abstract interactions, such as operations or streams (see figure 4.3).

Operations are probably the most common form of interaction between computational objects. An operation is an interaction between a client object and a server object, which is either an announcement or an interrogation. In this way, we distinguish between one-way and two-way (request and response) interactions.

Announcements are one-way interactions in which a client object requests a function to be performed by a server object, such that there need be no response from the server. The request is modelled by an *invocation*. In more detail, one signal marks the passage of the announcement from the client object to the infrastructure, and another signal marks its passage from the infrastructure to the server object. Using this fine-grained representation with signals, we can describe, for example, the transit time of the announcement, but for most purposes we can consider the announcement as a single nonlocalized interaction.

Interrogations are two-way interactions, in which a client object requests a function to be performed by a server object, and the server sends a response to the client, as in many RPC styles of interactions. The requests are modelled by *invocations*, and responses are modelled by *terminations*. The notion of a termination generalizes results and exceptions as found in many programming languages. Where necessary, operations can be defined in detail in terms of signals. For example, an interrogation operation between two objects that communicate through an infrastructure can be detailed as a set of four signals, which specify the sending and receiving of the invocation and termination individually.

The level of abstraction at which interactions are modelled depends on the specific needs of the system designer at each moment, and for each situation.

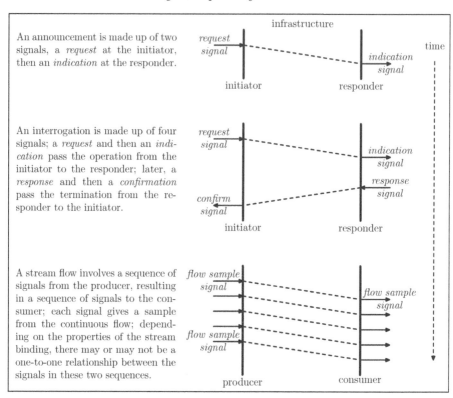

An announcement is made up of two signals, a *request* at the initiator, then an *indication* at the responder.

An interrogation is made up of four signals; a *request* and then an *indication* pass the operation from the initiator to the responder; later, a *response* and then a *confirmation* pass the termination from the responder to the initiator.

A stream flow involves a sequence of signals from the producer, resulting in a sequence of signals to the consumer; each signal gives a sample from the continuous flow; depending on the properties of the stream binding, there may or may not be a one-to-one relationship between the signals in these two sequences.

FIGURE 4.3: Expressing operations and stream flows in terms of signals.

The RM-ODP provides various types of interactions to enable designers to be precise at any required level. One example is the way that an operation can be refined into the set of atomic signals describing the individual interactions happening during the operation's invocation and termination. Another is the way a complex event distribution system can be modelled as a compound binding managing sequences of announcements, abstracting away from all the low-level details involved in the communications between the objects involved. The linkage of separate event management domains can then be modelled as a concatenation of compound bindings.

Finally, **streams** and their component **flows** are used to model continuous transfers of information, such as those used for exchanging videos and other kinds of multimedia streams. You can think of receiving a YouTube video or an internet radio broadcast as examples of this kind of interaction. A flow is a continuous transfer of typed information in one direction over a period of time. Flows can also be used to represent regular data flows, such as monitoring reports or the continuous flow of periodic sensor readings in a process control application, without explicit modelling of the steady sequence of messages involved. Properties of various kinds of continuous media are specified by stream interfaces that describe the nature of the data exchanged. This is done by declaring a collection of flows, each with an associated direction of transfer. This means that a conversational audio application could be described using stream interfaces in each of which there is a pair of flows, one in each direction.

ODP distinguishes three different kinds of communication pattern, each consisting of a pair of matched roles. In the first, the ***initiator*** is an object causing the communication, while the ***responder*** is an object that communicates with the initiator in consequence. Next, the ***producer*** is an object that is the source of the information conveyed, while the ***consumer*** is the sink for that information. Finally, the ***client*** is an object that requests that a service be performed by another object, while the ***server*** is an object that performs some service on behalf of a client object. Selecting the appropriate pattern lets us emphasize the most important properties of the communication being described.

4.5 Environment Contracts and Transparencies

The computational language also allows the specification of non-functional properties of computational objects and their interactions. Examples of such non-functional properties include quality of service (QoS) requirements, usage or management constraints, service level agreements (SLA) and so on. These requirements are specified using ***environment contracts***.

The way to specify and represent environment contracts depends on their nature and on the notation available for this task. For instance, in UML, environment contracts can be specified in various ways, ranging from timing constraints associated with object interactions to more sophisticated requirements expressed using any of the existing UML profiles for specifying QoS and real-time properties. One example is the *UML profile for MARTE: Modelling and Analysing Real-Time Embedded Systems* [35] proposed by the OMG. In addition, transparency schemata let us express quality of service requirements for objects. RM-ODP defines different kinds of transparency, including access transparency, failure transparency, location transparency, migration transparency, persistence transparency, relocation transparency, replication transparency and transaction transparency. Each of these allows the masking from the computational specification of the problems arising from the aspect named while still placing a requirement that these concerns should be addressed somewhere else in the system specifications. In ODP, the engineering viewpoint is the main place that provides the appropriate mechanisms for implementing them, and therefore it is normally responsible for clearly specifying how the requirements imposed by the transparencies selected in the computational view are fulfilled. Two of the set of transparencies defined by RM-ODP (the access and location transparencies) are always implied in every computational specification, and should therefore always be addressed by the engineering specifications. A more detailed discussion of transparencies can be found in chapter 9.

The selection of these transparencies simplifies the computational specification, hiding the problems and complications of having to deal with the replication of some components or connectors to increase the overall system reliability and availability, or with the need to know the location of services before you can invoke them, for example. In this respect, transparencies provide a very effective mechanism for achieving a sensible separation of concerns between the basic functionality of the system and other aspects that can be specified in a modular way and plugged-in according to particular user requirements.

ODP defines standard functions and structures to realize distribution transparencies, so that a conforming ODP system can implement those transparencies in accordance with the relevant standards. However, there are performance and cost tradeoffs associated with each transparency and only a selection of the transparencies will be relevant in many cases. Thus, not all transparencies are required for every system. It is up to the designer to select the specific distribution transparencies that need to be applied to each computational specification.

4.6   Writing Computational Specifications

Apart from relying on a set of well-defined concepts and mechanisms for expressing computational objects, interfaces and interactions, the designers also need some guidelines and structuring rules for writing the computational specifications of their system. This section offers some guidelines on how to do it.

4.6.1   Division into Components

We normally start by specifying the high-level software architecture of the application. Such an architecture will provide the big picture of the system, describing the key computational objects in the system, and how they interact to achieve the application's goal.

By software architecture we mean the structure and organization of the system, defined in terms of software elements (components, connectors), the externally visible properties of those elements, and the relationships among them [49]. This structure also defines the principles and guidelines governing how the design is to be allowed to evolve over time [71]. It provides the basis for satisfying both functional and non-functional requirements on the system [81, 82].

There are different approaches to designing the software architecture of the system. The first step is to select the architectural style that best suits the target application and user requirements (pipes-and-filters, client-server, multi-layer, blackboard, toaster and so on). The selection of the architectural style and the software methodology that helps the system designer make such a selection are outside the scope of this book. However, the RM-ODP is independent of these processes because it was designed to work with any of them.

In the case of the PhoneMob system, we can use a simple three-layered software architecture, which is typical of many web-based and SOA systems. This is an architecture in which the interfaces to users, the business logic and the persistent data storage are separated in independent tiers (or layers). Objects in each layer offer services to the other layers, creating a natural organization of responsibilities and separation of concerns for this kind of system.

However, in the enterprise specification we dealt with humans playing staff roles, and modelled their interactions with the ODP systems supporting them. We need to carry these interactions through into the computational specification, where they are refined to give more detail of the human-computer interface. To do this, we add a fourth layer to the architecture. Thus, the human interface layer represents human actors, and the presentation layer holds the software components responsible for interactions with the human users. The

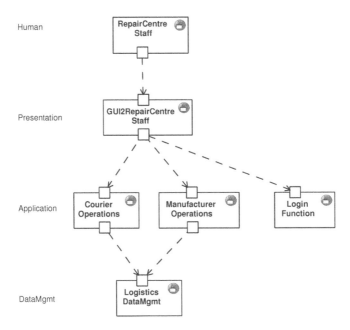

FIGURE 4.4: Division on one computational use case into the chosen tiers.

presentation layer communicates with the business logic layer, which provides the services that users require. The business logic layer controls the application's functionality by performing detailed processing. Whenever necessary, it accesses the data layer, where the persistent information of the application is stored and made available. This layer keeps data neutral and independent from application servers and from business processes and rules. Giving data its own tier also improves scalability and performance. The use of this structure to express a single use case concerned with organizing some logistics support is shown in figure 4.4.

Figure 4.5 shows a larger part of the software architecture of the PhoneMob system, described in terms of computational objects interacting at interfaces. Objects are grouped here in packages for organizational purposes, although the packaging is not critical: it is mainly used as a reference to identify the separate layers. The outer packages correspond to the architecture layers. Inside them, objects are grouped depending on the kind of services they provide. Auxiliary services (such as login, for instance) have been included because they provide a set of common functions to the rest of the objects. UML dependencies between the ports of the UML components that model the computational object types represent the requirement for bindings between them. Such UML dependencies are an abstraction of the more detailed way of expressing the

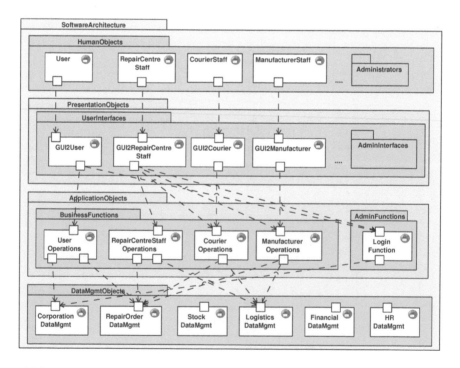

FIGURE 4.5: Part of the software architecture of the PhoneMob system.

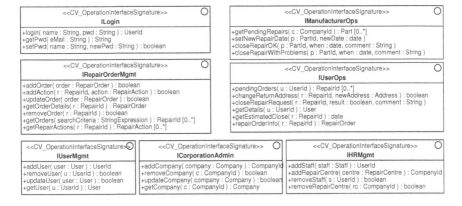

FIGURE 4.6: Detailed specification of operation interface signatures.

bindings that we showed in figure 4.1 or that we use later in figure 4.7, where the signatures of the interfaces are explicitly specified.

4.6.2 Object Interfaces and Action Signatures

Once the software architecture is defined, the next step is to refine the specific services that each object will provide to, or require from, other objects by specifying the interfaces of the computational objects. This involves both declaring the signature of their operations (see figure 4.6) and defining their behaviour (which will be discussed in the next section).

Computational interfaces are represented in UML4ODP by means of UML ports (see figures 4.5 and 4.7). The signatures for the services provided and required by each port are specified in UML4ODP by using UML interfaces. Thus, figure 4.6 shows the UML interfaces that specify the ODP interface signatures characterizing some of the system interactions. The use of these interface signatures is illustrated in figure 4.7, where the UML *ball-and-socket* notation is used to express primitive bindings between the corresponding computational objects.

Figure 4.7 includes further information about the components, such as some of their internal realizing classifiers. For example, component CorporationDataMgmt manages the information about corporations that are clients of the PhoneMob company. It represents a database that stores and manages the relevant information about them and thus contains a realizing classifier (the CorpMgmt «focus» class), which specifies its behaviour. This classifier owns the information about the set of companies and customers known by the system.

Note the use here of standard UML concepts and stereotypes for expressing some of the model details, in addition to the UML4ODP stereotypes. For example, UML classes stereotyped «focus» and «dataType» are used to make

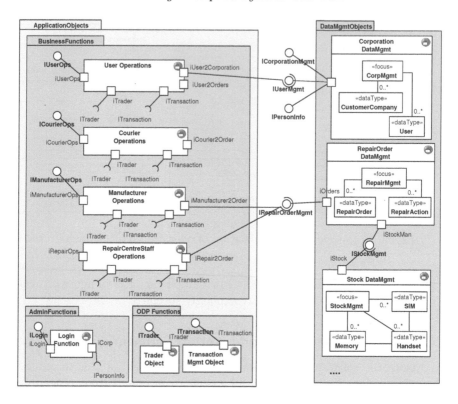

FIGURE 4.7: Refining the architecture by showing the operation interface
signatures for the computational interfaces.

explicit at this level the internal classes that provide the core logic of some of
the components and the main data types that they use.

The structure and contents of the data types representing the information managed by the computational objects are specified in the DataTypes
package, which is shown in figure 4.8. These data types are derived from the
corresponding information object types (which in turn came from the enterprise artefacts, roles and objects). However, this is not simply a matter of
copying the model elements concerned. The types do not need to be exactly
the same as in the other viewpoints, since refinement or abstraction may be
involved. For instance, some additional information has been added in this
viewpoint to store usernames and passwords of customers and other stakeholders. Identifiers have also been added to simplify object reference.

Just as in other viewpoints, computational objects introduced in the early
stages of the design can later be rewritten as smaller computational objects (by
refinement or decomposition), or combined with other computational objects
to form a larger computational object (composition). These mechanisms allow

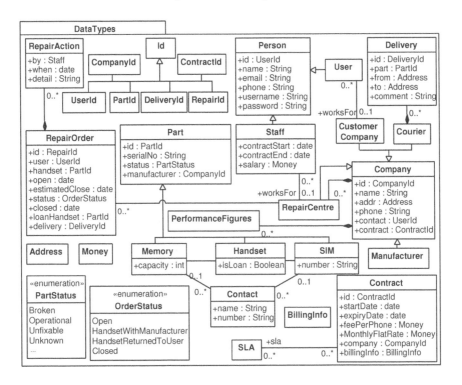

FIGURE 4.8: Data types used by the computational objects.

a computational specification to be created either top-down or bottom-up, or even from both sides using an iterative process (sometimes called *middle-out*).

So far, we have concentrated on a static structure to keep things simple, but a computational design typically involves a dynamically evolving structure. This involves the computational objects in instantiating further computational objects or computational interfaces, performing binding actions, using the control functions of binding objects, dissolving bindings, deleting computational interfaces or discarding computational objects. These mechanisms are modelled in ODP using the **factory** concept, which introduces an object that, when given an object type and any necessary qualifying parameters, creates a new object and returns a reference to it. This pattern is commonplace in systems nowadays, and found, for instance, in component factories in platforms such as .NET or JEE.

For example, the login process for a staff member typically involves an initial exchange with a generic presentation object, followed by the creation of a specific proxy object in the presentation tier to manage the interactions with that particular staff member. When the staff member logs out, the proxy object is discarded. Similarly, an object managing some volatile grouping may create a new interface instance for each new group member, thus enforcing separation of responsibilities, and it will delete this instance when the member leaves the group.

4.6.3   Behaviour: Operations

Apart from the structural aspects, we also need to specify the behaviour of the elements of a computational specification. UML state machines can be used to express the internal behaviour of any of the computational elements: ports, components and realizing classifiers. State machines are used to represent such behaviour, as has already been illustrated in the enterprise and information specifications.

UML activity diagrams are often used to express object interactions in this viewpoint because they provide the kinds of abstraction that we need to model the different ways in which messages are exchanged between objects. This is especially true when the interactions are defined in terms of signals or operations. Alternatively, when messages and interaction protocols are the focus of design, UML interaction diagrams can be more appropriate.

For example, figure 4.9 shows a sequence diagram expressing the interactions that occur between the components of the computational specification when a customer requests information about a pending repair order. The precise way in which the user interacts with the system and the information that is presented to her is encapsulated in the GUI2User object, and is not described here. Only the communications that result from those interactions with the system GUI are shown.

Figure 4.9 shows that, when the user decides to login, the presentation object (the GUI2User object) sends a request to login to the appropriate object in the business logic layer (the LoginFunction). That object consults with the corresponding database access object to check the username and password for

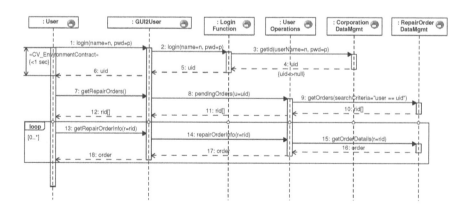

FIGURE 4.9: A computational interaction diagram, showing the steps in the processing of a query.

the customer, which returns the customer identifier to be used during that session (the alternative behaviour that happens when the name and password provided are incorrect is not shown for the sake of simplicity). The presentation object then enquires about the pending orders for the customer and presents these to the user. The customer selects one of them (which is identified by the appropriate Repairld) and the system is queried about this specific order.

It is also possible to incorporate environment contracts in the specification, expressed in terms of constraints stereotyped «CV_EnvironmentContract». For example, the duration constraint in figure 4.9 expresses the fact that the delay in receiving the response to the login operation should not exceed 1 second. This approach allows non-functional properties to be expressed so that they can be checked by supporting tools.

4.6.4 Behaviour: Flows

So far we have used operations to specify the interactions between the objects of our system. However, other forms of interactions are also possible. For instance, streams can be used to model continuous flows of information that are transferred from one object to another over an extended period of time.

Suppose that in the PhoneMob system there is the need for a dedicated teleconference application linking the service centres and the phone manufacturers. If we make this a videoconference, it becomes possible to show the handset and its parts to the manufacturer and to get advice, saving the time, effort and money involved in dispatching the handset to the factory, waiting for them to repair it, and then bringing it back to the service centre.

We will look at two ways of describing this, first by using primitive bindings, and then showing how the use of a compound binding can simplify the description.

The diagram shown in figure 4.10 represents the architecture of such a videoconference system, described using just primitive bindings; it is composed of two kinds of computational object (the repairer and the adviser). Each of these has three interfaces, two for control of the session and one for multimedia exchange. The control interfaces (named "ctrl") are like those we have seen before, and offer the operations described by the operational signature IControl.

There is also a stream interface (named "media") whose signature is specified by the interface signatures RepairerStream and AdviserStream. These stream interfaces define four flows for producing and consuming audio and video. The two interfaces form a complementary pair, with flows in the adviser stream interface being opposite in direction to those in the repairer stream interface. The repairer and adviser need separate complementary stream interfaces, so that audioln, for example, is produced by the adviser and consumed by the repairer.

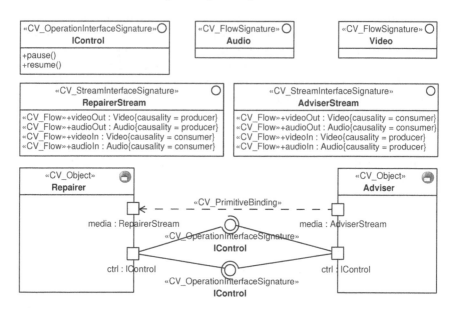

FIGURE 4.10: Using streams when specifying a multimedia application.

In this example, we assume that the control interfaces are bound by the infrastructure, whilst the stream interfaces are bound using an explicit binding action; in this first case, both of these are primitive bindings.

To create the configuration, the system at the service centre should initiate an interaction with the system at the manufacturer; this interaction causes the creation of the repairer and adviser proxy objects on each side, and exchanges the interface references of the control and stream interfaces on the created objects; the performance of the binding actions by the repairer completes the configuration. Either party can control the media flows by calling its peer's control interface. Once the conference is over, the proxy objects would be instructed to remove themselves and the references and resources used by these objects cleaned up.

Now let us look at the same application, but this time introducing an explicit binding object. The resulting configuration is shown in figure 4.11. There is a trade-off here; another object is added to the design, but the number of interface types defined by the application can be reduced. Now both the application components offer the same interface, MediaUserStream, so that both send audio out on their audioOut flow. The binding object offers a pair of complementary interfaces, with signature MediaBindingStream, which is derived from MediaUserStream by reversing the directions of all the flows in it. This signature is shown in grey in the figure to indicate that it is derived when the binding is created. The binding object would then have behaviour that consumes samples from audioOut on one side and produces it as audioIn

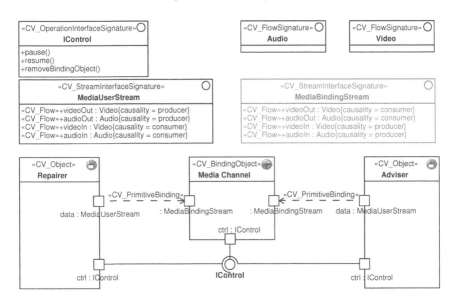

FIGURE 4.11: Using a binding object in a multimedia application.

on the other, and similarly for the other three flows, so that its two stream interfaces are cross-linked.

The binding action by the repairer creates the binding object, which then in turn creates the two primitive bindings to the media interfaces. The binding action returns a reference to the binding object's control interface, which is then provided to both the repairer and the adviser. All binding objects have such a control interface, which allows the binding to be shut down when no longer needed, but here we can enhance it to support the control operations. This is actually a cleaner structure than previously, since the binding object encapsulates the mechanisms supporting the flows, and it is these that we are trying to control. The repairer and adviser can independently bind to the control interface when necessary to gain access to the pause and resume functions.

The same system behaviour is being described here as in the first design, but the focus has moved to the binding object, which is generic, and so more likely to be derived from a reusable library.

The advantage of introducing the binding object becomes even clearer if the requirements evolve so that a multi-party conference is needed rather than just a two-way communication. If the description uses a binding object, all the parties involved can still use the same stream interface, while the rules for selecting or combining inputs are defined within the reusable conference binding object type, making the system design more flexible.

In more complicated applications, we can also use the ability to specify arbitrary behaviour as part of the binding type to define other useful building blocks that modify or filter the stream being carried. One can, for example, define bindings that link stream interfaces with different properties, so that, for example, a colour video source is linked to a black and white presentation object. If the flows are continuous sequences of report data, perhaps in a telemetry application, we can define bindings between flows of different data types to select a specific view, merge streams from different sources, or convert between different data formats. In this way, typed binding objects offer a powerful technique for structuring and reuse in application design.

4.7   Relationship with Other Viewpoints

As we have seen, the computational viewpoint specification is not normally designed in isolation, but is typically created after first drafts of the enterprise and information specifications are available (or, at least, in parallel with them).

For example, a first step in producing the computational specification of a system consists of deciding the right configuration of computational objects and the interactions among those objects that guarantee that the system functionality is fulfilled, as prescribed by the enterprise specification. The description of these computational objects and interactions should also be done at the appropriate level of abstraction, and they need to manipulate the information handled by the system as prescribed by the information specification. This is why the elements in the enterprise and the information specifications can be used effectively for identifying the computational objects and their interactions.

A different designer could also use a bottom-up approach if there are already good commercial off-the-shelf (COTS) or legacy components in the organization that can be used in the new system. Computational objects encapsulating the functionality of such legacy or COTS components are perfect candidates for the specification.

Once identified, computational objects may be grouped into packages following a particular software architecture, such as collecting business-oriented objects within the same layer, and common functions or UI objects in others. Such a structure is what constitutes and defines the software architecture of the system. For the behaviour, many of the computational interactions will be derived (using refinement, for instance) from the dynamic schemata in the information viewpoint specifications. Finally, enterprise policies relating to the system's business rules, together with information invariant schemata that control the state changes and integrity constraints on the system data, can serve as a starting point to specify the environment contracts for the computational objects and their interactions.

Where a policy is identified in the enterprise viewpoint, the associated behaviour is expected to be mutable, so the computational structure must reflect this fact. One possible technique is to introduce an explicit indirection, which invokes a policy value object that interprets the policy. The behaviour defined as part of the policy (see the description of the policy envelope in chapter 10) can then modify or replace this object without affecting the rest of the design. For example, a policy may be identified, based on marketing decisions, that varies the charge for repairs when the work is completed late. If there is a change in this policy from offering an immediate discount to giving credit for future repairs, the object that calculates the charge will need to be modified; this will be easier to do if the object is clearly separated from other parts of the billing process.

Of course, the three viewpoint specifications considered so far have constraints on each other, and usually each viewpoint specification is revised and refined as the others are developed.

Finally, not all elements in the computational specification need to correspond to elements in either of the other two viewpoints, and not all objects in the other specifications have computational equivalents. Each viewpoint focuses on a different aspect of the system, and is expressed using a different language. Therefore, their elements are different. However, they are all views of the same system, and therefore many of their elements represent views of the same system entities. This means that the view should be consistent and no views can impose contradictory requirements on the system. For example, the enterprise policies should be consistent with the invariant schemata of the information viewpoint, and with the computational environment contracts. In ODP, correspondences (see chapter 7) are used to specify in an explicit way the relationships between the elements of two different viewpoint specifications. Therefore, correspondences become essential elements for checking the consistency between the views.

Chapter 5

Engineering Viewpoint

"I'll have the ginger and mango sausage baguette with a latte," said Nigel, "and I'll pay for all four of us. We will be out on the terrace." This was one of his favourite places, just a little way upriver from the office, with a view across the broad sweep of the reach as it swung south away from the high-level bridge. They often came here on a Friday after the technical design reviews. Claire, Alex and Trudy were already walking down the short brick-vaulted passage leading to the old wharf that now formed the cafe's terrace.

"But if we have a stable middleware, why do we need to create a separate engineering specification?" asked Trudy, as they settled round one of the heavy scrubbed wooden tables. "Isn't all the information implied by selection of the middleware?" "Well," said Alex, "that depends on whether you have just one middleware, and on how stable you think your middleware choice is. A few years ago we thought we might use CORBA everywhere, but then web services and .NET came along. And you are still using much older ubiquitous platforms in the hardware repair workshop, with little prospect of any change. Who knows what another five years of innovation will bring?" "So how does the creation of another competing specification help?" "It's not direct competition, because the engineering language is taking a more abstract, architectural view of how the system is put together. What we want is a roadmap to guide system maintenance and transition planning if we do need to integrate a different middleware solution."

"What exactly do you mean by architectural, here?" asked Trudy. "It's not the same as a system configuration description, is it?" "No. It's more like a set of templates for solving the various platform problems found at different points in the configuration; and these solutions will depend on the level of reliability or robustness needed. Each actual interaction between the objects in our computational design needs to follow the appropriate prescription."

He looked across the terrace. "Hello, this looks like our order now." The waiter had come out with a loaded tray, and they were soon all eating. A tug with two barges worked its way up river, while a commuter ferry headed rapidly downstream.

After a bit, Claire put down her panini. "So if you want to change the requirements, you may end up using a different template?" Alex nodded. "Yes, the template selection can often be done by the tool chain, based on the properties required for the interaction; this is usually done based on the transparencies requested and the actual deployment details, since you need to know whether the objects involved are on the same system or on different ones, and if so what sort of communications are available." Nigel thought for a moment. "But that may change if the placement of the objects changes." "Sure, you need to know what changes can be foreseen. If an object is made mobile, for example, communication can change as it moves from using local access to interaction across a firewall." "So you have to plan for the worst?"

"Up to a point. But you may want to fix some configuration aspects in the design."

"I don't understand that, Alex," said Trudy, "don't you want to keep your options open?" "Not always. Think about cases where you want to express parts of the computational design using fine-grain data objects; a configuration of these objects may be generated by a factory object and may then be kept together throughout its life — a bit like a database table row. You know that these objects can always interact locally, wherever they are, because you have decided individual members of the configuration should not migrate away from the rest. The group form a unit, and are created together, migrated together, and checkpointed together. In cases like this, you can optimize the communications support."

"And how does this affect the engineering specification?" "Well, Claire, the engineering language offers a number of concepts relating to such groupings. A group of objects that share the same lifecycle is called a cluster, and the whole group can be manipulated by talking to a special cluster manager object. There are other useful grouping concepts — the capsule for relating objects with similar fault management and the node for relating objects sharing resources at the lowest level." "And the engineering language concepts let you express these as architectural requirements to be mapped onto whatever platforms you decide to use?" "Yes, Nigel, that's more or less how it's done."

They all thought about this while they finished their meal. At the end, Nigel pushed his chair back. "Well, this has turned out to be a very instructive lunch." Alex grinned. "Both tasty and profitable; oh, the joys of bookable time!"

5.1   What Is the Engineering Viewpoint For?

The goal of the engineering viewpoint is to identify and specify the supporting mechanisms for distributed interactions between objects. The focus is on specifying how distribution works — how objects are distributed over nodes, and how the structures of the nodes, and of the channels linking the nodes, are going to be modelled. It also defines common functions needed to support the required distribution transparencies. Clearly, this viewpoint is used by system designers who are particularly concerned with the infrastructure of systems.

Since this area has been a target of standardization for quite some time, a number of standards or specifications already exist to provide such mechanisms for specific technologies, such as Web Services, .NET, JEE or CORBA. The main value of the engineering viewpoint is in providing a technology-neutral architectural framework or reference architecture that can be used as a basic tool for designing new systems or comparing existing infrastructure technologies for distributed processing. In this way, infrastructure designs can have a much longer life than the technologies that support them; this allows these technologies to evolve without invalidating the system designs, which are a company's major asset.

Another important feature is that the information necessary for conformance testing originates in this viewpoint. Although the actual conformance testing may be performed against software and hardware artefacts specified in the technology viewpoint, the basic test requirements are defined in the technology-independent engineering viewpoint. For instance, observation of a SOAP message passing from a client PC technology object to a departmental server technology object may be used to check conformance by comparing it to the interactions expected at an interface between the corresponding engineering objects that has been identified as a conformance point.

5.2   Objects and Distribution

The major objective of the engineering design is to support the distribution transparency requirements of the computational objects. As explained in the previous chapter, computational interactions are at least access and location transparent. However, more transparency attributes may be specified in the computational transparency schema specification.

Basic Engineering Objects (or BEOs for short) are a special kind of engineering object, which are used to give a representation of each computational object in the engineering viewpoint. We are concerned here primarily with the engineering of machines and of network communication. Some computational objects may represent human actors, but for these there is just a simple placeholder BEO; the engineering of communication with them is a matter for HCI standardization, but is not detailed in this reference framework and so is not discussed further here.

The set of BEOs can be seen as abstractions of the computational design. The resulting description hides distinctions between objects with similar communications requirements, and retaining only the information about the computational objects that characterizes them as users of the distribution platform being provided. Therefore, the BEO is the primary object to be placed on a particular node, and which initiates communication across the network. All other engineering objects are secondary elements defined in a node or channel architecture, whose goal is to provide the functions necessary to support distribution. This includes a variety of supporting objects, like repositories or directories, which are drawn from a set of common functions called the ODP functions.

In the PhoneMob computational specification, we established a multi-tier design (see figure 4.5) in which human objects were supported by presentation objects, which in turn used application objects that accessed data management objects. In the engineering viewpoint, we place these objects on specific nodes (see figure 5.1).[1] Thus, the User and RepairCentreStaff objects will each be supported by their own presentation objects, and these will be on different nodes. This is done by placing the BEOs corresponding to the computational presentation objects on nodes that are local to the people concerned. Although this sounds complicated, in practice, it will generally happen quite naturally because these objects are created by an initial login agent object on the appropriate node that acts as a local factory.

The BEOs representing the application and data management objects are then placed on suitable backend service nodes; these may be replicated to achieve enhanced performance or reliability. They are generally placed explicitly for reasons of performance and load balancing. This distribution of engineering objects and the way they are connected through different channels has a strong influence on many other key concerns about any system and, in particular, on most of the so-called non-functional aspects (such as reliability, high availability or security).

For instance, the diagram in figure 5.1 shows a design with a dedicated node for interfacing to each business activity at the branch repair centre. The rest of the business objects are run on a separate node. Similarly, there are dedicated channels via which the repair centre interface objects access the main server and others to support backend distribution. This allows the imposition of different requirements for each one. There is a channel (the PhoneMobDedicatedChannel) with strict security requirements and high performance to connect the repair centre interface objects with the PhoneMob main node, in order to guarantee fast and secure communications between them, instead of using the same kind of channel as the other presentation objects.

The performance requirements are specified in an *environment contract*. Environment contracts are expressed in UML4ODP using OCL or timing constraints attached to the appropriate nodes or channels. Alternatively, use can be made of a dedicated UML profile such as MARTE [35] to specify these non-functional requirements.

The actual nature of the nodes is not determined here, but will be identified in a technology viewpoint configuration, identifying the customer or courier

---

[1]In UML4ODP, NV is used as an abbreviation for engineering viewpoint.

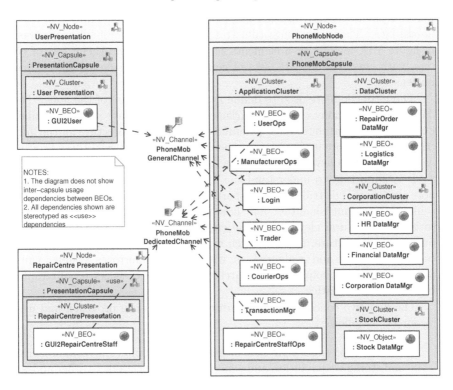

FIGURE 5.1: A high-level description of engineering object distribution.

support as thin clients running on a PC, Mac or smart phone, and the nodes supporting the application objects as resources within the PhoneMob service centre, where a web server validates and, when appropriate, forwards those incoming requests to services running behind the firewall. These nodes might, for example, be enterprise systems running PhoneMob applications on top of JEE or various other frameworks with legacy database systems connected.

5.3 Node Architecture

The node architecture identifies a number of functions that are commonly found in the platforms supporting application objects. Providing a technology-neutral architecture for describing them helps to identify the commonalities between different infrastructure solutions, such as JEE or .NET, and so makes the integration of different platforms simpler. Several of these functions are concerned with groupings of objects that are important when managing essential system properties, such as resource consumption, fault tolerance or persistence. These groupings (illustrated in a much simplified configuration in figure 5.1), include such elements as nodes and, within them, sets of clusters, with cluster managers, sets of capsules, with capsule managers, and a nucleus.

These concepts are used to define the logical structure of the node. These days, there are many complete packages of infrastructure support available, but it is still important to have a common functional architecture for the infrastructure to support interoperation and interworking between these products, or to extend it to new technologies as they appear.

It is important to understand the kinds of functionality required to support provision of distribution transparencies, the basic mechanisms needed to achieve those functionalities, and how they can be structured and assigned to the architectural elements of the engineering viewpoint. This provides a reference architecture, against which existing distributed processing systems can be compared and evaluated, or with which tomorrow's systems can be designed. Using it helps technical architects specify or select required infrastructure characteristics.

The first two concepts make the distinction between provision and use of resources, as follows:

- A *node* represents a physical object that has computing, communication and storage capabilities, and generally has connections to other nodes. A node will therefore have one or more network addresses, and the elements deployed on the node can become network accessible. Your laptop, your office PC, your mobile phone and your organization's server machines are all nodes. However, this is a slight simplification because a node does not actually have to be a separate, physically tangible object; a virtualization of such a resource (see section 9.1) can also be considered to be a node.

- An *engineering object* is any object of interest in this viewpoint. These objects support computational requirements, distribution transparencies or infrastructural aspects of the system. We distinguish here between BEOs, which represent computational objects, and other engineering objects, whose aim is to provide basic engineering functions, such as managers, interceptors and directories.

The engineering viewpoint language also defines three other concepts that describe the principal controlling elements involved in any engineering specification:

- A *nucleus* represents the basic mechanisms needed to make a node function at the lowest level, typically representing an operating system kernel that manages and allocates processing capabilities, communication capabilities and storage capabilities. Fair scheduling and accurate timing both depend on the centralized control of the node's resources offered by the nucleus.

- A ***capsule*** is a unit of independent processing and storage. Faults within a capsule can affect all of the objects in it. The capsule supports a collection of engineering objects managed by a ***capsule manager***. Capsules are isolated from one another by some protection mechanism, so that incorrect behaviour in one capsule does not damage other capsules. One of the consequences of this is typically that, because of the extra checking involved, communication across capsule boundaries is much more expensive than communication within a capsule. An example of a set of capsules is the set of independent processes, each with its own address space, run by an operating system (a nucleus). Another example of a capsule is a JEE or CCM [29] component container.

- A ***cluster*** is a collection of BEOs that have closely coupled lifecycles, and so can be activated, deactivated or migrated as one single unit. The record of objects that makes up a JEE or .NET component is a cluster. Another example is the aggregation of small primitive objects into a larger configuration to form a row for database update.

Every nucleus, capsule or cluster contains a managing object that is responsible for it and which controls its membership. An outline of this structure

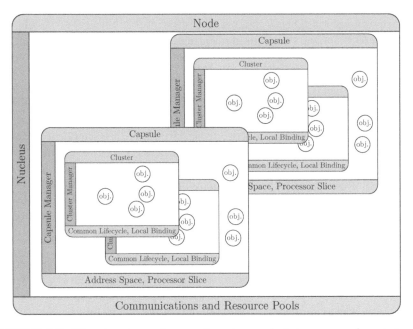

FIGURE 5.2: The structure of an engineering node into managed containers, each with associated properties and resources.

is shown in figure 5.2. The nested components are typically instantiated in sequence as the system is initialized.

At first, the node is configured by its nucleus. The nucleus then allocates resources to a capsule and its capsule manager. The capsule manager then creates any necessary clusters with their cluster managers. When doing this, the capsule manager allocates resources to the cluster manager. Finally, BEOs are instantiated, either inside a cluster or directly in a capsule, to perform the tasks specified for the computational objects they represent.

When a BEO's work is done, its resources are returned to its direct manager. If this is a cluster, the cluster manager may decide to terminate and, when all its work is done, a capsule may terminate, releasing its resources back to the nucleus for reallocation so that the system returns to the initial state in which there is just a node and a nucleus.

5.4   Channel Architecture

The second main set of concepts in the engineering language is concerned with defining a channel architecture that represents the communication infrastructure, which allows engineering objects to interact.

The basic element is the *channel*, which is the engineering equivalent of a computational binding. A channel consists of stubs, binders, protocol objects and interceptors and links communicating basic engineering objects, generally residing in different nodes. Figure 5.3 shows an example of the channel that connects the GUI2User and UserOps BEOs of the PhoneMob application.

Normally there is no need to specify these elements in detail because they are provided by the underlying middleware platform (some of which are themselves standardized [13]). However, there are occasions in which we want to model them functionally, in order to specify some of a channel's properties, or to express requirements on it — such as performance requirements on the channels or security constraints on the protocol objects or interceptors.

All channels involve the same functions, using specialized engineering objects to implement the required functionality in an ordered manner. However, different specific communication architectures may each organize or interleave these functions in their own way.

- *Stubs* transform or monitor information in the channel. This includes, for example, the marshalling and unmarshalling of message elements, the translation of local interfaces into interoperable interface references, or provision of message content encryption. Stubs are the elements that enable access transparency in the communication between two objects written in different languages (such as C++ and Smalltalk). The client object talks to its local stub, which is in charge of translating the request

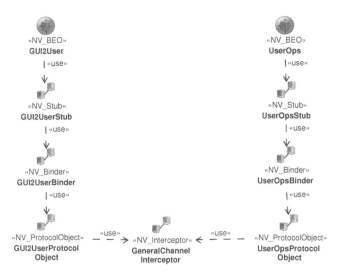

FIGURE 5.3: A channel from the GUI2User BEO to the UserOps BEO.

into a neutral format that is sent along the channel and that the server stubs understand. The received request is then translated by the server stub to the language of the server, and passed to it. The response from the server follows a similar route back to the client, with the stubs again translating the messages. The result is that the client and server objects both think that they are talking to local objects written in their own language.

- **Binders** provide services to establish a distributed binding between the BEOs communicating through the channel and to provide the transparency functions that coordinate replicated object instances. There can be a number of different dialogue styles involved in this. Thus, for instance, the client and server binders can set up the communication channel and the server binder can wait for requests before activating the server object. In fact, the server binder can exhibit different behaviours depending on the activation policy required for the server object; the binder can create one object for every request received, or instantiate only one object to take care of all incoming requests when the channel is started, or it can create one server object that takes care of all requests received during a period of time, but which terminates if it receives no requests for a while; many other instantiation policies are possible.

- A **protocol object** is an encapsulation of the communication capability of the protocols, which may be a full stack of layered protocols for a specific task, such as support for the Web Services protocol SOAP. At a lower level, protocol objects might exploit IPv6 roaming support to keep in contact with mobile devices in a way that does not involve the recreation of bindings. A protocol object may also encapsulate an implementation of some special purpose protocol, such as a driver for a noise resistant satellite link or a quantum cryptography channel.

- When there is a need to cross any organizational, security, system management, naming or protocol domain boundary, some kind of gateway is needed. ***Interceptors*** are the elements provided by the engineering language for this purpose. The fact that all the messages exchanged go through the channel interceptor also enables the addition of interesting management functionality to the system. For instance, messages can be observed in order to carry out quality of service and performance monitoring, or even reordered or filtered for security or other reasons. Another use is where two objects live in different networks, each following some local communication protocol; one uses OSI's seven layers architecture and the other one follows a vendor's proprietary protocol, for instance. The task of bridging these differences can be carried out by an interceptor within the engineering channel that connects them. Interceptors need not analyse all the layers of encapsulation in the communication; they can just pass on information unchanged if it is already understandable to both sides. This is discussed further in chapter 11.

Each of these objects usually has a control interface to allow the coordinated management of the different aspects of the channel and the dynamic reconfiguration of the communication facilities.

5.5   Common Functions and Processes

In addition to allowing the engineering objects to be placed on different nodes, the engineering viewpoint identifies some common functions, called ODP functions, that are needed to support the transparency requirements. Broadly similar sets of functions are found in the various distributed systems available today, although they are generally implemented in a technology-specific way. The engineering viewpoint defines an independent vocabulary, offering a technology-neutral description of them. These functions allow the hiding of system failures, resolving the location of objects from their names, finding service offers (by trading), managing events and so on. Some of the ODP functions can be considered as providing basic processing patterns to achieve the common functionalities for distributed systems, and the basic building blocks for designing distribution infrastructures in a reusable manner.

ODP defines a set of fifteen common functions, organized in four main groups:

- Management functions: the node management, object management, cluster management and capsule management functions.

- Coordination functions: the event notification, checkpoint and recovery, deactivation and reactivation, group, replication, migration, transaction, ACID transaction and engineering interface reference tracking functions.

- Repository functions: the storage, information organization, relocation, type repository and trading functions.

- Security functions: access control, security audit, authentication, integrity, confidentiality, non-repudiation and key-management functions.

This book cannot deal with the detailed definition of the full set of functions, so we restrict the description to a selection of them, which we use to illustrate how they can be combined together to provide useful composite functions to the application designer.

Let's take a look first at the transaction function. Note that this function is more general than the ACID transaction function that is normally used in most bank account management systems. In a real distributed processing environment (think, for instance, of any system built over the Internet), parties involved in a transaction may be spread over different cities or countries, and the transaction may be a long-running process, lasting for days or even weeks. An object providing this function, therefore, will need to communicate with all the participating objects or parties involved in the transaction to monitor the relevant actions and to check for possible inconsistencies.

If an inconsistency is detected, the object will schedule the initialization of some compensation actions, which are usually local transactions at each node to remove the changes and effectively bring each object back to its initial state. For instance, if some money is withdrawn from an account in a transaction, the compensation action means explicitly depositing the same amount back into the account, which is different from the typical implicit rollback action defined in an ACID transaction. With this approach, the states of the objects may become temporarily inconsistent but will eventually become consistent again. This function has been defined in detail in several subsequent standards including a part of the CORBA specifications called *Additional Structuring Mechanisms for the OTS Specification* [39] and OASIS standards called *Business Transaction Protocol* [42] and *Web Services Coordination Framework* [43].

Another relevant example is the ODP trading function. This function originated from the idea of a Yellow Pages service provided by telephone operators; it allows service providers to export their services to a trader (representing the set of objects providing the ODP trading function). The consumer objects can then look up the service, based on a given set of constraints, to get references to the objects providing it. This function will sound familiar to many readers because it has since been at the heart of the SOA architecture and is the basis for the Web Services specification for UDDI. The ODP trading function standard was also adopted by OMG, becoming the *CORBA Object Trading Service* [27].

ODP functions can also be combined to implement certain transparencies. For example, let us look at how system failure can be hidden from computational objects in two different ways by using a selection of the ODP functions.

- One approach is to save the state of the system from time to time, and restore operations from this saved copy whenever necessary. To do this, the checkpoint and recovery function is used to checkpoint a key part of the application state (held, for example, in a cluster), and then later recover the information when it is needed.

- Another approach is to use the replication function; this allows the management of a behaviourally compatible object group. If one replica fails, it is replaced by a new replica that is integrated into the group. Meanwhile, the service is maintained by the remaining members of the group.

ODP functions can also be used to provide other transparencies. For example, the migration function allows an application (cluster) to migrate to another process (capsule). This can be done in two ways. One is to use the replication function to extend a service into a new node by forming a group of two objects, and then removing the original member, leaving one provider at the new node.

Alternatively, migration can be achieved by using the deactivation and reactivation function. A cluster manager first deactivates its cluster, which is then checkpointed. The checkpoint is moved to a new node where it is reactivated in a new capsule.

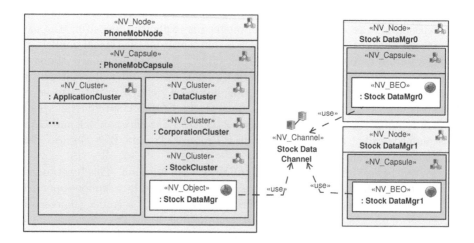

FIGURE 5.4: A storage object is replicated on separate nodes to increase its availability.

Another use of replication transparency, this time to increase both availability and performance, is shown in figure 5.4. This is a refinement of figure 5.1 in which the original Stock DataMgr basic engineering object has been decomposed into a supporting object that remains in the PhoneMob node and coordinates two replicas of the original BEO, each in separate nodes.

Further details of the selection and use of transparencies and migration functions are given in chapter 9.

5.6 Writing Engineering Viewpoint Specifications

The RM-ODP is agnostic with respect to the methodology used to develop the system viewpoint specifications. However, in the following list we provide some guidelines that could be used when writing engineering specifications:

1. Examine the computational viewpoint specification of the system and identify the computational objects needing support; define BEOs corresponding to each of these computational objects.

2. Analyse the required transparency schemata and identify any necessary transparencies and the ODP functions required to implement mechanisms for handling them.

3. Identify the nodes and elaborate the node structures.

4. Associate the BEOs with nodes.

5. Associate the ODP functions with nodes.

6. Add engineering objects where needed to support the groupings of objects identified above (cluster managers, capsule managers and so on).

7. Identify channels and design channel structures.

8. Identify basic conformance points where testing is to be carried out.

The last of these steps forms an important link to the testing process. Conformance points are positioned primarily in terms of interfaces in the engineering viewpoint, although sometimes they may be identified in more abstract viewpoints. Where this is the case, the abstract model elements concerned must be linked by a chain of correspondences to engineering interfaces. RM-ODP defines four kinds of conformance point: interworking, programmatic, perceptual and interchange conformance points (see section 8.3 for details), any of which can be nominated and positioned in an engineering viewpoint specification.

As we will see in the next chapter, the technology viewpoint then says how conformance requirements are to be documented and what additional requirements for conformance to implementable standards should apply. This involves making reference to the conformance points defined here and providing statements about how tests are to be carried out at them.

The full list of steps will lead you to an initial version of the engineering viewpoint specification, following a top-down approach. However, you may also have requirements on artefacts in the engineering and technology viewpoints that require a bottom-up approach. For instance, you may need to use given COTS packages, legacy systems or sets of network channels existing in your organization, or developed for it by third parties, and then include them in your engineering specification.

5.7   Incorporating Current Technologies

When some of the ODP functions and their associated mechanisms are embodied in a specific technology, they are refined to meet the additional requirements originating from the target technology. We have seen that some of the ODP functions, or their adaptations, are found in CORBA, Java or Web Services technologies. These include, for example, naming, event notification, trading, transaction and security support.

There are other situations in which the distribution infrastructure is provided by a third-party organization or company. This happens, for instance, when cloud computing is used. The implications of the adoption of this technology are simply that our engineering specifications should be mapped to the specifications of the transparency mechanisms and common functions implemented and offered by the cloud provider. The details of how they are provided are encapsulated within the cloud provider and so do not form part of our design.

5.8   Relationship with Other Viewpoints

The engineering objects play a part in fulfilling the objectives established in the enterprise viewpoint by supporting the interaction and management of computational objects, which are represented in this viewpoint as Basic Engineering Objects. In addition to this indirect coupling, the various engineering objects will also be subject to generic rules and policies established in the enterprise viewpoint, which control the configuration of the system as a whole. Thus, an enterprise policy may determine performance or security goals affecting the behaviour of nodes, nuclei, capsules, clusters or other ODP functions. In particular, enterprise artefacts may need to be represented by basic engineering objects so that references to them can result in implicit interactions to determine their state or properties.

The designers producing a computational specification focus on computational objects representing the basic functionality of the system, and the interactions at the interfaces of those objects. They do not care how this basic structure is distributed, replicated, migrated or made persistent. It is in the engineering viewpoint that this distribution and the mechanisms necessary to support it become the principal focus.

In general, a computational object has one corresponding basic engineering object, and a computational interface will have one corresponding engineering interface. However, there are exceptions:

1. When a computational object is a binding object, that computational object will result in a corresponding local engineering binding or engineering channel instead of a basic engineering object, and

2. When the given transparency schema requires use of a replication function, multiple basic engineering objects will be introduced to support the required transparency.

Finally, the objects and interfaces in the engineering specification need to be grounded in real resources, such as processors and networks. This involves declaring a set of correspondences between, for example, the engineering nodes and suitable technology objects defined in terms of implementable standards. This is the subject of the next chapter.

Chapter 6

Technology Viewpoint

"The King is dead; long live the King," muttered Alex as he stared at the huge notched axe in its glass case. He had insisted on coming here when Trevor and Trudy had admitted that neither of them had ever been inside the White Castle, even though they worked only three blocks away. It was well worth a Saturday morning to see their reaction to the scale of the place.

"I never did understand that saying," said Trevor. "Surely either he's dead or he isn't. He can't be both." "It's making a deliberate contrast between two views of kingship," said Alex. "The office of king continues, with the heir taking over instantaneously when the old king dies. So one instantiation of the king terminates, but there is still a king, even though it's not the same individual." Trudy grinned. "It sounds more like a Hydra in this case," she said. "But it seems a bit of a funny way of looking at it."

"Do you think so? Think about the specification of a call centre operator we were reviewing on Friday. The operator deals with one customer at a time. A particular dialogue is terminated and the customer description in the operator's state is destroyed. The immediately following action responds to a new customer by instantiating a new description. In our specification, it was still a customer, but a different instance."

"But hang on," said Trevor, turning from an array of crossbows to join the conversation, "aren't both the operator and the customer just roles?" "Yes they are, but my point is that rules for filling them are different, because one operator deals with many customers over a session, but there is a level of continuity in the model. Even if we bind a specific employee to the operator role, there is still a steady flow of different customers, and their identities are chosen by the environment."

They walked through into the banqueting hall, its dark vaulted roof hung with banners. "If you don't like that one, think about the system configurations we have been describing. The elements in the description have quite different lifecycles and ownership. The main servers are fully determined, and we know all about them, right down to their serial numbers and the colour of the cabinets. The local networks are under our management, but are reconfigured and upgraded all the time; we try to track the changes, but they are largely self-configuring at the detailed level, so we concentrate on capturing major properties, like VLAN structure and security domains. The customer systems outside, across the wide area, are beyond our control. We often don't even know what kind of equipment is involved, and must be satisfied with laying down minimum capabilities for things to work. Yet they are all elements in the same configuration specification."

"But if most of the configuration is shifting sand, how about testing? We need a firmer handle on things to test and to monitor for correct operation on a day to day basis." Trudy paused to stare at the huge reveals, which showed the full width of the massive walls. "Yes, the configuration detail influences not just where to test, but also how to test," added Trevor. "But that's why we need to declare conformance points explicitly in the specification, so that we will know which points we have to make accessible in an agreed way. As to how to test, we need information from others, either implementers or deployers of parts not directly under our control. They must provide us enough detail to access the conformance point and understand the choices they have made so that tests can be interpreted correctly."

"OK, Alex, I'm beginning to see now," said Trudy, "but how do we ensure that the right information is provided?" "Well, that's part of procurement or, internally, of direction by senior management. The first requirement is the establishment of clear standards, which was traditionally one of the responsibilities of the monarch. Long live the King!"

6.1 Linking to the Real World

Most software designers would prefer to live in an ideal world that allows them to specify, develop and deploy their systems for any vendor platform without any technological or cost constraints. However, we all know that this is never the case, and the technology viewpoint addresses this problem. In most situations, the designer needs to take into consideration the IT infrastructure already available in the company, their budgetary requirements and the existing commercial policies or strategies that might force (or forbid) the use of particular vendor technologies. For example, a particular corporation may require the use of the huge, shiny blade array that was acquired only a couple of years ago. Given that such a large investment has just been made, they cannot afford to buy different hardware machines or software applications not compatible with their current platform. Another company may have a corporate policy that forces the use of open source software in all their applications. Others may require the use of low-cost PCs for running all their IT applications.

These requirements pose very strong constraints on the system implementation, and so, as a result, on its software architecture, the programming languages in which applications are developed, and the way the system functionality is distributed. However, such requirements do not form part of any of the viewpoint specifications described so far, and are overlooked by most specification approaches. Thus, they end up being incorporated very late in the development process of the system. This is normally too late, when almost no significant changes to the system specifications can be tolerated.

A second concern that is often ignored when preparing the specifications of a large system is the need for establishing different conformance and compliance criteria and tests. Conformance tests are those which check that the components, languages and protocols used by an implementation conform to the specifications and the standards listed in them as mandatory for the system. For example, we may need to check that system services are implemented as web services whose interfaces are described using WSDL and which communicate using REST protocols, or that our operating systems are ISO/IEC/IEEE 9945 POSIX conformant. Conformance tests are specified in ODP using conformance points, where it is possible to check that the real implementation matches the specification. Compliance tests are of a different nature. They are concerned with checking that the system specification is consistent with the architecture or design framework being used. Chapter 8 deals in more detail with these two kinds of tests.

Finally, any system specification should also include some plans for the technology selection processes and for the evolution of the system parts (that is, the software and hardware products that together comprise the system implementation). We are all aware that current technologies change rapidly, and therefore the kinds of changes foreseen and how to cope with them need to be explicitly described and documented somewhere in the system specifications.

The developers of the RM-ODP introduced a dedicated viewpoint to address these issues, namely the technology viewpoint, which is concerned with all aspects related to the choice of technology to implement the ODP system.

6.2   The Elements of the Technology Language

The main goals of the technology language are to provide concepts and constructs to specify the hardware and software products from which the system is built, to test that such an implementation complies with the specification as prescribed by the rest of the viewpoints and to specify the plans and processes for the selection, acquisition and evolution of the system parts (hardware and software products) during its lifetime. The technology language defines four main concepts: technology objects, implementable standards, implementation and IXIT (Implementation eXtra Information for Testing — a name derived from the earlier protocol specific OSI concept of a PIXIT).

6.2.1   Technology Objects

The technology specification describes the implementation of the ODP system in terms of a configuration of *technology objects* (representing the hardware and software components of the implementation) and the interfaces between them. These objects are constrained by the cost and availability of satisfactory technology products.

Technology objects are normally specified in terms of their types. Examples of such types include the kinds of PCs, servers, ATMs, printers and other hardware devices that can be used to implement the system and execute its functionality. Giving a clear definition of these types helps in answering questions such as whether we are going to count on there being colour printers available or not, or whether our system will run some particular services on a central server, on a PC or from an external cloud computing system. The technology specification also describes the types of operating systems and applications (such as browsers or text editors, for example) and the types of connections (LANs, WANs, intranets and so on) that will be used for deploying the engineering channels.

For example, figure 6.1 shows the technology configuration of the PhoneMob system using the UML4ODP notation. It is described using a UML deployment diagram that specifies the deployment architecture of the system by showing the different technology object types that will be used and how they can be connected. In a deployment diagram, a computer node is expressed as a node and lines are introduced to express interfaces between the nodes. Different types of network are also depicted as nodes. The diagram shows that there will be three different kinds of computing resource (PCs, enterprise application servers and backend business servers), two different kinds of communication media (LAN and WAN) and, as special peripherals on the PCs, printers and barcode readers. PCs and enterprise application servers can be connected to LANs and WANs, whilst backend business servers can only be connected to isolated LANs under the control of a firewall. Connections to the WAN are also achieved through the firewall.

The technology selection has clear consequences. For example, the types of the technology objects used may affect the provision of quality of service. They determine the performance costs of interactions and thus, indirectly, the quality of service which can be achieved by the behaviour defined in other viewpoints. The selection may also affect the way in which functionality needs to be developed, and even the software architecture of the application. For example, some technological platforms such as JEE or .NET impose particular architectural styles (such as client-server or multi-layered) and provide some common functions and services. Other platforms may not provide all the necessary services and thus any that are missing must be implemented by adding code each time they are needed.

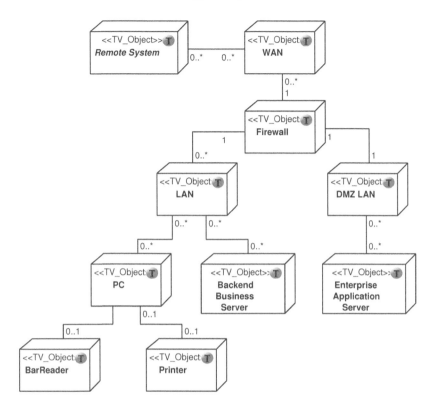

FIGURE 6.1: An overview of the node configuration.

6.2.2 Implementable Standards

Although the level of interoperability between vendor platforms is increasing nowadays, there are still some incompatibilities that force the use of particular applications that match the operating system selected in the specification (Linux, MacOS, Windows and so on). This is why there is the need to specify the ***implementable standards*** to which technology objects must conform. Examples of such implementable standards are the application programming interfaces for *ISO/IEC/IEEE 9945 (POSIX)*, or for *ISO/IEC 9075-10, SQL — Object Language Bindings (SQL/OLB)* and media format specifications like *ISO/IEC 13490 CD-ROM filing systems*. Figure 6.2 shows a schematic view of the business server technology object, which contains other technology objects that represent the CPU, memory, middleware and so on, and the implementable standards to which some of these objects should conform.

Implementable standards are effectively templates for the technology objects. Thus, the technology viewpoint provides a link between the set of viewpoint specifications and the real implementation by listing the standards

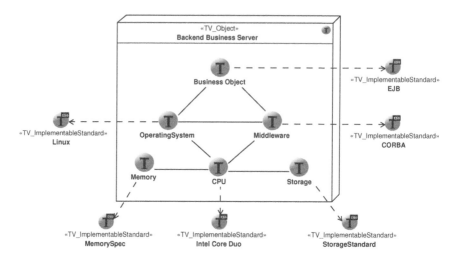

FIGURE 6.2: Internal node structure and implementable standards.

used to provide the necessary basic operations using the chosen languages, operating systems or hardware platforms.

6.2.3   IXIT

The technology language also plays a major role in the conformance testing process. Conformance testing is based on the observation of the system implementation at certain points defined in the specification to be conformance points. These points are a subset of the set of reference points established in the specification which need to be accessible for testing (see chapter 8 for more detail). Although how they can be found is documented in this viewpoint, the points themselves are typically associated with various kinds of accessible interfaces defined in the engineering specification. Four classes of reference point at which conformance tests can be applied are defined. The first is a programmatic reference point representing a software interface, observable via operating system logs or by the installation of portable interceptors. The second is a perceptual reference point observed by direct inspection of the physical system, looking at a screen or a mechanical actuator. The third is an interworking reference point, checked by examining the messages passing between systems, and the last is an interchange reference point, checked by reading some portable medium produced, such as a CD-ROM or external hard drive.

However, since a specification typically does not define a complete protocol stack, but leaves some detailed choices to the implementer, an implementation needs to be accompanied by some extra explanation from the implementer about how the implementation is structured and how the tester is to access the conformance points declared in the specification. This body of information is called the implementation extra information for testing, or IXIT. The technology specification gives a proforma stating minimum requirements for the information the implementer must include in the IXIT. This information is then used to interpret the observations a tester can make in terms of the vocabulary and concepts defined in the other viewpoints. For example, it allows valid interactions to be recognized, so that their appropriateness can be checked against some specified object behaviour (see chapter 8).

Proformas indicating the information that an implementer is required to include when producing the IXIT can be attached to any technology object or interface; figure 6.3 shows an example of the association of requirements for this additional information with two technology objects. Another example might involve the technology specification saying that the implementer is required to state the precise version number of any mandatory platform components provided, such as the EJB environment in an application server.

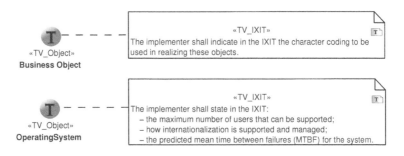

FIGURE 6.3: Some requirements for elements in the IXIT.

6.2.4 Implementation

The technology viewpoint defines an ***implementation*** as the result of a process that instantiates a specification, the validity of which can be subject to test. These processes not only cover development, but also other activities related to the system deployment, configuration and evolution. They include, for instance, configuration guides, deployment plans, change management plans, criteria for the selection of technology and of service providers, maintenance processes, and so on. In UML4ODP, these processes are expressed using activity diagrams stereotyped «TV_Implementation».

Figure 6.4 shows an example for the selection of a technology object. It assumes that the owner and operator of a system need to add some functionality; they perform a search for components that meets their needs and, if they already have the elements of a suitable solution, they select and deploy them. However, if nothing suitable is available, they specify their requirements as a supply request and issue it to a subcontractor who will implement the com-

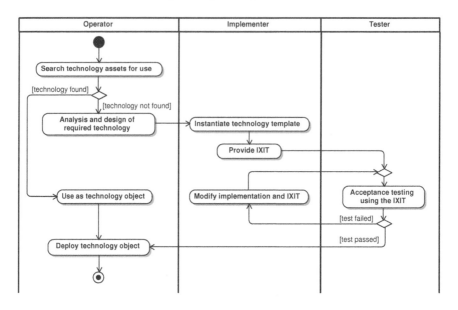

FIGURE 6.4: A TV_Implementation activity selecting a technology object.

ponents and describe the solution in an IXIT. An acceptance tester acting for
the operator then uses this information to test the new component. If the
test is successful, the component is deployed, but otherwise it is corrected and
tested again.

6.3   Relationship with Other Viewpoints

The technology viewpoint is primarily related to the engineering viewpoint
because it specifies the hardware and software components that have to implement the engineering objects, including the nodes and channels identified
in the engineering specification. Thus, there is a technology object corresponding to every atomic or composite engineering object. Note that the
relation goes both ways: engineering objects provide the entities that need
to be implemented, and technology objects provide the information on the
specific technology used to implement them and the standards to which these
implementations should conform.

Chapter 7

Correspondences — Joining It All Up

Nigel stepped back from the whiteboard. "Well, at least we agree we need to have users and sessions in the specification." Claire pursed her lips. "I'm not sure we mean the same thing, though," she said. "In my computational model a user has a name and credentials, but in your engineering model it's just anyone sitting at a browser. My sessions can be suspended, but yours map directly to network connections, if I understand this constraint here."

Neither of them wanted to change the way they worked and they looked defiantly at one another, each searching for an opening. This was going to be difficult.

"Wait a minute, people," said Alex, "this is quite usual, and it is exactly why I said correspondences are not just a matter of matching names. It seems clear to me that the correspondences you need here establish a subtype relationship." They all relaxed slightly. "But how does that cover the difference in session lifetimes?" asked Claire. "Well, look at your session states. If a session exists, it can either be active or suspended. So Nigel's sessions correspond to your active sessions. We can handle that by putting an extra constraint on the correspondence between the states." "I think I see," said Nigel, "so that means we have a subtype relation between the session types and a constrained equivalence relation between the states, but not a one-to-one relation between the instances." "Yes, that's right. The instance relation is one to many." Claire smiled. "Actually it's going to be many to many, isn't it? My model has sign out and sign in operations that can be used in a single communication session, so that it can carry more than one user session, one after the other."

Nigel walked over to the window and gazed out at the roofline opposite for a moment; the sun picked out the brilliant orange of the rings of lichen on the slates. This was another change the cleaner air was allowing back into the docklands, and he wondered if the moths were changing back to their old colour to compensate. "What I don't see," he said, turning back to face the others, "is how changing these constraints works through into implementation changes in the running system." "Well," Alex began, "there could be a number of routes, but they all depend on the tools picking up the constraints and deducing that they imply the choice of suitable engineering templates. The simplest way is probably to make communications session reuse one of the selection criteria for picking a binder template. If there is a computational action that changes the user identity, this will imply use of a multi-user binder. And there will have to be such an action, because the detail of the sign-on operation will involve it."

"We are asking a lot of our tools, aren't we?" said Claire, tilting her head. The same sun picked out the highlights in her blond hair. "But we should!" Alex replied. "The tools are much better than the programmers are at spotting simple logical implications from different parts of the design, and for doing boring but crucial consistency checks as the design develops." "And if the logic isn't simple, or the side effects not obvious?" She was teasing him, and he knew it. "Then heaven preserve us from clever programmers. If the system depends on a line of code so obscure you want to put it on a T-shirt, I'm betting the system will be a pig to maintain."

7.1   The Need for Correspondences

So far, we have concentrated on the set of five viewpoint languages. It is all too easy to leave it at that, but we need to relate the different viewpoints so that they are woven together to give a unified system specification. This chapter aims to redress the balance by concentrating on the correspondences between elements in different viewpoints.

If the viewpoints are seen as representing the areas of concern of the different stakeholders, then the correspondences represent the agreements between these stakeholders about how their views of the world overlap and what entities are to be found in multiple views.

Each correspondence in ODP links a pair of viewpoints, and so has two endpoints, one in each viewpoint. All the **correspondences** between a particular pair of viewpoints together form what is called a **correspondence specification**. It would, in principle, be possible to define multi-way correspondences, but these are more difficult to understand and manage, so a mesh of binary relationships is used for simplicity. As a result, with five viewpoints, there could be at most ten correspondence specifications, but there is not necessarily something significant to say in every possible case, so in practice there are less than ten. However, there cannot be less than four sets of correspondences in total, or the overall specification will not be completely connected and will fall apart.

The idea of a correspondence in ODP is deliberately kept quite general because the various viewpoints may be specified using different languages, satisfying their individual needs. A correspondence is therefore a general link between specification elements with an associated rule or constraint indicating the way the elements in the two different viewpoints are related. The linkage of the two specification elements can be made independent of the languages involved, although the expression of the additional rules to be applied generally does require some knowledge of the languages being used. We shall return to this point later.

The simplest kind of correspondence is to say that two elements refer to the same thing. Thus, for example, we can state that the enterprise object filling the role Branch staff corresponds to the computational object Repair-CentreStaff, meaning that they are two representations in different viewpoints for one and the same individual in the real world. Of course, in our simple example, we could have aligned these names, but, in large-scale specifications drawing on different existing libraries, this may be much more difficult.

7.2   Different Kinds of Correspondence

Most modern modelling languages have some concept of an object as a representation of the entities that are being described, and an object has attributes representing the properties of the real-world entities and behaviour indicating how it interacts with its environment and evolves over time. While the statement at the end of the previous section that a correspondence shows that two descriptions are referring to the same entity may seem straightforward, it does not follow that the way the description is expressed is the same in each case. The properties expressed may not be exactly the same; indeed, they may be completely different.

So, even in the simple case of declaring that two objects represent the same entity, we also need to be clear whether there is a correspondence between their types as a whole or between individual attributes, and if so whether the attribute types correspond. Even if two specifications are dealing with the same entity, they may be describing quite different properties of it.

In fact, the types used in the different viewpoints will generally be different because they will have been chosen to express different concerns, and so represent different abstractions of the same entity. For example, the enterprise description of a phone may express its value, service bundle and ownership, while an information description of the same phone may express its memory capacity and SIM number.

Often, the two viewpoint specifications deal with similar properties but at different levels of detail, so that an attribute in one description corresponds loosely to a different attribute in the other, which may have a type that is a subtype of the one used in the first description (because it needs to provide more detailed information).

The correspondence can also add information to the specification by stating a correlation between attribute values. For example, we could make a correspondence between phones with the premium service bundle and those whose memory size is bigger than two megabytes. This now means that all premium service users have phones with enough capacity, which is a fact that could not have been expressed in either of the viewpoints being linked on their own.

Correspondences can, in fact, be established between pairs of specification elements of any relevant kind. In addition to objects and attributes, we may, for example, establish correspondences between actions or states, and here it is more likely that the two viewpoints as a whole will be using different levels of abstraction. One viewpoint may talk about broad business actions, while the other expresses fine-grained computational actions. In such a case, the correspondence will involve a *part-of* relationship, since we can say that observing the business action implies that the computational action has occurred, but the computational action just implies that the business action is in progress, not that it has completed.

Another kind of correspondence is found between viewpoints that deal primarily in specifying types (such as the information viewpoint) and viewpoints dealing primarily with instances (such as the computational viewpoint). Here the correspondence can be the familiar type-instance relationship. Examples can be found in links between the types (or templates) defined in the information and technology viewpoints and specific configurations defined in the technology, computational or enterprise viewpoints.

7.3   Correspondences Required by the ODP Architecture

The ODP reference model defines the concepts and rules that make up the five viewpoint languages, but it leaves as much flexibility as possible for designers to use them freely to express the system that best meets their requirements. One consequence of this is that it places very few constraints on exactly what correspondences there should be; they will be decided primarily by the properties of the problem domain. However, the reference model does, itself, lay down a few mandatory correspondences, and these are the result of areas where there are architectural concepts spanning or linking viewpoints. These correspondences ensure architectural integrity.

We consider two areas where there are architectural constraints. The first of the areas where correspondences are stated is between the information and computational viewpoints. Here there is a requirement that the constraints of the invariant and dynamic schemata, which represent required information state transitions, should be traceable in the computational view as either interactions or internal actions of the corresponding computational objects. This is necessary to demonstrate that the requirements are being met.

The second area is between the computational and engineering viewpoints, and deals with a set of constraints to ensure that transparencies can be provided without introducing unexpected snags or side effects as a result of unexpected feature interactions. The resulting correspondences are sketched in

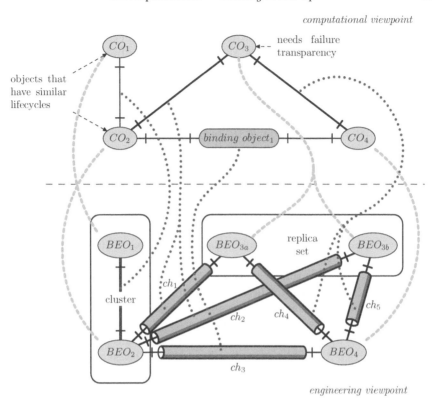

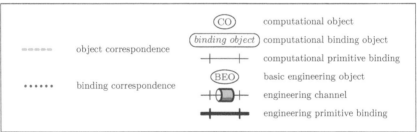

FIGURE 7.1: Mandatory computational to engineering correspondences.

figure 7.1. The aim here is to create an engineering structure that will be able to evolve in a flexible way to deal with changes in the environment and map cleanly at all times onto the computational design it is supporting.

One of the mechanisms that may complicate this mapping is the support of replication. The various constraints therefore enforce simplicity in the cases where there is no replication so as to avoid adding extra complexity to the replicated situations. This is achieved by saying that, unless there is replication, there is a one-to-one correspondence between computational objects and their supporting basic engineering objects. If there is replication, one computational object corresponds exclusively to a single set of basic engineering objects; in figure 7.1, for example, the computational object CO_3 corresponds to the set containing BEO_{3a} and BEO_{3b}.

This deals with most computational objects, but not all. Computational binding objects are special because they encapsulate communications facilities. Binding objects, or primitive bindings of interfaces, are required to correspond either to engineering channels or to local interactions within clusters. There are also rules to ensure that computational actions are refined in a consistent way when elaborated as more detailed dialogues.

These are very simple constraints, but there will also be many more domain-specific constraints. To help the specifier organize these, the UML4ODP standard includes a number of checklists, in the form of metarules for identifying the kind of correspondence statements needed to link the different viewpoints. As an example, it states that, for each enterprise object in the enterprise specification, the specifier shall indicate the configuration of computational objects that realizes the required enterprise behaviour. Similarly, for each interaction in the enterprise specification, they shall provide a list of those computational interfaces and operations or streams that correspond to the enterprise interaction, together with a statement of whether this correspondence applies to all occurrences of the interaction, or is qualified by a predicate. It is then up to the specifier to apply these rules and, in doing so, generate a set of domain-specific correspondences.

7.4 Anatomy of a Correspondence Specification

The UML4ODP standard brings all this together by defining a metamodel for correspondence specifications. This is outlined in figure 7.2. The specification itself is a separate model, linked to the viewpoint models but standing outside of all of them.

The two viewpoints characterize the specification that is to tie them together. The specification itself is built up from a set of *correspondence rules*, members of which are referred to from a set of *correspondence links*. Every correspondence link has two *correspondence endpoints*, which are each associated with some set of *terms* in the viewpoint concerned.

The element Term in this metamodel can be associated with any language element in the viewpoint concerned. In the UML profile, this is done by the use of tags, so that there is no commitment to the properties of the namespaces concerned; this results in the minimum of impact on the writers of the viewpoint specifications.

Correspondence rules express constraints that must be enforced for the set of elements from the two viewpoints being linked. One example is the

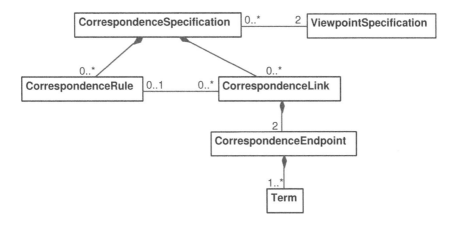

FIGURE 7.2: The elements of a correspondence specification.
Taken from the UML4ODP standard; for copyright, see Preface.

constraint we mentioned earlier about phones with premium service bundles needing to have a memory capacity above a certain threshold. In UML4ODP, these constraints are usually expressed in OCL. Correspondence rules can also serve to provide information about the kind of relationship that links the elements; a few examples are *use, runsOn, affects, implements, realizes* and *replicates.* These kinds of relationship are not predetermined, but are normally defined by the system designers. This definition must include their semantics, indicating what they are to mean in this system specification. For example, in the PhoneMob specification we use a runsOn constraint to indicate the technology object types used to run particular BEOs, or replicates to indicate the correspondence that links a computational object with the set of replicated BEOs that support it.

7.5   Taking a Formal View

The set of viewpoints defines an associated set of domain-specific languages. Each of these languages is formally defined in terms of a mapping of its elements onto some very simple supporting model, often some form of labelled transition system representing the way the system's state evolves. If we are to unify the different viewpoint languages, we must first produce a unified supporting framework. This brings us back to the importance of unifying the set of primitive types assumed, and the combination of different languages is much simpler if they share a common set of primitive types. Fortunately, there is now a quite broad consensus on the primitive types such as boolean, integer and string; part 2 of the reference model also provides a uniform foundation for the object modelling concepts needed.

We then need to express the evolution of the system as a whole by combining the interpretations of all the corresponding items in the different domain-specific languages to give a set of rules for the evolution of the complete system's state.

It is important that the coupling between the viewpoint specifications should be kept as lightweight as possible. This is why we have stressed the need to separate the namespaces associated with the different viewpoints. We need to be able to add elements to a particular viewpoint without incurring the overheads of ensuring the names being used in the additions are unique across the whole design, and we need to be able to carry out significant refactoring of the design within a viewpoint without requiring matching changes to be made elsewhere.

All this may sound rather heavyweight, with the potential for more correspondences than model elements in the viewpoints themselves. However, things are not quite as bad as they may seem. Although there is a need for a great deal of information in the correspondences, a very high proportion of it can be inferred from some quite simple rules.

Firstly, despite what was said previously, we can identify certain contexts in which name equivalence can be taken as implying correspondence. Although, in general, the namespaces of the different viewpoints are unrelated, and accidental name matches can occur, an organization will often choose to align parts of these namespaces to aid its own internal communication. In these situations, stakeholders agree that, as long as there are correspondences at the type level, names will not be reused for different purposes within the scope established by the type relations. If this is the case, two elements in different viewpoints that have the same name can be taken to have an implied correspondence.

Secondly, we can go even further by asserting correspondence not just at the type and instance level, but at the level of a complete type system or subsystem. This may be done by importing a family of type definitions from one viewpoint into another (or into two viewpoint specifications from an external library), so that there are automatic correspondences wherever the shared definitions are used. This kind of sharing is often based on a set of type definitions from the information viewpoint; these are then used either directly or via local refinements in other viewpoints.

However, we cannot lose sight of the fact that the correspondences bind the viewpoints together into a coherent whole, and that the whole, once constructed, shows the problems of scale and complexity that led us to opt for viewpoints in the first place. So what have we gained, after all? Well, the main design work is carried out in the viewpoints, where life is simpler, and we can then exploit strong tools to check the consistency of, and derive implementation components for, the complete system. Once we have the correspondences, either by explicit definition or by derivation from some higher-level rules, we can use them to run checks and analyse the behaviour of the system we have specified.

Correspondences also have other important uses. For example, since they identify the related elements in a multi-viewpoint specification, they can help to identify the elements that would be affected by a change. Thus, they can be useful in performing some kind of *what-if* or impact analysis: which information and computational elements will be affected if I decide to change a policy in the enterprise viewpoint? Will a change in a set of engineering objects affect any particular service level agreement or environment contract in the enterprise or computational viewpoints?

Similarly, the constraints associated with the correspondence rules can be used to maintain consistency in the viewpoint specifications. Consider, for example, a consistent set of models related by a set of correspondences. If we make a change in one of the models, in many situations it is possible to propagate that change through the correspondences, thereby changing the other models so that the consistency is restored. Think, for instance, of a correspondence that establishes that the name of a binding object in the computational viewpoint is the same as the name of the corresponding channel in the engineering viewpoint. If the designer decides to change the name of the channel, the change can easily be propagated to the computational binding object, and vice versa.

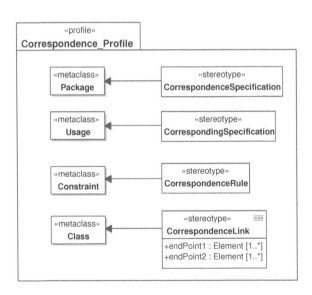

FIGURE 7.3: The correspondence profile from UML4ODP.

Taken from the UML4ODP standard; for copyright, see Preface.

7.6   Examples of Correspondences

We can demonstrate the principles involved in defining correspondences by looking at some simple examples. They are shown here using the UML profile defined for correspondences in the UML4ODP standard, which uses four stereotypes as shown in figure 7.3. Correspondence endpoints are represented as tag definitions, providing great flexibility to refer to any model element in the specification.

Let us show some examples of use. First, figure 7.4a shows the correspondence between the binding object and the engineering channel depicted in figure 7.1. Another correspondence (shown in figure 7.4b) establishes the relationship between the Stock DataMgmt computational object from figure 4.5 and the replica engineering objects which support it, introduced in figure 5.4.

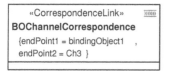

(a) A binding object and the corresponding channel.   (b) A computational object and its engineering replicas.

(c) An enterprise task and the computational operation it uses.

FIGURE 7.4: Three examples of correspondences.

A more interesting correspondence defined for the PhoneMob system (shown in figure 7.4c) establishes that a task defined in the enterprise viewpoint is related to a specific operation signature defined in the computational viewpoint specification. Here, the correspondence indicates that a particular computational operation type is to be used to support the business process step in the enterprise specification.

7.7   Tool Support for Specifying Correspondences

Usability is one of the limitations of most current UML tools. Writing large systems specifications becomes a tedious and cumbersome task; in particular, the specification of tag values of stereotyped elements normally implies a long sequence of interactions with the tool. This is especially relevant in the case of the specification of correspondences in UML4ODP, given that the number of correspondences is normally large and the related elements need to be selected individually for each correspondence. Tools can be a great help in such a situation.

It is possible to define correspondences in a more succinct and visual manner, using stereotyped dependencies between the related elements (although the direction of the dependency is not significant). For example, a tool can extend the UML4ODP standard notation for expressing correspondences, providing a shorthand notation that is easier and quicker to draw, while, at the same time, providing a more intuitive representation. Using it would allow the relations between elements to be shown very quickly, with the core facilities available in most UML drawing tools. The diagram depicted in figure 7.5 shows an alternative representation of the correspondence between a binding object and an engineering channel that was shown in figure 7.4a.

«CorrespondenceLink»

«CV_BindingObject»   «NV_Channel»
bindingObject1   **Ch3**

FIGURE 7.5: A simpler representation of the binding object to engineering channel correspondence.

A tool can take care of the model transformations required to convert automatically correspondences specified in this way to correspondence specifications that conform to the UML4ODP standard notation, and vice versa.

Similarly, the user does not need to specify all correspondences manually in all cases because a tool can easily specify all correspondences between the elements in different viewpoints that are closely related according to some given criterion (for instance, having the same name), or defined in an implicit way using rules (expressed, for example, using QVT relations — see chapter 15). It is normally easier to fine tune a set of correspondences produced automatically from a small set of implicit relations than to start from scratch and then have to specify a large number of individual correspondences one by one.

Part III

Using ODP

About Part III

Building on the viewpoint structure, this part examines a number of ways in which requirements can vary, and shows how system designs can be made more resilient and more broadly applicable by applying suitable architectural techniques.

To set the stage, chapter 8 explores the concepts of compliance and conformance, which provide the bridges between architecture, design and implementation. It shows how the different levels of design can flow through naturally into conformance assessment and testing.

Following this, a series of chapters each examine different kinds of variation and how they can be coped with. Chapter 9 looks at variation in the environment in which the system may be deployed, and how the use of transparencies can decouple the application-specific concerns from these variations. Chapter 10 looks at the way changes in management thinking can be accommodated by using the idea of mutable policies.

The following chapters, dealing with the federation of different organizations, incorporation of existing components and response to changes in requirements, each look at different ways the architectural framework can enable the smooth evolution of systems. These aspects are all concerned with the way systems change over time, and how the lifetime of a design can be extended in a changing environment.

Chapter 8

Conformance — Does It Do the Right Thing?

Nigel had paused at Trudy's cubicle to say hello, and had got more than he bargained for. Her desk was covered with pieces from printed documentation, and there were about a dozen windows open on her screens. They were all covered with pieces of highlighting and notes, and the whiteboard was a tangle of circled references linked by arrows. One particular looped set of arrows was traced in red marker.

"It's no good," she said, "they just don't say what the rules are." "What's the problem?" "They claim to be market leaders for CRM systems, but they don't make it clear what the package really needs. It's just like that transaction abort problem last year, where we found that all the messages had to be mapped to full SOAP. The obvious REST equivalent just didn't work, but there was no warning in the installation guide."

Nigel ran his fingers through his hair. Indeed he did remember. It had delayed an important upgrade and Marcus had not been best pleased. "But these aren't transactional components you are looking at here." He waved towards the whiteboard. "No, this is a different problem, Nigel, to do with registering interests. I just want to know whether this operation has to be called by a descendent of one of the package's workflows, or whether it can be called by anyone. It all depends on the definition of parent activity and propagating action here, but the definitions are circular, as you can see. But the real problem is that this other step in the circle can't be checked unless we know what supporting mechanisms qualify — the same problem again, really — and their documentation *just does not say*." Her voice had a slightly desperate edge to it as she hammered each word out.

"It sounds to me," he said, "as if they don't have a clear conformance model for their product, which in turn means that the consortium writing the so-called standard they claim to be following didn't know they should be insisting on one." He thought for a minute. "Look, all you can do at this stage is ask their support line what it does, and be sure the lawyers put the answer into the Memorandum of Understanding so that we get some insurance. But it's a classic case of *I wouldn't have started from here*. Come on, I'll get you a coffee."

8.1   Compliance and Conformance

When using a framework like the ODP reference model, we need to have ways of assessing whether the interpretation being made is correct. There are two concepts that can be used here — ***conformance*** and ***compliance***. The distinction depends on whether there needs to be some testing of a physical product, or whether reasoning about the consistency between two pieces of specification is enough (see figure 8.1).

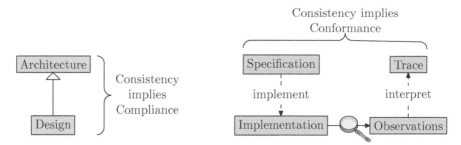

FIGURE 8.1: Assessing compliance and conformance.

Whenever we take a reference model, such as the RM-ODP, and use it as a starting point and create either a more detailed framework or a complete design, we need to check that the result complies with the reference model. The same is true when we use any other similarly abstract architectural standard. In effect, this involves looking at the reference model and the new material together and asking whether they still make sense. A composite model is formed by tracing every use of a concept back to the corresponding reference model definition and then doing some logical analysis to see if there are any contradictions. If there is a contradiction, then the new specification is not compliant.

The situation with conformance is much more complicated. Here we want to ask whether some product does what a specification says it should. This cannot be done by reasoning about descriptions. It requires some kind of ***testing***.[1] Testing is a process that involves observation of what a system does; the result of the process is a set of test results — statements of what was observed — and testing conformance is essentially equivalent to checking the compliance of the test results to the original specification.

---

[1]Of course, we can only ask questions about conformance if the target specification is itself consistent.

8.2   A Conformance Community

The idea of conformance can be applied very broadly in many different areas, from product manufacturing through service provision through to the application of management guidelines. ISO work on conformity assessment [19] aims to be sufficiently general to cover this entire range, but for our purposes we want a more specific framework, concentrating on open distributed systems.

Part 2 of the RM-ODP provides a conformance architecture, which you can think of as an enterprise model of the design, implementation and testing activity (see figure 8.2); it defines three main roles, identifying the specifier, the implementer and the tester. As usual, an object can fulfil more than one of these roles, but it is simpler to describe the case where the roles are distinct — the so-called third-party testing scenario.

The *specifier* produces and publishes a specification. Not only does this specification say what an implementation should do, but it also constrains how the implementation can be tested by defining where its behaviour can be observed. This is necessary because many different styles of specifications can represent the same intended object, and the implementer should be left with as much freedom as possible to produce something that works efficiently.

For example, a business process might describe the packing and dispatch of a repaired phone as involving a sequence of steps: wrap the phone, print a test report, print a label on the box, fill the box, perform a final check and seal the box. It may or may not matter exactly in what order these happen. If the specifier is just using the sequence for simplicity of description, but would accept other sequential or parallel behaviour as doing the same job, we don't want to be unduly restrictive.

However, for assessing some of these activities, such as the final check, it may really matter that all the earlier steps have been completed. In this case, the specifier declares the interaction between the checker and the previous steps as a *reference point*. This means that it is a place where correct behaviour may potentially need to be observed.

UML4ODP provides a simple profile that allows elements in the specification to be stereotyped as «ODP_ReferencePoint» and qualified by suitable comments stereotyped as «ODP_ConformanceStatement».

A specification will generally be intended for reuse; the final decision about what needs to be tested may vary when it is reused. A specification may therefore identify quite a lot of reference points, indicating where testing is possible, and the final integration of the full product specification will then involve selecting a subset of these as *conformance points*, where it is stated that final product testing is required.

The *implementers* obviously have to produce an implementation that behaves according to the specification, and this involves them in making im-

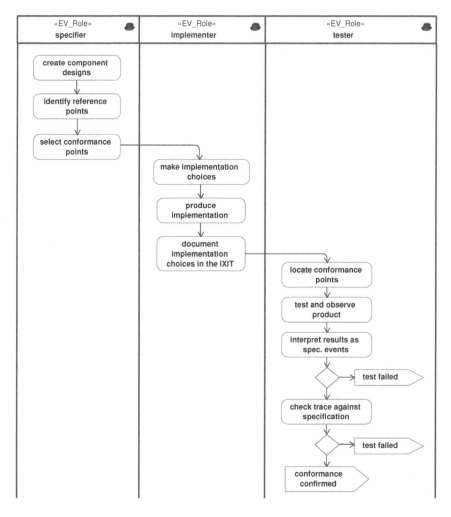

FIGURE 8.2: A simplified view of the testing activity.

plementation choices where the specification does not go into full detail. However, they also have various obligations to provide information about what they have done. They have to declare what specifications, and what options, they are implementing; this will often involve confirming what they have been contracted to do, but it may not be so clear for off-the-shelf offerings. Secondly, they have to declare how the conformance points can be located, in terms of the access a tester has to the physical or software artefacts being supplied. Finally, the implementer needs to say how the atomic concepts in the specification are realized. This last obligation may involve them in providing a lot of information. For example, a computational specification may be expressed in a quite abstract way, in terms of high-level interactions or messages. The implementer needs to state how these interactions are supported, which may involve reference to other standards or provision of additional pieces of specification.

The *tester* stimulates and observes behaviour at the conformance points. The observations are necessarily at a very detailed level, in principle observing, for example, electrical or optical signals being exchanged with the system under test. These have to be interpreted in terms of the symbols they represent, and then these in turn interpreted as complete messages, and so on. Eventually, this process results in detection of one of the atomic concepts from the specification being tested (or an error in the implementation being detected if the observations cannot be interpreted or make no sense). The tester then knows that an event in the specification has occurred, and the sequence of events detected so far (called a trace) can be checked against the behaviour that the specification allows.

8.3 Types of Reference Point

The testing process can take a number of different forms, depending on the nature of the reference points involved. The RM-ODP identifies four important kinds of reference point, as follows.

An *interworking reference point* is associated with some physical communication channel, such as a network link or a connector between subsystems. The physical signals passing between the communicating systems can be observed. For instance, when a pair of protocol objects with SOAP interfaces are bound together, an access cable to a network over which they communicate can be specified as an interworking reference point.

A *programmatic reference point* indicates a software interface where interactions can be observed for testing purposes. This implies some support from the local system infrastructure to report events, such as calls to kernel or middleware services, or provision for installation of some software monitoring component, as might be provided by a modified class loader. For example, a BEO may need to use an event notification service provided by an engineering object within the same cluster. This interaction will be local and therefore checks at the interface will involve use of a programmatic reference point.

A *perceptual reference point* is a point where the system interacts with the real world. This may be via a keyboard and screen, or with some more specialist device, like an ATM terminal, or through sensors and robotic devices; there are many other examples. Testing at such a point involves watching what happens when the system reports it is taking an action; if the control system for a chemical plant reports a valve is being closed, can we actually see this has in fact happened? Alternatively, a security audit function

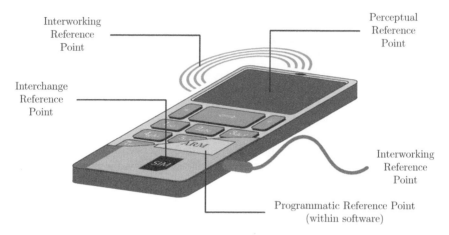

Interworking
Reference
Point

Perceptual
Reference
Point

Interchange
Reference
Point

Interworking
Reference
Point

Programmatic Reference Point
(within software)

FIGURE 8.3: Conformance points for the mobile phone.

may be required to generate a pop-up message when it detects unusual event traces. Checking that this actually happens must be performed at a perceptual reference point.

An *interchange reference point* is a point where some portable medium is read or written, and this process can be checked by observing the state of the medium before and after a known series of operations. For example, the specification might state that, in certain circumstances, configuration details on a removable SD memory card are updated; the tester can remove this card and see if the change has in fact been recorded. Or a customer's confirmation of order information may be written onto a smartcard, and subsequently this recorded copy can be checked for consistency with the system's state.

To illustrate these ideas, consider the provision of a phone tester by a subcontractor (see figure 8.3). A test SIM is loaded into the repaired phone, which is then connected to the tester, using an external interface provided by the handset manufacturer. A software harness is loaded into the phone's memory. The tester orchestrates a series of tests, in which the functions of the phone are exercised, including reading and writing the SIM, presenting patterns on the phone's display and exercising the wireless receiver and transmitter. At the end of the test, the SIM is plugged into the tester and its contents checked.

In this scenario, the tester is connected at an interworking reference point; the wireless interface provides another interworking reference point. The loading and running of the test software depend on there being a programmatic reference point at which a particular set of operating system services are available. The checking of displayed patterns takes place at a perceptual reference point, and finally the SIM checks require an interchange reference point.

8.4   Conformance to Viewpoint Specifications

We explained earlier how conformance test results need interpretation to identify the actions that are defined in the standard. Nowhere is this more important than in the enterprise viewpoint, which deals with quite abstract actions and events. We therefore conclude this chapter by looking at how this mechanism works in more detail.

Consider an interaction performed by a specific role in an enterprise specification — perhaps the transfer of billing information from the Branch system to the HQ system. This interaction should be observable at a reference point positioned on the communications path between the two systems, such as the HQ system's network access link. However, there is a big gap between the arc in the activity diagram representing the enterprise behaviour and the optical fluctuations on the access link.

Let us look first at the series of design steps involved in narrowing down the requirements. Within the enterprise specification, we need to identify the object that is playing the role that is being considered. The arc in the enterprise behaviour can then be associated via some correspondences with a transition in a state machine expressing the computational behaviour. In fact, both the behaviour of the Branch system and the behaviour of the HQ system will have such a transition, but, since we are focusing on the HQ system in performing the tests, we will concentrate on its behaviour. Note, however, that the transition may not be directly involved in a correspondence, but might need to be inferred from correspondences involving the states it links; even so, there is still a chain of logic pointing to it, which, in turn, identifies a computational interaction.

The way this interaction is performed will depend on the selection of an engineering template that satisfies the transparency requirements in the particular environment, and this will prescribe an appropriate message format, protocol and series of message exchanges. How these exchanges are carried out then depends on the implementable standards identified for communications in the technology viewpoint. Each of these choices is recorded in the system's documentation, either in the viewpoint specifications, the correspondences or, for the last stages, by the implementer making statements within the IXIT (see chapter 6).

The analysis of the results of a conformance test reverses this sequence (see figure 8.4). First, knowledge of the communications standards in use allows the physical measurements to be interpreted, yielding a bit stream and then a series of raw messages. Knowledge of the protocols and formats in use lets these be interpreted to identify the computational actions being performed and the parameters they convey. It is common for monitoring tools in current use to do this; anyone who has carried out a hand analysis of a binary dump knows how valuable such tools are.

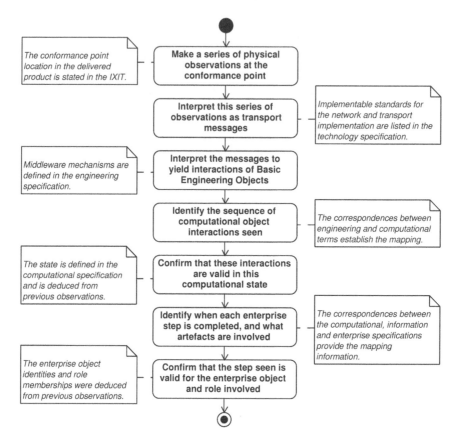

The conformance point location in the delivered product is stated in the IXIT.

Make a series of physical observations at the conformance point

Interpret this series of observations as transport messages

Implementable standards for the network and transport implementation are listed in the technology specification.

Middleware mechanisms are defined in the engineering specification.

Interpret the messages to yield interactions of Basic Engineering Objects

Identify the sequence of computational object interactions seen

The correspondences between engineering and computational terms establish the mapping.

The state is defined in the computational specification and is deduced from previous observations.

Confirm that these interactions are valid in this computational state

Identify when each enterprise step is completed, and what artefacts are involved

The correspondences between the computational, information and enterprise specifications provide the mapping information.

The enterprise object identities and role memberships were deduced from previous observations.

Confirm that the step seen is valid for the enterprise object and role involved

FIGURE 8.4: Checking conformance in the enterprise viewpoint.

We now have our observations in terms of a sequence of computational signals. The next step is to interpret these as operations performed by particular processes. This is a nontrivial task, since it is necessary to pair-up requests and responses and disentangle concurrent threads of execution, and it may involve building up the necessary context by finding suitable correlators, like session or transaction identifiers. Finally, these computational interactions must be interpreted using the next set of correspondences to identify the enterprise interactions and the roles that are responsible for them.

As we move up to progressively more abstract representations, we need to draw upon knowledge of the context involved that has been acquired by analysis of earlier observations. In some cases, the initial analysis may be ambiguous, with further observation being necessary to determine, for example, which of the roles an object holds is responsible for its rejecting a request.

Of course, anywhere in this chain, the analysis may fail. Such failures indicate a failure to obey the rules of the view concerned, and so indicate a fault in the system, making the communication meaningless before questions about its relevance to the enterprise can be asked.

Finally we should note that paralleling this behavioural and observational analysis, there is a chain of obligations relating to the testing process. Tests can only be made mandatory if performed at conformance points, which must have been declared as reference points in sufficient detail to allow the tester to locate them. Thus, if the access link to the HQ system was declared by the implementer as a conformance point, this percolates through to other views, thereby making it possible for corresponding model elements to be involved in the conformance assessment. On the other hand, if a conformance point is declared in the enterprise specification, there is an associated obligation to identify conformance points in other viewpoints so that chains of reasoning, like that as outlined previously, can be constructed for all the valid refinements of that enterprise design.

8.5   Claiming Compliance or Conformance

When a detailed specification claims compliance with a broader framework, it should include a statement asserting this compliance and making it clear which terms and concepts are derived from the framework. The claim should indicate exactly what revision of the framework is being referenced.

A claim that a product conforms with a specification is made as a part of the product documentation. This claim will generally form part of the IXIT, and should include the instructions for locating all conformance points defined in the specification. The specifications and the IXIT together must always provide all the information needed for carrying out tests and interpreting their results.

In this book we normally assume that a full set of viewpoint specifications is being produced. However, in some cases where products are being targeted at some existing environment, the specification may detail only a subset of the viewpoints so that it includes, for example, full specifications for just the enterprise information and computational viewpoints. In such cases, links to the missing detail must be made via the IXIT, and there will always need to be at least a vestigial technology specification for this purpose.

Chapter 9

Transparencies — Hiding Common Problems

"It's no good," Trevor said, shutting his laptop with an air of finality. "We just can't meet the performance and availability targets with our current server platform, and what's probably needed is some kind of nonstop platform that would put us well outside our budget."

The four of them were struggling with resource plans in one of the small meeting rooms. These rooms had been carved from the drawing office when the old dockside works had been converted as a home for cleaner, higher tech activities. There were windows on both sides, now partly blocked by extra whiteboards, but still looking down, to the left over the cubicles of the open plan development area and to the right over what was now the repair lab, shipping areas and stores. The skylights that used to illuminate the drawing boards now showed the hurrying streamers of mares tails, orange in the setting sun.

"Well," said Nigel, "what about sharing the load by replicating the logistics server on independent platforms? We could put replicas at regional centres so that no local service failure took everything out, and get better local response at the same time." "Please," said Claire, bristling, "have you any idea how much trouble we would have in coordinating and synchronizing those replicas? Last time we tried to get our developers to produce a structure like that we lost almost two months in test." "And ended up needing three platforms rather than two to compensate for the extra cost, as I remember," added Trevor. "Mind you, it would mean we could use the existing equipment, so it would certainly be cheaper!"

"Hold on," said Alex, who had been listening quietly for some time. "You don't want the application programmers involved in writing code to manage replicas. That's too hard a job to want to do it more than once. What you need is an infrastructure solution. Put it in the engineering view and then use it as a generic service." Claire looked unconvinced. "But we would still need to get the application people to pick the right style each time they call for an access; any misunderstanding would result in chaos." "But remember what I told you about using transformational tools. Don't worry about the accesses. Mark the data objects that need special treatment and then use those markings to guide a transformation that rewrites all the critical accesses to use the replication options." "And we do that marking throughout the computational view?" "Better still, mark the key types in the information view, if you can," said Alex. "That way there will be less scope for error, as long as the same requirements apply whenever a sensitive type is used; and that's often the case."

As if to punctuate the discussion, the buildings smart lighting system chose this moment to respond to the gathering dusk by fading up the concealed ceiling spots.

9.1 What Is a Transparency?

Distributed systems are inherently more complex and unpredictable than monolithic ones. As Leslie Lamport is widely reported to have said, "A distributed system is a system in which I can't do my work because some computer that I've never even heard of has failed." Distributed systems are subject to all sorts of problems, from clock skew to uncoordinated change management. There are well-known solutions to many of these problems, but some of them are subtle and easy to get wrong, and all of them make the designer's life more difficult. There are just a lot more potential kinds of error to be considered when distribution is present. It would be nice if we could hide some of this complexity.

But there is no magic bullet. We can hide transmission errors by using acknowledgements and repeating lost material, but the result is a less predictable transit delay. We can safeguard against local power failures by keeping non-volatile copies of data, but this slows the system down, and is unlikely to be effective against flood or earthquake.

However, we can still make things simpler by reducing the number of kinds of error, hiding some errors completely if we accept the potential costs, and acknowledge that there will still be some rarer but more serious errors that get through. We express this by using the idea of a *transparency*. When designers request a transparency, they are stating that they wish to work in an environment where a corresponding class of problem will not be seen. Either the problem will be fixed by the infrastructure or, if this process fails, a single more serious kind of error will be reported. More formally, this simplified view of the infrastructure is requested by declaring a *transparency schema* that says what language features used to express the design (or, equivalently, the virtual machine supporting it) should hide selected exceptions from the designer. Figure 9.1 illustrates how this hiding takes place.

The infrastructure then configures itself based on this request for the transparency. What it actually does depends on the environment in which it operates. Consider a request from an application designer that *migration*

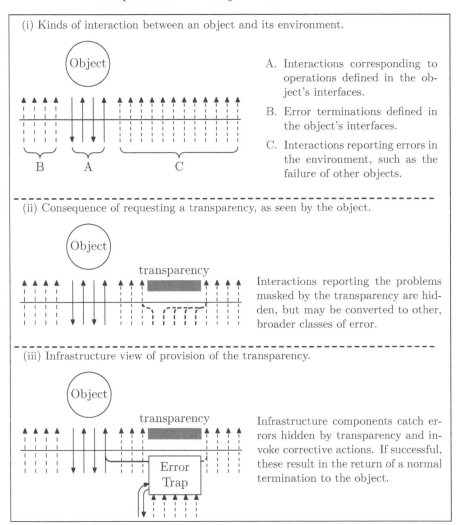

(i) Kinds of interaction between an object and its environment.

A. Interactions corresponding to operations defined in the object's interfaces.

B. Error terminations defined in the object's interfaces.

C. Interactions reporting errors in the environment, such as the failure of other objects.

(ii) Consequence of requesting a transparency, as seen by the object.

Interactions reporting the problems masked by the transparency are hidden, but may be converted to other, broader classes of error.

(iii) Infrastructure view of provision of the transparency.

Infrastructure components catch errors hidden by transparency and invoke corrective actions. If successful, these result in the return of a normal termination to the object.

FIGURE 9.1: How transparencies change an object's environment.

transparency should be applied to a particular server. That is to say, the application should not need to take any special action if the server object moves to a new network location, as might, for example, be necessary to balance load. The infrastructure's configuration control will assess the request. If the server is indeed mobile, it will need to deploy extra components in the channel from this client to the server, perhaps to trap server-not-found exceptions, search for the new server location and then reconfigure the communications support to link to that location. On the other hand, it may be the case that the server concerned is incapable of migration because it is closely coupled to some physical resource, such as a huge data archive. If so, the infrastructure can omit the extra components, since it is clear they will never be needed, and costs can be reduced by their exclusion. However, if in the future the server is redesigned so that it does become mobile, the transparency schema for the application is still on record, and so the infrastructure supporting it can then be modified to include the recovery mechanisms needed.

This approach of separating the assumptions about the infrastructure from the way they are satisfied is particularly useful when a widely distributed application needs to operate in many different kinds of environment. For example, a user interface client may operate on a desktop or within a mobile phone. It has the same failure transparency requirements in either case, but the complexity of providing them differs considerably, with more mechanisms needed to compensate for the wider range of threats and failure modes in the mobile case. This is not just a basic communications issue, as the mechanisms needed to safeguard the persistent state in the client might be quite different in the two cases, requiring completely new communication paths for the mobile client to log its transactions at a base location; the static desktop could be much simpler while providing the same quality of service.

This last example hints that figure 9.1 is an over simplification. Many of the supporting mechanisms need some additional parameterization; for example, transaction transparency mechanisms are likely to need to add transaction identifiers to interactions under their control. Others need to transform existing parameters; one example is location transparency, which will need to transform naming parameters from a location-independent to a location-specific form. In general, adding a transparency will involve the analysis and, potentially, the modification of the parameters of any interaction for which the transparency is responsible; this is equivalent to a set of interaction rewriting rules applied by the supporting virtual machine.

It should be clear from these examples that there is a close relationship between provision of transparency and virtualization, which is one of the basic techniques for the support of cloud computing. Transparency aims to simplify the virtual machine a designer sees, in terms of its management and failure behaviour; virtualization does the same thing by providing a virtual machine that offers a slice of some shared resource as if it were provided by a physically separate platform, independent of other users. Both of these may involve providing software support that guarantees a particular user view of the services or resources offered, simplifying the designer's life.

9.2   Types of Transparency

There can be many types of transparency, some of them being domain-specific or applicable to general aspects such as security. The RM-ODP itself defines a standard set of transparencies covering common distribution problems. These are:

- **Access transparency** hides differences in representation and programming model between different environments, allowing language-independent distribution. Almost all popular middlewares provide access transparency.

- **Failure transparency** masks failures of objects or their supporting environment; its provision usually involves some mechanism, such as checkpointing or replication, which allows the recovery of the object's internal state.

- **Location transparency** involves the provision of object identifiers or other names in a form that is independent of the physical location of the resources concerned, so that there is a decoupling between application structure and the physical configuration supporting it.

- **Migration transparency** hides the fact that an object has been moved from both its current and potential users. Thus, a management function can move an object to a new platform without worrying about causing errors elsewhere in the system.

- **Relocation transparency** is concerned with preserving the binding of interfaces. It involves the updating of bindings so that existing communications are not disrupted when an object moves.

- **Replication transparency** hides the fact that a particular interface is supported not by just a single object, but by a cooperating group of objects in order, for example, to achieve increased performance or availability.

- **Persistence transparency** hides from an object and its users the actions a system manager may take to temporarily suspend and then resume execution of an object; the state of an object, or a container for a whole collection of objects (such as a cluster), may be moved to some secondary storage to conserve resources, or to give the impression of continuous availability following system crashes. When persistence transparency is present, the application's state is nonvolatile, surviving failures of the supporting platform.

- **Transaction transparency** conceals a whole group of concurrency and consistency measures needed to ensure that independent threads of behaviour can share resources in an orderly way. The transparency schema identifies groups of related actions, leaving to the infrastructure the bringing into play of appropriate transactional and compensation mechanisms.

9.3   Transparencies and Viewpoints

The transparencies play an important role in the linkage between the management of infrastructure mechanisms in the engineering viewpoint and the design constraints established in the computational, enterprise and information viewpoints. The relationship between the computational and engineering specifications is particularly significant because the computational design establishes the potential for distribution by specifying the constraints on the behaviour of specific implementable objects. The enterprise and information specifications impose broader, more generic, constraints on this computational structure. However, the shift from the computational to the engineering viewpoint introduces the properties of particular infrastructures and distribution environments.

The computational designers mark their objects or interfaces to indicate any special properties they are to have. The engineering specification then defines a set of **templates** that give reusable solutions to the various distribution problems, together with the necessary rules for selecting the appropriate templates to satisfy the computational requirement in whatever environment actually applies. Instantiating the selected templates produces the various components needed to provide a binding and hence a supporting channel with the right properties.

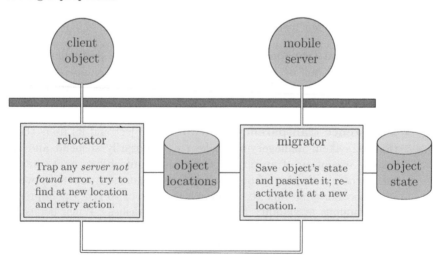

FIGURE 9.2: The supporting objects that are needed to provide migration transparency.

Consider, for example, the provision of migration transparency for work tickets in the PhoneMob system (see figure 9.2). The aim, from the computational point of view, is for the object representing a repair task to be visible anywhere in the application, without worrying about its actual location, which may change as the phone concerned is shipped between depots or departments. The application designer simply marks this object as having migration transparency by creating a corresponding transparency schema for that object type, perhaps in the computational viewpoint, because, in this case, the information type concerned is a supertype, which deals with a wider range of task types. Note, however, that at this stage UML4ODP does not support the specification of transparency schemata on individual objects or types.

This results in the selection of a corresponding engineering template suitable for the platforms in use. It provides for the checkpointing, passivating and reactivating of the object at a different location. It also requests the establishment of relocation mechanisms for each of the object's interfaces, so that existing clients do not see errors if they attempt to access the object while it is moving or after it has moved. In addition, it may be necessary to update registry or directory entries with the new location if the object was offering published services.

Another example is the provision of persistence transparency. The PhoneMob designers may decide that the state of a user dialogue in their web interface should persist across session failures. This can be achieved by asking for transparent persistence of this state, resulting in the recording of the dialogue state to nonvolatile storage at each step and restoration of the state at the start of any new session.

However, there may be a need for some additional computational design features as a result. There may have been an implicit assumption that the application starts in its initial state at the start of a session and that session restart is the way to escape from consistency problems. If so, some additional interactions will be needed to allow for the explicit cancellation of the dialogue to prevent the user being trapped in a neverending series of failed sessions, in which some incorrect state is restored on every new attempt. Similarly, if persistence across processor failure is provided by checkpointing, it will be necessary to have some process that allows faulty checkpoints to be abandoned.

Finally, we might ask whether there is really a need for the marking in the computational specification. Migration transparency sounds like a useful thing to have, so why not make it mandatory for all objects? Life would be simpler. The answer is that there is no free lunch. Adding the additional mechanisms has an associated cost, and so including these mechanisms everywhere, including between objects that are strongly interdependent, may result in an unacceptable performance hit. By marking only those objects that the designer can conceive of as moving at some stage, we can reduce cost, since we can leave out a lot of expensive activity where it is not really needed.

Chapter 10

Policies — Tracking Changing Requirements

"It still just says delayed," said Nigel, after walking over to check the monitors outside the departure gate. "I'm not sure we are going to get out of here tonight. Anyone want a coffee?"

They were supposed to be on their way to a conference; Alex had persuaded Marcus to let him take Nigel and Eleanor to attend the industry experience track at EDOC, the premier event for the kind of enterprise modelling they were now doing, and so expose them to more new ideas. However, there were problems with an air traffic control centre on the route, and they had already been waiting for almost two hours.

Alex opted for a cappuccino, and Eleanor a Christmas special crème brûlée latte. Nigel got himself a plain filter coffee. "It's interesting," he said, as he put the tray down, "when we got here the queues were much longer, and everyone got two of those little almond biscuits. Now everyone gets the fancy design stencilled on top of the coffee, but only one biscuit. It's not random, I watched four or five customers in front of me each time." "It must be a policy," Alex said. "They let the duty manager vary the prescription depending on the load."

"We could use that idea," said Eleanor. "We need to vary the discounting algorithm every time marketing has a brainwave; now we can just tell them they are changing a policy. It would be good for their egos." "Any more ego and those guys would explode," said Nigel. "But I've heard that term used in network congestion management, and in security. Is it the same idea?" "Yes," said Alex, carving a spoonful of chocolate and froth from his drink. "It's a common pattern that shows up all over the place. It's really useful to highlight the places where you expect to have to make changes. It lets you make tomorrow's job easier." "But is it the same idea in the network and in the enterprise?" asked Nigel. "Is Eleanor's crème brûlée the same as the stuff I had last night in a ramekin?" "Certainly not," said Eleanor. "This is just getting them to put brown sugar in and them not bothering to stir it." They all laughed, but Alex went on. "It's the same pattern, but different detailed mechanisms and timescales. But if you stick to the pattern, you don't have to reinvent all the possible mistakes people make."

Just then, the flight was called. "Just wait," Alex said, as he picked up his bag, "you will be hearing a lot more about policies in the conference, I'm sure."

10.1   Why Do We Need Policies?

Often, when working on a design, decisions need to be taken where the designer is aware that the best answer will change as things develop. This may be because of changes in the organizational goals, the supporting technology, or the environment in which the activity is to take place. The designer can insure against any of these changes by saying that the parts of the specification that are likely to change involve *policies*. This is a warning that the system should be constructed so as to make changes easy to incorporate, and lets the designer make it clear how much freedom should be allowed when planning subsequent changes.

A system's properties do not generally change steadily throughout its lifetime. Rather, there are periods of stability punctuated by events in which the rules governing system behaviour are modified. The ODP Reference Model defines an *epoch* as being a period of time when something, be it an object, a component or a system, has a particular kind of behaviour or obeys a particular set of rules. One example of an epoch is the period during which a policy applies. Policy change events mark the boundaries between different epochs.

There can be many variations on this general picture. Occasional change as part of the management of a running system is one, but similar considerations apply when widely used components, such as beans or shrink-wrapped packages, are deployed; the design envisages that the artefact produced may be used in many different circumstances, and allows for a controlled degree of tailoring as part of the deployment process when it is brought into use. The adopter of such reusable components must define and install a set of deployment policies. A typical system life history is outlined in figure 10.1.

Some of the things a system is expected to do are determined by broadly based decisions about how the organization it serves is to operate. Thus, for example, most organizations have some form of pervasive security policy determining what level of control is to be applied in handling different kinds of information, and who is to be trusted with what. The team that delivers a major system that is unable to track changes in these access control rules quickly and accurately as situations change will generally have a miserable time, so tailorable security policies are almost, but sadly not completely, universal. There are many other examples, such as transaction approval policies, discounting policies or delegation policies.

Another reason for introducing policies is to allow a system design to be exploited in a number of different jurisdictions, or to respond to changes in

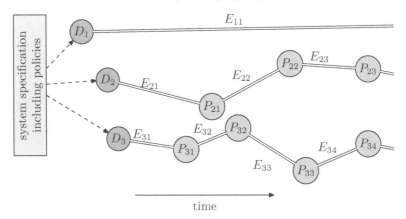

This figure shows the way behaviour derived from a specification evolves. Here one specification is instantiated three times, giving three distinct systems.

D_i is the deployment of system i, with establishment of an initial set of policies for it.

E_{ij} is the jth epoch of system i; it is drawn as a straight line because the behaviour specified by the policy is constant.

P_{ij} is the jth policy setting event for system i; the change in direction of the system's trace indicates that the system's behaviour has changed at these points, but remains constant throughout the following epoch.

FIGURE 10.1: Epochs and points where policies are asserted.

regulation affecting the system's behaviour. Thus, for example, a financial system may need to be tuned to satisfy a particular national tax law, or a set of audit requirements. The original designer will be aware that there are certain key points in a business process where tax is due and must be calculated, but the details depend on the locale, and may be changed by legislation that was not even drafted when the system was first created.

Policy is a general concept, applicable to any of the viewpoints. However, as these examples have shown, it is particularly heavily used in the enterprise language, where there is a need to satisfy requirements both for agile business processes and for stable and reliable provision of IT systems.

Policies, then, are a vital tool to let an organization make changes to the behaviour of a system or subsystem in a controlled way, and, by so doing, to let it respond to changing requirements and challenges.

10.2   What Is a Policy?

Loosely speaking, a policy is any point of potential variation in a specification that has been identified by the designer or the other stakeholders concerned. The idea of introducing a policy to increase flexibility is generic, and so can be applied in any viewpoint. Each policy has a number of pieces of information associated with it, and these constrain the behaviour of the system in different ways. We can distinguish the following terms.

- *Policy* is the term used when referring to the whole collection of information or referring to a variation point in the specification.

- The *affected behaviour* is that part of the system behaviour that is modified or controlled by the policy. A policy might, for example, control the conditions that must hold before a loan handset is issued, perhaps based on the previous reliability of the user. The step Get Loan Phone would then be the affected behaviour.

- A *policy value* expresses the constraints applied at the variation point during a particular epoch. Changing the policy value changes the system's behaviour. Policy values for an access control policy, for example, might select suitable mechanisms, so that one policy value might require password validation, while another that replaces it requires presentation of a valid certificate.

- *Policy-setting behaviour* is the behaviour that modifies the policy value. If no such behaviour is defined, the policy cannot be changed by mechanisms within the running system. It could still be changed by actions not forming part of the system's specification, such as choosing deployment information before the system is first started, or changing it and then reinitializing the system. However, it is expected that most systems will need to be able to evolve dynamically, and so there will be definitions of the way policies can be changed, and of any constraints on when such changes should take effect. For example, a change in financial policy should not become visible within the scope of a compensatable transaction! The designer also needs to decide what should happen if a change of policy would leave the system in what has just become a forbidden state; it may be necessary to define some transitional rules to deal with such situations.

- A *policy envelope* indicates limits on what policy values are acceptable. If system managers are given complete freedom to install absolutely any policy value, it becomes impossible to reason about the correctness of the system design. Any required system property may be invalidated by sufficiently draconian policy values. However, if the policy envelope expresses constraints that must be true for any acceptable policy value, the impact of changing a policy can be limited and so meaningful deductions about system behaviour can be made that are true whatever valid policy value is applied.

Policy envelopes can be expressed in a number of ways. The most restrictive approach is to limit the setting of policy values to selection from a declared enumeration of possible pieces of behaviour, although this is generally too inflexible. Other approaches limit the policy values to expressions in a given language, or to restrictive classes of algorithms. Restrictions can be placed on which aspects of the system state can be accessed or changed by the policy value, or more complicated constraints applied.

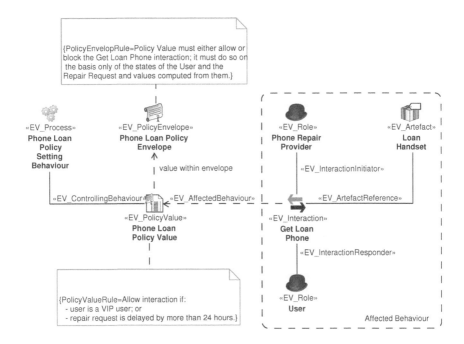

FIGURE 10.2: A policy that controls the issue of loan handsets.

We can see these concepts at work in the example given in figure 10.2. This shows the policy that controls the circumstances when a handset should be loaned to a customer. All the related pieces of information are gathered together into a single diagram, so that the policy can be seen as a whole. The affected behaviour is identified as being a specific interaction, namely the interaction in which the handset, seen as an artefact, is transferred from the phone repair provider to the user. In any particular epoch, this interaction is constrained to happen only if the guard expressed by the policy value is satisfied. The policy value can be changed by the policy-setting behaviour, represented in the figure as a process. The definition of this process will state what roles can change the value, and in what situation this can happen. This might involve an agreement between a branch manager and someone at headquarters. Finally, whatever change is proposed, the policy value must satisfy the constraints given in the policy envelope. Here, these state that the value must be a boolean guard and must draw only on information about the user and the progress of the repair request that the user has made. In the example, both the value and the envelope are expressed informally, but these rules would have to be expressed in a more precise notation than this in an actual specification.

The presentation of the policy concepts in figure 10.2 differs somewhat from that given in UML4ODP, in that greater prominence is given to the way that the affected behaviour is constrained by the policy value and the way that the policy-setting behaviour is constrained by the policy envelope. In UML4ODP, these were implicit, being derived from the transitive closure of other relationships. The original version also showed the value as being contained in the envelope, illustrating just the simplest situation, where a specific list of values is given; here, we show that the relationship is, in general, based on constraining the value with a statement in some policy language. The enumeration of possible values would just be a trivial case of this.

There have been many proposals for languages to express policies. Many of them are based on an event-condition-action model, in which the policy value is a set of expressions stating what action should be taken (or forbidden) if a given action occurs while an associated condition is satisfied. The same basic structure can be used to express both permissions and obligations. One of the best known of this family of languages is Ponder [64], which has a number of useful features for structuring sets of policy rules. Other proposals have been based on deontic logic (see chapter 14).

For communication between systems, *eXtensible Access Control Markup Language (XACML)* [44] is an XML language specialized for the representation of access permissions in an event-condition-action style. It allows sets of permissions to be constructed from individual statements, stating how they are to be interpreted together; for example, access may depend on any statement being true, or all may be required. Individual statements express details about the subject requesting the action, their target and the nature of the action to be performed. Subjects and targets are identified by the matching of sets of attributes; again, various options for their combination are available.

The *Semantics of Business Vocabulary and Business Rules (SBVR)* [33] is the result of recent work within the OMG, and provides a framework for defining business vocabularies and business rules. As such, it has the potential for expressing the supporting semantics of subject and targets that are often glossed over by policy languages. It has been produced with use in a model-driven environment in mind, making it a potentially useful element of tool support for requirements capture and design.

10.3 Implementing Policy

To be an effective tool for system evolution, policy values must be easy to change. This implies the selection of a structure that allows a loose coupling of the policy representation to the rest of the system. This can be achieved in a number of ways. One approach is to interpret the policy representation at run time, so that it can be retrieved from a suitable repository (as, for example, in directory enabled networking [59, 96]); this allows changes to be made by updating the repository since the various system components will retrieve the new version next time they need to interpret the policy. Another alternative is to provide the policy as a plug-in object within a suitable component management framework, or as a service identified by a reference that can be rebound dynamically when necessary.

One well-known architecture for applying policies is defined by the IETF, and involves the identification of sets of control points for each class of policy. There are two kinds of control point (see, for example, figure 10.3).

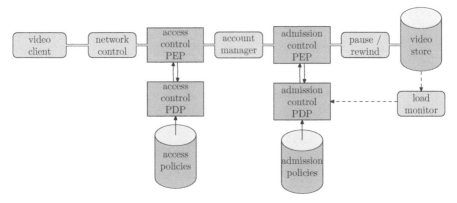

FIGURE 10.3: The use of policy execution points and policy decision points to control policies in a streaming video server.

The policy execution points (PEPs) are points at which choices have to be made based on the policy in question. When a decision is needed, the PEP communicates details of the request to a policy decision point (PDP) which interprets or otherwise consults the policy and determines what the outcome should be. It then returns the result to the PEP, which behaves accordingly, permitting or prohibiting the request. The advantage of this structure is that the policy value is interpreted by comparatively few PDPs, which may be serving very many more PEPs, each associated with individual fine-grained resources.

The PEP/PDP structure assumes that there is a need for controlled enforcement of a policy whenever it applies. This is what is known as a pessimistic policy enforcement approach. The system is constructed in such a way that the enforcement points make it impossible to violate the policy. However, this is not the only way of handling enforcement. There is another approach, called optimistic policy enforcement, in which the policy is published and the system then monitored, possibly on a sampling basis, to check that the policy is being observed. If the policy is seen to have been violated, some corrective or punitive actions are taken. This is the case in many enterprise policies, and also where policies take the form of legal regulations; the system is expected to obey any relevant laws, and violation may lead to interested parties seeking redress from its owners through the courts.

Chapter 11

Federation — Talking to Strangers

The sun glinted on the winding river in the valley below the hotel as the group gathered round the table on the terrace. Marcus had specified that this off-site planning weekend should be informal, but serious business, nevertheless. They had spent the afternoon before reviewing their current position, and had been treated to an excellent dinner as a thanks offering for the progress they had made. The morning session was gnomically labelled as *new business models* on the agenda, and frustratingly vague compared with the clear topics of the previous day.

"Well, I hope you all enjoyed your breakfast," said Marcus, "but I want to share some important news with you now. I didn't give you any preparatory material because this is very sensitive, not for us, but for our new collaborators, who could be in deep trouble with the market if their involvement became known at the wrong time." He certainly had their attention now, although Eleanor had a self-satisfied look that indicated she knew what was in the wind. "We have been in discussions over the last couple of months with Factotum, the market leader in bespoke luxury travel packages. They want to include access to our services in a portfolio of benefits to take the hassle out of travel. They are making a big thing of these extras in their advertising; to be honest, they are being hurt by the fringe benefits some of the top-end credit card companies are offering to their platinum cardholders, and need to fight back."

Claire looked puzzled. "I'm not sure I get it," she said. "Will the volume be enough to make a difference to us, and are they going to be in the centres we are planning to cover? Aren't they going to be in the tourist centres, not the business hubs?" Marcus nodded. "Quite right, but think about it a bit more. To take your second point first, a lot of their business is in historic cities where we do have an interest, and they already have a very slick courier network for handling tickets and delivery of luxuries to the isolated areas they cover, so we can ride on that. As to the volume, that's not really why we are interested. To be perfectly honest, I don't expect huge extra volume; we will break even, but the real opportunity is that it's a perfect opportunity for viral advertising. We want people who matter in our real market — the CEOs and CIOs of companies we want to sign up — to hear at dinner parties how their friends had their holiday rescued from disaster by the PhoneMob. We want them to look at the Factotum flyers and think they should be giving their sales teams support like that." He paused while this sank in. "It's a variation on the exemplary service idea."

"OK, Eleanor, tell us what is needed to make it happen." She looked round the table, and smiled. "It's not that big a change, really. Most of what we need to change is in the customer relationships area. We need to accept requests based on the traveller's Factotum identifier, and this needs to be validated with their itinerary records. We will need to interface with the Factotum courier services, and supply delivery details in their terms. And the billing will be different, of course."

"So, the two main external links into our system will be from their traveller database into our headquarters customer accounts system and from their courier workflow management into our logistics control subsystem."

Nigel leaned forward, putting his elbows on the table. "What do we know about their infrastructure? Can they handle inter-system links? Do they use the same middleware we do?" Ira chipped in, "Do they have the information we need in their systems already? Do we know what their information schema looks like?" "What I want to know," Claire added, "is whether they will be committed to making any changes to their systems that are needed to make it all work together." "Yes," Eleanor agreed, "are they really going to give this the right priority — you said it was just part of a package of new benefits, so they will be being pulled in different directions. Are they up to it?"

"OK, everybody," Marcus spread his hands for silence. "That's the aim of this session, to brainstorm and find out what the issues are. I want to go home with a list of questions for the management at Factotum and a rough idea of the size of the task involved for us. But first, I would like to hear something from Alex. In particular, do we have to talk them into using the same framework that we have been working with?"

Alex leaned back in his chair and paused for a moment, looking out across the valley. Then he glanced round the table. "This is a familiar kind of federation problem," he said, "and it's no different in principle from any other design activity. We start with a federation community, with our two organizations filling roles, and capture the obligations of each side in a federation contract. This needs to be as formal as we can make it because it will form part of a real legal contract this time. Then we can work through the viewpoints, looking particularly for significant differences. At some level, we need to be sure that we share an information model, but we must keep that as simple as possible, and it's up to each side to ensure this simple description is consistent with both our local views."

"And what if it's not?" asked Ira. " Are we going to have to slug it out until someone changes their system?" "No, it's not as bad as that. At least, not for the detail. At some abstract level, we need to have a shared understanding or we cannot communicate; after all, that's how communication works. But then if there are differences in how we express things, we have to fight about whose version we exchange, but it's like arguing with a foreign partner about who pays the translator; we don't need to change the way we think, just be sure the other side hears what they expect to hear."

"But how does that work if the infrastructures are different?" Nigel asked. "You remember those interceptors in the engineering channel model? Well, that's where the work is done. They are the translator, and they do whatever jobs we find we need, subject to preserving our agreed high-level view. If the middlewares are different, or the message formats, or any other detail, the interceptor works its way up a process of interpretation to the point where there is common agreement, and then works back down the stack translating the common concepts into the other side's concepts."

"OK," said Marcus, "that sounds simple enough; let's just do it." "Well, we'll find out, won't we," said Eleanor, "five gets you ten we aren't finished by lunchtime." There were no takers.

11.1   How Does Interoperation Work?

The objective of a *federation* is to allow two or more separate organizations to cooperate while maintaining their fundamental independence. They can each still go on doing what they want, managing their separate activities, except that they must observe some minimum constraints in the narrow area where these are needed to make the cooperation work. Generally, any of the partners can opt out of the federation if it no longer matches their objectives, although there may be some penalty, so as to compensate the other partners if this happens.

Forming a federation is a particular case of forming a community, which is the basic building block of the enterprise language. Like any community, a federation is described by a contract — in this case, it is known as a *federation contract*. It also has an objective, representing the purpose for which the cooperation was formed.

The necessary degree of independence is ensured because each of the parties to the federation is an organization represented by its own community. The federation community overlaps with these, so that the behaviour of the complete system is the result of the composition of the constraints from the federation with the constraints within each organization. Strictly speaking, this is done by having the partners' communities fill roles in the federation community. The definitions of the roles to be filled by the parties in the federation contract are made as abstract as possible, so as to avoid unnecessary constraints on their ongoing activities. Remembering that a role is a formal parameter to be instantiated by some object, it is clear that the role type constrains the type of the object that can fulfil it. In this case, the federation role type is significantly less detailed than the object type of the community object for the party filling it, and abstracts away all aspects of the business not involved in the federation (see figure 11.1). Each party should then only depend on the abstract view of its peers captured by the role types found in the contract; anything else may be changed without warning by the local management.

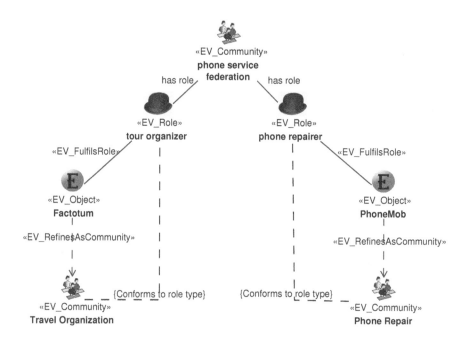

FIGURE 11.1: How organizations fill roles in a federation.

It is often helpful to use the concept of a **domain** to make issues of ownership and accountability clear in these circumstances. A domain, in general, is a set of objects with a characterizing relationship to some controlling object, but the term can be used to express responsibility for resources, corresponding, for example, to all or part of the area of authority of some partner. Defining a suitable domain containing the resources to be committed to the federation makes the scope of the contract clear.

The community behaviour of a federation covers two areas. First, it defines the interactions between the parties that are necessary to achieve its objectives. For example, Factotum sends a list of its customers to the PhoneMob, requesting that they be given phone repair services for a specified period; later, the PhoneMob bills for the cover and the actual repairs performed. Second, the federation contract covers detailed responsibilities for establishing, maintaining and terminating the federation. This covers organizational matters, like periods of notice and penalties on withdrawal, but also defined technical responsibilities and infrastructure matters, such as interchange formats and conversion responsibilities (see section 11.4).

Like any other community contract, a federation contract can include the definition of policies, and these allow the management of the federation to be carried out by changing some of the constraints placed on members dynamically during the federation's lifetime. The policy-setting behaviour will define the process for making changes, and what say the various parties have in agreeing to the changes.

Because of the loose coupling between federated organizations, it is quite likely that either the basic behaviour or the policies applied will give rise at some stage to conflict and inconsistency. It is therefore usual to find that a significant amount of a federation contract deals with the handling of violations, exceptions and compensation terms.

11.2 Interpreting and Sharing Information

One of the main issues in establishing a federation is the decision of what the form of the communication between the various parties should be. Whether we are talking about humans or automated systems, any communication of information between two entities depends on a basic shared level of understanding between them. The receiver of a message needs to be able to interpret it, recognizing the terms it contains and the implications of the context resulting from their position in both the message and the broader dialogue. Without this understanding, no communication can take place.

We can express this by saying that the communicating entities must share a common ontology, so that they agree what categories of things exist and can therefore be referred to. They must also share some understanding of the grammar or structure of their communications. If there is a core agreement, it can be used to exchange further rules and definitions so as to broaden the scope of the exchanges, although the state of the art only allows fairly straightforward enhancements of machine communications. Humans are much more flexible, and use many subtle clues from the local context to remove ambiguity. This can be seen in the extensive use made of local context in natural language, as in Susumu Kuno's [83] "Time flies like an arrow, fruit flies like a banana," or of wider context needed to understand Noam Chomsky's [58] "The police were ordered to stop drinking after midnight," with its four possible interpretations.

At present, we rely on the federation contract to give us an agreed core grammar and ontology, to which suitable domain-specific packages can be added to cover the exchange of other categories of information. One of the thrusts of current interoperability research is to develop more flexible extension mechanisms for use in loosely coupled communication.

So far, we have concentrated on the interpretation of terms as having intrinsic meaning, but there is another, equally important consideration, and that is with the use of terms for referring to entities; that is to say, the understanding of terms as names. The problem here is that, even within one language community, there may be many local differences in the way things are named. You may call your cat Fred, but in the house next door Fred may be most immediately understood as the name of the householder. In such cases, if I stand at my back door and call for Fred, I may get either the cat or the neighbour.

Sorting the problem out lies at the heart of the so-called context-relative approach to naming. This whole area is dealt with in detail in *ISO/IEC 14771: The ODP Naming Framework* [16]. The standard gives a model of the passing of names through a series of naming domains, explaining how the names should be interpreted and transformed so that the communicating parties understand them as references to the same thing, even though they have different forms in each domain.

One particular topic described in the naming framework is the use of special naming domains, or contexts, to support federation. These can be used both to facilitate the intended communication within the federation and to prevent unintended access by limiting the external visibility of local resources.

First, a partner in a federation can create a specific **export context**, which contains the names of services it has agreed to make available. If all external communication is restricted to be in terms of names in this context, any other local services cannot be named, and so cannot be accessed by users outside the organization.

To ease communication within the federation, a single shared naming context, called the **federation context**, can be created as part of the federation agreement. This context ensures that the various partners have a common set of prefixes for each others' resources, so that, in this form, their names are never ambiguous.

Finally, an **import context** can be defined within an organization to provide explicit control over the external services that local users can access. In many cases, of course, an organization will forgo this level of control and import the whole Internet naming structure into its local naming context, so that all connected systems can be accessed by name, but there is a powerful control mechanism available here for use if necessary.

11.3   The Basis of Interoperation

The full federation of separate organizations needs creation of a federation contract which involves agreements in several viewpoints. Some aspects, given in the following list, will be concerned with what the federation is for and how it will work, and others (in the second list) will be concerned with how the activity is managed. Thus, there need to be, at least:

- An agreement in the enterprise viewpoint that the federation is necessary, with a clear statement of its objectives and the level of resource sharing and devolved control needed, in terms of management and security policies. This agreement needs to be confirmed at the highest management level of the participating organizations. *In the example, a memorandum of understanding (or MoU for short) stating the objectives is prepared by the two CTOs and signed by Marcus and his opposite number.*

- The agreement of the joint business processes, and of any associated business services, that will articulate the federation. *Eleanor works with her counterpart to document the required business processes and the situations in which they are to be invoked.*

- The development of a shared information model for the activities covered by the federation agreement. *Ira extracts a subset from the PhoneMob information model, dealing with the properties of customers and users, and agrees it with technical staff from Factotum, who do not yet have an integrated information model for their systems.*

- An agreement in the computational viewpoint on the resource discovery mechanisms and the publication strategy for services and on the computational interfaces to be supported by each participant. *This federation links two specific parties, so open publication is not needed. The two organizations can simply exchange service description, involving computational interface signatures in a suitable language, such as WSDL or IDL specifications; there is no need for more visible publication mechanisms in the computational view. The PhoneMob computational model is extended to include a mapping to the agreed interface definitions.*

- Decisions on the engineering and technology solutions to support the actual communication between participants and assignment of responsibilities for any message transformations required to match the internal conventions of the participants. *Nigel has no problem here at first because the communication between organizations uses normal web services conventions, but some of the information items being transferred have different representations from the PhoneMob's internal usage. These need to be transformed, and an interceptor is introduced into their web services support platform, tightly bound to it.*

These considerations are primarily concerned with the design of the federation. There also need to be plans for its deployment and ongoing management. These include:

- Agreement, in the enterprise viewpoint, of a maintenance procedure for the federation contract; this should include the agreement of testing and validation procedures and phased plans for implementation, initial testing, deployment and use. *A joint working party from the two organizations documents agreed procedures, and these are added as a codicil to the MoU.*

- The federation should also have an enterprise-level exit strategy, stating what is to happen if the federation has to be wound up. *Periods of notice for dissolving the federation are agreed, and arrangement for completing work in progress added. Penalties reflecting lost investment for termination within two years and lost opportunity for abrupt termination are added. This is also attached to the MoU.*

11.4   Engineering the Federation

Once the federation community has been defined, we know the abstract view of the information to be exchanged and the structure of the dialogue. However, we still need to establish the communication technology, the way links are established, and how the communication formats to be used over them relate to local usage in the systems run by the individual federation members. There may be incompatibilities between the way types in the abstract information model are refined to concrete representations, or differences in local usage, either in the selection of middleware or in the supporting protocols. There may also be a need to invoke additional management functions to ensure access or security policies are applied.

What is needed is a way of placing the necessary extra functionality for access control or data transformation into the communications path. The engineering channel architecture provides the concept of an interceptor for precisely this purpose. An interceptor can act as an intermediate system up to and including the highest level at which there is an incompatibility between the engineering solutions in use. Messages received on one side of the interceptor are interpreted using the rules on that side until an element of the shared abstraction is recognized, and this is then recoded and sent on its way in the format of the domain on the other side of the interceptor (see figure 11.2).

The complexity of the conversion to be done by the interceptor depends on the nature of the incompatibility to be dealt with. If the incompatibility is at a comparatively low level, affecting only the supporting communication protocols, the interceptor is reasonably straightforward because it does not need to be concerned with application-specific aspects of the dialogue, and can just pass application messages through without interpreting them. This

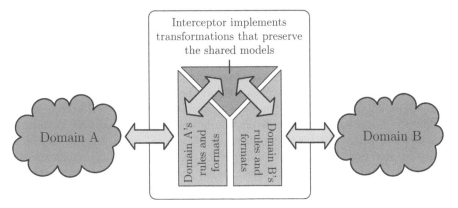

FIGURE 11.2: Operation of an engineering channel interceptor.

means that it maintains comparatively little state, and so the interceptor can be placed anywhere between the domains, and can be restarted or migrated easily.

If, on the other hand, the conversion involves the formats handled by the stubs in the peer systems, the situation is much more complicated. In order to be able to interpret and modify the messages being passed, the interceptor needs to be aware of the interface types in use, and to maintain more dialogue state. For example, it may need to transform between local representations of some abstract type being communicated, and so must analyse the messages and be prepared to reformat them. In some cases, there may be differences in dialogue structure, where one system negotiates a local context, so that information need not be repeated in a series of messages, while the other includes the information explicitly in each message. In such cases, the interceptor must be aware of the dialogue state and add or strip out information where necessary. It needs to know the interface type to do this, which implies that it must have an intimate involvement in the binding process.

If the domains use different publication and resource discovery processes, the interceptor that is needed is even more complex because it must translate between these different processes, acting as a proxy for the registry or trading services involved in resource discovery. It must then be prepared to maintain rather long-term state in the form of mappings between equivalent services. If, for example, there is a need to map between a web services domain and a CORBA domain, there is a need to collate information from a number of different sources because the two resource discovery systems each package together different architectural functions, with WSDL addressing more concrete information and CORBA IDL being more modular. In fact, the OMG has produced a specification called *CORBA to WSDL/SOAP Interworking (C2WSDL) Version 1.2.1* [34] describing how to do this.

11.5   Federating Type Systems

One way of simplifying the management of federated domains is to introduce type repositories. The idea behind the type repository is to make all the type definitions used in the domain accessible from a well-known service. The same repository also registers the location of external type definitions, indicating where the type repository for their local home domain can be accessed, and registers mapping information, in terms of subtype relationships, so that potential users can reason about the types and deduce whether or not an interceptor can be expected to convert them into a form that can be understood locally.

The technical details of how this is done go beyond the scope of this book, but details of the ODP type repository can be found in *ISO/IEC 14769: The ODP Type Repository Function* [15], which is also available as *ITU-T Recommendation X.960*. This standard laid the foundations upon which the OMG later defined its specification for the *Meta Object Facility* [28].

11.6   Federating Identity

Another area of considerable practical importance is the federation of identity, which allows the creation of broadly based single sign-on schemes. Here the aim is to support the establishment of distributed trust models and the management of access tokens or pseudonyms. The federation approach to these requirements is supported by technologies like *WS-Federation* [45] and *WS-Trust* [47].

The general structure needed is very similar to the model underlying interoperation. First, there needs to be an agreed conceptual framework for expressing identity and trust, and a negotiated set of trust relationships between the various domain authorities. These may be either direct or indirect; they are indirect if domains are linked by some third party, such as a trusted peer or an acknowledged authority.

A federation community is then formed involving roles for the domains and for the third-party broker if there is one. The federation contract defines the behaviour used to export names with appropriate credentials, or to generate linked tokens of pseudonyms. It expresses the properties that generated identities will have, such as their lifetime and any constraints on whether further federation steps should be allowed. It also captures the way violations are signalled and the penalties associated with them. These days there may also be obligations to disclose identity mappings on demand to the legal authorities, so that criminal activity can be traced.

11.7 Legacy Systems

As well as their use in inter-organizational federation, it should be noted that these ideas can also be used in the planning and execution of legacy integration. Linking legacy services to a more modern infrastructure involves management decisions about what services need to be retained and which are obsolete and can be phased out [54]. The resulting decisions can be captured by specifying what role the legacy system is expected to play and how this relates to other roles within the organization.

The actual integration involves establishing a shared ontology and process model, which may have to be reverse engineered from the existing usage of the legacy components. Based on this, the nature and location of any necessary converters are determined, and an engineering plan for their realization and commissioning written. Finally, a plan for the eventual transition away from the legacy components and for their decommissioning will be needed.

11.8 Interoperability or Integration?

How is the decision whether to federate or to integrate related systems to be made? It is a difficult trade-off involving a variety of costs and depends on assumptions about the way the organizations will evolve.

Firstly, stronger integration allows more informed management, which results in more efficient and more reliable operation. There will be more complete sharing of information models (although legacy barriers will persist) and so more consistency and better planning follow.

On the other hand, this close coupling means that the different systems depend on each other, so that withdrawal of any party damages the remainder of the organization. If there is significant autonomy of the components, changes of their objectives may result in the necessary level of cooperation and sharing being lost. However, the strongest reason for concentrating on interworking is that, as organizations evolve, their groupings change, and integration measures have to be repeatedly reworked, placing an intolerable burden on an organization with many business links, while a good implementation of a standards-based interworking strategy will support an evolving set of partners with lower maintenance and thus much lower total cost. Integration creates longer range ordering, which physics tells us is a sure sign that a fluid system is about to freeze solid. In a nutshell, federation reduces threats from changes of the partners' objectives, and integration allows more rationalization, but limits the partners' freedom of action and the system's future flexibility.

Chapter 12

Using Existing Products

"Next item," said Marcus. They were back in the old drawing office area, and had spent some hours working their way through a technical audit report. This audit had been one of the results of the ongoing negotiations with Factotum, and most of its concerns were about resilience.

"Recommendation 27b identifies problems of consistency between the instances of repair orders that are duplicated in different service centres," Eleanor read from the pink sheet in front of her. "They are right; there is potentially a problem here, but it means adding transactional controls to all the order update steps. It will be a huge job, particularly when taken together with the improvements to archiving and disaster recovery we talked about before coffee."

"What about replication transparency? That worked well for the logistics server, as I remember," said Nigel, hopefully. "Maybe," Eleanor looked out, for a moment, over the cubicles on the floor below. "But I don't think so; we would still need to factor in the channels to archival, and linking that whole subsystem with replication would be too damaging to performance." "Just explain that to me again will you," broke in Marcus, looking puzzled. "I thought transparencies hid all that sort of thing." "They hide complexity from the programmer, but the problem here is the real runtime costs of coordinating a larger number of objects. In any case, what we want from archival is resilience, which means keeping the boundary to it as clean as possible." There was another pause.

"We could try a different approach," said Alex, quietly. "If we don't want the complexity of all these archive-based resilience mechanisms, can't we avoid them completely?" "But we spent half the morning identifying reasons why we must have them," snapped Claire. "Not quite. We have shown that we need consistency and resilience, not that we need to implement all those horrid mechanisms ourselves." "So what's the alternative?" "Don't build the subsystem; buy what you want as a service. There have been a lot of developments recently in cloud computing. You could buy resilient, consistent storage from one of the global suppliers and use it as a secure mailbox between the local centres. That way the external supplier has to worry about the coordination and the disaster recovery. You agree on a suitable SLA with them, and they already have all the resources needed to provide it. All you have to worry about is the local centre access, and you can still use the replication transparency dodge to avoid visible complexity there."

"OK," said Marcus, "what's the down side?" "You have to allow for the risk and the recurrent cost. Costs shouldn't be too far from a realistic total cost of ownership for the in-house solution, and may well be cheaper. There are always hidden costs you miss when assessing doing a job in-house. Risks are more difficult. You have to plan for commercial failure of your supplier, but they are a big player. You should look at a lower quality fallback system in the local centres and set up a commercial hedge." "You mean betting on the commercial failure of the biggest bookseller on the planet?" asked Ira. "This is serious dealing." "Indeed, but it has to be considered. More important, I think, are the risks to security, confidentiality and loss of control it implies. Do you trust your supplier to maintain a really stable service offering without changes in the specification? There is always the risk of over-enthusiastic upgrade." "Surely upgrades are safe?" Marcus looked puzzled again. "Improving a service can't be a problem, can it?"

"Oh yes it can," said Eleanor, ruefully, "remember that online sales tax system a couple of years ago? We had just got it nicely bedded down when they upgraded it and added a whole extra level in their data model. It took weeks to get the miscodings out of our financial data and the internal audit people still remember all the special reconciliations."

"OK, I remember that, but the idea still sounds interesting. Let's talk about the detail."

12.1   What Does This Product Do for Me?

One of the practical problems in using an architectural framework like ODP is that the world is seldom as simple as the textbooks assume. The picture of development taking place in isolation, from requirements to deployment, is far from reality. Rarely can a design team produce the specification of a complete enterprise system as a self-contained activity. Usually, they identify at least some components that are available elsewhere. The incorporation of commercial off-the-shelf products (COTS subsystems) shows the clearest separation of design responsibility and gives the best illustration of the issues. However, use of legacy components involves the same problems.

In essence, the problem to be solved arises from the need to retain the advantages of a clean architectural approach while incorporating subsystems that have already been produced, outside your control, and based on a different framework, or even with no clear framework at all. To be specific, how can components from a non-ODP culture be incorporated into our ODP world?

When you purchase a COTS product to perform some function, you surrender control of the detailed design. On the other hand, you get a working solution immediately and benefit from the supplier's economies of scale. Or at least, you do if you select a well-established, reputable supplier. You also get ongoing support, maintenance and periodic upgrades. However, such upgrades can be a mixed blessing because they may introduce changes that invalidate the way you have integrated the product into your system.

There is certainly no magic bullet in this area. The customer wants guarantees of product stability from the supplier, but the supplier has to balance the conflicting demands that many different customers place upon them. They also need to innovate to attract new customers. The balance between these conflicting requirements will depend on the nature of the supplier's business. A supplier who uses a family of components to offer individually tailored, bespoke solutions to respond to individual invitations to tender from their customers will be more likely to take account of individual customer constraints than one selling a generic product in shrink-wrapped form to thousands or even millions of customers.

A lot depends on the way the suppliers document their products, and how seriously they take the maintenance of this documentation, on the provision of advanced warnings of changes in the product and on the supply of transition tools to make the customer's life easier. At the core of these documentation issues is the need to create suitable models, both of the product and of the way it is to be used; these models themselves need to be positioned within the ODP framework.

12.2   Supplier and User Views

The supplier will have its own specifications used in designing and constructing the product, but these include much private detail, so we concentrate here on a set of models related to its use. These have a number of jobs to do.

In an ideal world, the process of assessing the available products and deciding which to use will involve confirming the relationships between these various models (as well as many other factors involving value for money and commercial credibility, of course). We illustrate these relations in figures 12.1 and 12.2, by showing the observable behaviour as Venn diagrams, so that subsets of possible behaviour are shown as included within their supersets. A product is suitable if the services it offers are a superset of those the user requires, and if the infrastructure support available in the user's environment is a superset of the product's requirements.

First, let us consider the infrastructure. The supplier will have a model, in functional terms, that describes the infrastructure needed to support the product; this model will, in general, describe several alternatives because it will cover a range of different environments in which the product can be deployed.

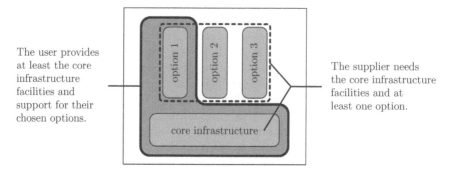

The user provides at least the core infrastructure facilities and support for their chosen options.

The supplier needs the core infrastructure facilities and at least one option.

FIGURE 12.1: The infrastructure services a product needs and the services its user makes available.

However, there will be constraints on the choices of environment to ensure that the choices made by the user result in consistent operation. For example, the supplier may state that the necessary communications can be supplied in a number of different ways, corresponding to a variety of common fixed and mobile technologies the user may want to exploit. Figure 12.1 shows, in a schematic form, that a product needs some core infrastructure and at least one of three possible technology options.

The user will also have an infrastructure model, this time indicating the supporting services that they actually make available when deploying the product. This model will be more restrictive than the supplier's infrastructure model, since it only covers the specific choices of technology the user has made, but, within these limits, it will be more general because it describes the full capabilities of the technologies chosen, which will generally be broader than the specific requirements of the product. This is what is shown by the provision contour in figure 12.1, which shows that the user can support the core facilities and option 1, and more besides. For example, the supplier model may require only point to point communication, while the actual infrastructure provides both this service and some form of group communication or multicast.

The second model the supplier has is one describing what the product can do for the user. This is a classical component model, indicating the widest range of things the product can do in its least constraining environment; that is to say, it describes the union of all the possible styles of use envisaged by the supplier. The supplier may also provide as part of their documentation a number of use case models, suggesting productive ways of exploiting the product, but these are likely to be illustrative, rather than definitive, and give no guidance as to why the user actually bought the product. There may also be a basic core of mandatory user behaviour, such as initialization and registration of security credentials, which must be engaged in if the product is to function correctly. In our Venn diagram, this can be reorganized into a separate region, separating behaviour the user must initiate from that the user may initiate when it requires specific services. In figure 12.2, the inner contour

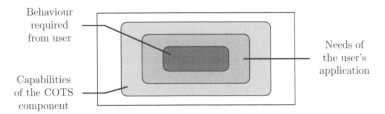

FIGURE 12.2: Broadest and narrowest behaviour envisaged by the supplier and the behaviour needed by the user.

shows the behaviour the user is obliged to initiate and the outer contour shows behaviour the user is permitted to initiate.

The user will also have a model of what the product is to do for them. Again, this is a subset of the actual capabilities of the product, this time indicating what subset of the features available is actually to be used (see the middle contour in figure 12.2). It may also indicate whether particular features are essential to the user's business processes or are merely desirable.

Of course, the supplier may not make the product models available in a form suitable for assessment, or in extreme cases may only describe the product in the broadest marketing terms. In such cases, the potential customer will need to construct their own description of the product, filled in where necessary by asking the potential supplier questions.

The provision by the supplier of a rigorous model showing what they claim their product does is also important in considering conformance. Once the supplier has claimed that a given model represents what their product does, the user can apply it both as a conformance target, checking test observations against it, and in the validation of their own designs, to check that the services they are building on top of the component will match their business needs.

The above discussion gives an idealized and simplified sketch. For example, each of the models described may be manifest in more than one viewpoint. Using viewpoints will help to organize the required assessments, but there may be differences in interpretation in the various supplier and user organizations, reflecting their own internal structures and stakeholder responsibilities.

To position this information in the ODP framework, the product and user models discussed previously will, in general, need to be restructured to create the necessary sets of viewpoint models. We can consider the key features of these for each viewpoint in turn. Firstly, this process will have little impact on the enterprise viewpoint because most products will be generic from the user's point of view. The product's information viewpoint will need to be related to the broader user model by establishing a series of correspondences, mostly in the form of subtyping relationships from general supplier definitions to specific user ones. The computational model describing the intended uses of the product will be a subset of the computational model for the application as a whole, and the user technology model of support provided will be a superset of the product's requirements. From an engineering point of view, there will be correspondences at a broad functional level, but there is not much of an issue here because the details of the product's engineering will be largely hidden from the users. The focus is on the support of the product's interfaces.

The introduction of COTS products will also impact the tool chain; there will be a need for tools to police all these new relationships, and for them to provide planning support for the supplier's commitments about the evolution of the product.

12.3   Competing Sets of Viewpoints

So what happens if both the producer and the user of a component are using ODP? They will each have a set of viewpoint specifications, but are these aligned with one another? Each of a set of viewpoint specifications contributes to a complete and consistent system specification. That is to say, the set is concerned with the capturing of different stakeholder concerns, but they are unified by being concerns about a single target system.

When two independent groups specify different systems, they each define their own logically distinct viewpoint specifications. If the two groups are operating within the same organization, the enterprise specifications may be quite similar, but the emphasis and level of detail applied to particular aspects will differ, and some features in one of the specifications may be omitted as irrelevant in the other. Indeed, as we saw when discussing federation, one of the problems in establishing interoperability between systems is that each of the systems works with a view in which the other is expressed in quite abstract terms as part of its environment.

The key point here is that the content and level of detail in a specification is determined by the role the system is to play. If the system is to interact with some other system in its environment, it is necessary for the nature of these interactions to be expressed. If the system is to act as an intermediary, perhaps receiving a reference in one interaction and passing it on to a different partner in another interaction, then the details of the object referred to are not of concern to the intermediary, so long as the reference type is correct and any assertions about the quality of the object referred to are fulfilled. Again, it all comes down to satisfying the stakeholders' concerns.

12.3.1   Applying Viewpoints to Components

The analysis of incorporation of COTS components can be quite confusing because the specification of a component required to provide services exists in parallel with one or more specifications with broader scopes, each of which describes one way it is to be used.

For example, an information exchange service component may be obtained to integrate information provided by a group of contributing peers. From the point of view of providing this service, it is the coordinating activity which will form the focus of its enterprise specification; the objective is to generate and distribute a common shared image from information contributed by members of a group. Why they should wish to do this is not of any concern to the component provider.

Associated with this view of the product, there will then be a set of shared data types in an information view, a computational access procedure, and supporting engineering and technology constraints.

Such a component could be used in many ways. In coordinating a committee, or a project group, the information exchange is a specific kind of interaction between the community roles being specified, and the service for doing so is therefore visible in the enterprise specification; however, the exact way the service is accessed forms part of the computational specification. On the other hand, in a survey application, the coordination may be implicit, expressed via requirements on one particular role to provide statistical information, but without reference to the enabling service until the detailing of the computational specification. Finally, if a scientific modelling activity needs to exploit distributed simulation tools, the same coordination component might be used as a collation mechanism in the engineering viewpoint but be completely invisible in the computational design.

To achieve this, the viewpoints of the component and the user applications are related in different ways, but retain their independence. A practical example of this can be seen in the standardization of the ODP trader function (ISO/IEC 13235-1), a general-purpose service publication and resource discovery mechanism [9]. This standard describes enterprise, information and computational specifications of trading, but leaves the engineering specification to a platform designer (although one specific engineering realization, supporting the use of directories, is standardized in ISO/IEC 13235-3 [10]).

The trader function is visible in application designs only in their computational view as a service accessed by well-known interfaces, and in the definition of selected information data types and constraints. This reflects the difference between the stakeholders involved in an organization that uses a service and the organization that provides it.

12.3.2 Changing Technologies

As a product evolves, it acquires new features and exploits new supporting services. The supplier maintains upwards compatibility if no service is withdrawn and no additional demands are made on the infrastructure. At each step in the evolution, there is a corresponding set of models describing capabilities and requirements. In practice, many vendors offer a more restrictive guarantee of compatibility, in which, at every release, a statement is made about how many steps back down the release chain the compatibility relationship holds, perhaps with an associated warning about what the situation is expected to be following the next upgrade, so that users have time to respond to impending changes that would otherwise cause them problems.

If new product features become available, the user first has to decide whether they offer sufficient benefits to merit a migration campaign. Such a campaign will normally start with an assessment of whether the changes would offer local usability improvements within the existing business processes, or whether a change to the business processes themselves is going to be needed. Consider, for example, a workflow management system. This might have its user interface upgraded, replacing a coarse-grained web forms interface with a more dynamic AJAX-basedinterface without making a significant difference to the business process, but requiring changes to the interfaces of a number of decision-support plug-ins. Or, on the other hand, dynamic work rescheduling features might be added to the same service, resulting in significant changes to the business processes because they make possible finer scale targeting of premium services to critical markets.

Once a level of abstraction has been identified at which the proposed enhancement is no longer visible, this level can be used as an overarching invariant and the change becomes a refactoring exercise aiming to maintain this target description. This analysis helps to identify the scope of the changes with confidence, since the invariant elements essentially limit the degree to which consequential changes can propagate in the design. There is clearly a strong parallel here with the discussion of federation in chapter 11.

12.3.3   The Changing Views of a Stakeholder

One of the consequences of opting for the use of externally purchased products and services is that there is a shift in the local stakeholder concerns, and this, over time, results in evolution of the viewpoints used to model the system as a whole. Something that was previously a major concern for engineering design may cease to be of interest at all if responsibility for some particular set of mechanisms is outsourced.

Consider, for example, the change in emphasis if an organization decides to buy in a trust management solution from one of the specialist suppliers. A whole range of encryption key-management technologies for which local skills had been needed in the past become simply background information required for risk assessments of the use of the external supplier, and the servers and plug-ins needed become just black boxes. However, in consequence, there is a strong dependency on the external supplier, and, in some respects, a reduction in agility. Accepting this is as much a business decision as a technical one.

Chapter 13

System Evolution — Moving the Goalposts

Eleanor handed Claire a glass of chilled Sancerre from the tray by the door and they both moved on into Marcus's office. The papers from the side table had been cleared away and in their place sat an architect's model of the proposed redevelopment of the east warehouse area.

"I think I'm going to like this new layout," said Claire, "particularly the way she has managed to stagger the floors in the main space, so that you get both small-scale spaces and a share of the views." "Yes, and without losing all the original decorated ironwork; it's a good thing we scotched the misapprehension early on about programmers not wanting to be distracted by outside views; she actually believed that we preferred to be staring at a screen in an enclosed space."

Marcus joined them. "Well, what do you think of the plans now? How do you think your people took it? Was it what they were expecting?" Claire thought for a moment. "I would say they are positive about it; I'm already getting queries about who gets what space, but it's cherry picking stuff, and not at all defensive. When are we going to see schedules and transition plans?" "When you've all contributed to writing them, of course. We have to be sure the changes happen smoothly and don't impact our work; we can't afford the muddle we had when we first moved here from the incubator site; we've got real customers this time." Eleanor grinned. "Don't remind me — nobody knew where anyone else was or who to go to for help. It was chaos."

Alex joined them, twirling an empty glass. "We just treat it like a major system enhancement. The same principles apply, you know; we identify dependencies and get supporting services up and running first. Then we transfer functions as their needs are satisfied. In fact, this is easier than most upgrades we do because it's just a migration and the business processes remain the same."

"Not like introducing a new travel booking system, then, is it Marcus?" "OK, Claire, I should have told the finance people about the new forms before you started submitting them, but I was negotiating for additional capital at the time, as you well know; anyway, it's not the same." "Actually, I think it is," said Alex. "There is a key rule in migration planning that says you never send a message unless the recipient is already able to interpret it. It's called the no surprises rule, and is the key to the management of distributed upgrades. You always upgrade the receiver before the sender, and only let your clients make requests the server is able to satisfy. We always need to keep the principle in mind."

"Any more words of wisdom, Alex?" "I think that just about covers it; now you just need to put it into practice. Always have the next bottle open before the guests need it; I'd like some more of your fine Sancerre."

13.1   Coping with Change

No organization remains unchanged, and so business processes and infrastructure requirements are continually evolving. The ODP architecture tries to limit the impact of technical innovation to be within the engineering and technology viewpoints, and this can be done as long as the basic functionality provided to the organization remains the same. However, new technology enables new ways of doing business, and so technology can be a stimulus for business process reengineering.

More crucially, however, there are continual new opportunities for business innovation, arising from the opening up of new markets, mergers or acquisitions, and internal organizational changes. These all lead to changes in the IT requirements, and are generally more pressing than the cycle of technology adoption. No manager will willingly accept being told that they must wait for IT changes before entering a new and potentially lucrative market.

The RM-ODP does not have a lot to say directly about such unforeseen changes (as opposed to its provision of policies at predictable variation points, as described in chapter 10) because it describes systems as they exist, not the dynamics of the process by which they are developed. However, the reference model is structured to make evolution easy; this is a result of the separation of concerns it offers to the various stakeholders. Separating the system specification into a set of viewpoints, loosely coupled in a clearly understood way by explicit correspondences, allows various aspects of evolution to be carried out separately, as long as overall consistency is maintained.

13.2   The Importance of Tool Support

One of the problems with business-driven evolution is that it is difficult to predict how pervasive the impact of a given change will be. Technology-driven change usually involves the modification of the way some concept representing a business abstraction is supported, and so the change is transparent as long as the abstraction is unchanged. Business-driven change involves modification to the goals and design of the system at a quite abstract level, and the changes can trickle down to any part of the supporting infrastructure. A good design will still be quite robust because the infrastructure will offer services that are sufficiently general to support a large proportion of organizational changes, but there is less confidence that the impact can be predicted; the acid test involves extensive checking that the infrastructure is still fit for purpose.

If this checking has to be done by human beings, it is tedious and error prone. However, if sufficiently powerful tooling is available, a large amount of the checking can be automated. The same is true of the subsequent implementation. In cases where the change involves the application of a well-established pattern to new abstract data structures, so as to generate appropriate storage and access mechanisms, a very high proportion of the work can be automated. It is where new logic is introduced that there tend to be more design decisions to take, and so more human intervention needed.

It is here that the benefits of adopting a model-driven engineering approach (see chapter 15) really show themselves. If changes in requirements can be expressed in terms of modifications to abstract models, and transformations to merge and refine such models have been established, then a great deal of the work in creating the complete system specification can be automated.

This level of automation of specification management also allows evaluating the impact of proposed changes to be made a much simpler and more efficient process, so that it is possible to associate accurate transition costs with proposed changes as part of the decision-making process.

13.3   Making Changes to Viewpoints

Some of the implications of handling system evolution in a framework of linked viewpoints can be illustrated by considering a simple example. Suppose that the PhoneMob organization decides to introduce a new business service, in which repaired phones can be collected at the airport if doing so suits the user's plans better. An agreement with an established franchise for the supply of mobile phone accessories is made to give access to suitably placed outlets.

First, the changes to the business processes are expressed in the enterprise specification. This involves introducing an airport outlet role into the Phone Repair community, and adding the logic to the repair process to decide whether the logistics provider should deliver to the user directly, as at present, or to the airport agent.

Supporting this change will have immediate consequences; new model elements will also need to be added to the information model, representing the new agents and extending the delivery information needed to describe a repair order. Some of the dynamic schemata will also need to be updated to represent the new paths and artefact states in the enterprise processes.

The consequences of changes to the information objects will flow through more or less automatically to the computational specification, which already bases its view of business objects on the information objects. However, it will also need to flesh out the dialogues involved in interacting with the new agent role, and design work will be needed, for example, to extend scheduling algorithms and interactions with the logistics supplier to support the new activities.

In this particular example, the engineering specification is unlikely to be significantly affected because it deals with reusable solutions to the problems of providing interactions, and the kinds of interaction with the new agents are not fundamentally different from those that are already being supported. However, new solutions may be needed if introducing novel styles of computation implies that there are new problems to be solved. One area that might need some extension is security, as the balance of trust and threat may be different from what was previously accepted.

Finally, the technology specification will need to be extended to describe the new form of terminal needed in the agencies and to capture the enlarged configuration that results.

At each step in this process, change will be triggered by the discovery of any inconsistencies. Where there are established patterns of correspondence, these can be used to discover when new elements in one viewpoint require addition of corresponding elements in another viewpoint to maintain the pattern. Again, this change propagation can be automated using suitable tools.

13.4   Avoiding Synchronized Transitions

Even in the smallest distributed systems, it is difficult to make changes that need to be applied to multiple components at the same time; for configurations of any significant size the strategy of turning everything off, updating all components and then restarting is both too disruptive and too high a risk to contemplate. It is taking a step into the unknown, and is just too much like a novice attempting Olympic ski jumping. Any practical evolution strategy needs to be based on the application of incremental changes in such a way that it is possible to introduce any particular kind of change to the individual component systems one at a time. Even with the best planning, problems will be encountered, and it must be possible to roll back local changes as these problems are identified.

One way of achieving the required incremental development is to ensure that the interfaces that are bound together in a design always comply with the so-called no surprises rule. This states that no component should ever be placed in a situation where another correctly functioning component sends it a message that it cannot interpret. One example of the application of this rule can be found in the computational language, where a series of constraints on computational interface types is laid down in the reference model to ensure that evolutionary changes in interface type can be carried out in a smooth and orderly way. These rules describe the relationships between client and server operational interfaces that must be satisfied in order for a binding to be created between them; they state that:

1. The operations defined in the client interface must be a subset of those defined in the server interface and must have the same number of parameters;

2. The parameters generated by the client must be subtypes of those expected by the server; and

3. The terminations issued by the server must be a subset of those understood by the client, and their parameters must be subtypes of those the client expects.

What these rules (summarized in figure 13.1) amount to is that neither party will receive anything they are not expecting, although they may not receive things they could well handle because the sender still lacks the capability to generate them.

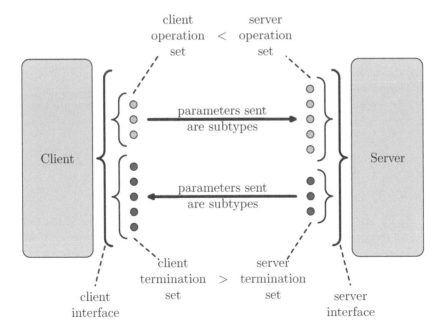

FIGURE 13.1: Computational interface type compatibility rules.

So, how does this help? Well, suppose that, in the PhoneMob system, changes in regulations governing the sending of phones to certain countries result in a need to extend the list of repairOrder status values to include *awaiting export clearance*. If we update some service centres before others, the later ones may receive status messages with an unknown value. If, on the other hand, we perform a two-phase update so that each service centre is first updated to accept and store the new value but not to generate it, there will be no problem with communication between new and old versions. Once this change has been made and become stable, we can make a second change to each system in turn so that they begin transmitting the newly defined value, and the new functionality becomes effective.

Although this example is trivial, much more complex transitions can be organized as a complex sequence of groups of updates, organized so as to ensure that all subsystems are ready to handle new functions before they are activated. This will generally involve quite a number of steps in order to ensure that functional dependencies are observed. Checking that the update schedule is sound and robust is a complex task, and is another area where tools can be used to create and validate suitable sequences from the specifications of the system before and after the change.

The computational language contains specific rules for supporting this kind of evolution because it is by the creation of computational bindings that we link subsystems that are at potentially different stages in the required sequence of updates. However, similar analysis and reasoning can be applied in the other viewpoints, although in the more abstract viewpoints we take a less localized view of the system's behaviour and so just have models of the states before and after the change. It is in the computational viewpoint that we introduce the interfaces at which distribution may potentially take place, and so it is here that the management of system evolution has to take account of interaction between domains in which different sets of updates have been applied. It is therefore natural that this is where the corresponding rules are positioned.

13.5   Evolution of the Enterprise

So far, we have considered incremental modifications. Some of the changes to an enterprise and its infrastructure can be much more drastic. Consider the large-scale changes involved in the big events in an organization's history, such as mergers and acquisitions, or significant divestitures. At these points there is a major upheaval in the provision of IT support, and sometimes this severely damages the organization.

We can treat mergers in many ways as being similar to the establishment of a federation. The key is to establish a clear enterprise model of the organizations that are to merge, and use this as a reference throughout the process.

First, we need to build a plan based on the loose coupling of high-level views, with conversion by interceptors at the domain boundaries to solve detailed incompatibilities, and then follow this up with an incremental campaign of rationalization and alignment. This is a good strategy because time is of the essence. The CIO of a new telecommunications startup once told us, off the record, that they had "the most modern legacy system in the business" because time pressure had forced them to clone the billing system of one of their competitors, rather than deciding all the detail of what they really wanted.

The most difficult part of this process is likely to be predicting who the major stakeholders will be and how responsibilities will be assigned in an organizational structure that is very likely to be fluid for some time. This suggests that there are benefits in aiming for a looser coupling than usual between the viewpoints. It also places emphasis on tools again, this time in support of the refactoring that is bound to follow.

Refactoring is also a key ingredient in divestiture, but here the sequence is reversed. Once the possibility of detaching some business unit has been identified, its interactions with the rest of the organization need to be codified and then processes refactored to weaken mutual dependencies. Domains need to be established clearly, and interceptors introduced, not because of any deliberate intention to introduce incompatibilities, but because the domain boundaries will become points at which the assumptions of trust change, and so management controls will be needed.

It is clear that this topic is more a management issue than a technical one, so the reader should look to sources in those areas and we say no more on the topic in this book. However, we do stress the importance of having a proper architectural framework, like ODP, providing a robust enterprise model for use as a roadmap when planning and carrying out any such large-scale transition activity.

13.6 Version Control

As we indicated previously, the management of system evolution takes us beyond the scope of the ODP reference model, since the model concentrates on capturing one particular design for the system. However, considering how to support system evolution raises a number of significant issues, and it should already be clear that there is a requirement for powerful modelling tools to support evolution.

One of the limitations of current specification languages and tools is that, like ODP, they concentrate on a single specification of the required enterprise system. In the future, these tools will need to be integrated with powerful version control mechanisms and evolution planning aids, so that a designer can produce a revised version of the system specification to support proposed organizational changes. The designer can then be supported by their tools in turning this target design into a series of safe migration steps which put the changes into effect.

Such a version management system needs to be the point at which the major development projects of the enterprise meet; the different development activities will overlap and update key components in different ways. These activities need to be merged and checked for potential conflicts. Senior management also needs to be able to set priorities, so that mission critical changes are given priority in the deployment process. This whole area is one where there are many opportunities for the introduction of new standards and products to support the complete process.

Part IV

Moving On

About Part IV

The last part takes us beyond the material contained in the ODP reference model standard itself. It does this in two main ways.

First, we look at the way the reference model is formulated, aiming to answer some of the questions a reader might have as to why particular approaches were taken and what assumptions are being made about the conceptual framework that underpins the various modelling activities. This gives a brief glimpse of the theoretical basis of ODP, and raises some fascinating questions, but is not essential reading for straightforward users.

Chapter 15 concentrates on the tool chain. The ODP work assumes a powerful set of tools and a considerable degree of automation in support of the design process, but the ODP standards do not cover this area or indicate how such tools are to be constructed. This chapter makes up for this by reviewing some of the key directions taken in the rapidly moving world of model-driven, tool-supported design and development.

Finally, chapter 16 looks briefly at where more information on the topics covered can be found and identifies a number of other proposals for enterprise architectures. This chapter also mentions a number of areas of work that ODP has influenced in recent years.

Chapter 14

Modelling Styles

"What kind of world do these people live in?" Claire asked. They were still sitting in the back row of the lecture theatre, but most of the audience was already filing out. A small group at the front were gathering round the speaker, still carrying on a heated discussion. Alex grinned. "Didn't you like it? I thought he made a good case." "But what use is it? I mean, does it matter whether we distinguish between something being necessarily necessary, or just necessary? And when he said 'In a world with no future, everything is necessary,' I really wondered what the point of it all was."

At Alex's suggestion, they had come up to the University, on the hill overlooking their office, to listen to an inaugural lecture in the Computing Department by the new Professor of Modal Logic, who was well-known for applying his theoretical ideas to industrial problems. He had talked about the importance of putting modelling on a formal basis, illustrating his argument with examples of how simple statements about requirements could be interpreted in many ways.

"I'm still not sure if some of the subtle points really matter," Eleanor added. "Can't they be sorted out by applying common sense?" "Well," Alex thought for a moment before continuing, "a lot depends on what sort of cooperation we are trying to support. If we are all sitting round a table talking about a problem, any differences in the way we look at it can probably be sorted out as we go, but if we are writing down a design for others to interpret, it's not so easy. And it really gets to be important when we start trying to automate things, particularly if the misunderstandings are about how the languages we use are supposed to work." "But that's why we use standardized languages, isn't it? Surely languages like Java are universal these days?" "Not really, Claire; they are not as formally based as you might think, and the real problems come when we look at languages that deal with requirements and rules of behaviour. A statement that sets b to $a + 1$ is generally well understood, but one that says the customer ought to pay within seven days is much more difficult to be sure about. The closer to the real world we get, the more difficult it is to be precise about how all the tricky cases are to be handled. That's why the lawyers rely on the idea of the reasonable man and what such a man might do — it gets them out of a lot of difficult detail in predicting all the possible situations. Our tool builders can't do that."

Eleanor looked down at the worn wooden bench, where some young wit had recorded his ignorance of biology. "But what about all that necessity of necessity stuff? It can't have any real effect, can it?" "Well, he was talking about the way the behaviour is modelled and how the way the model is expressed changes the range of behaviours you would consider as being the same. If you can show a rule for simplifying the description of behaviour always holds, even if it is seemingly quite obscure, it may be the key to simplifying the description and so proving it satisfies the objectives. If I know that I can just replace *necessarily necessary* with *necessary*, then I've got a tactic for rewriting the description in a simpler form, where it may be more obvious that two terms are the same." Eleanor was still not satisfied. "But isn't it obvious they mean the same?" "Unfortunately not. There are a number of formal descriptions of necessity and possibility, which can be arranged as a family depending on the assumptions you make. Unfortunately, this very point is one of the distinguishing features of subfamilies you get by including or excluding particular axioms."

By now it was dark outside the high windows and only the group round the whiteboard remained, and it was thinning out. They were now drawing complex expressions consisting almost entirely of stars, arrows and brackets.

"OK," Claire said, "but what about the worlds with no future?" "One of the ways of clarifying what possibility and necessity means is to talk in terms of what is sometimes called a possible-worlds model. It is made up of nodes representing possible states of the system as a whole, expressed as frames giving a list of statements that say how the state is expressed and markings saying which of these are true in a particular situation. These nodes are then linked by arcs that indicate whether one description can evolve into another. If we have such a model, we can define our terms in a simple way. Something is possible in a given state if there is at least one way the system can evolve that would make it true, and it is necessary if there is no way evolution can make it false. This is a very powerful way of analysing properties of behaviour, and is very important for toolbuilders. The tag he quoted is not very useful in itself, but helps students remember the definitions. If a state can't evolve at all because it has no outgoing arcs, it clearly has no successor where a statement is false, so anything you want to consider is necessary."

A porter had come in at the lower door and was cleaning the boards.

"Come on, they want to turn the lights out, and I've talked for long enough. Let's go and have a drink."

14.1   The Importance of Formal Models

So far, we have described the basic conceptual tools needed to describe a system. Here, we look behind the scenes a little, to explain how some of the assumptions made in this kind of modelling differ from those that are familiar in traditional software engineering. In particular, this chapter looks at specific requirements underpinning enterprise modelling. There is no room in a book of this sort for a lot of supporting theory, so we concentrate simply on giving the flavour of the issues that come up when we are designing a modelling framework.

It should be remembered, however, that we are talking throughout about formal systems; that is to say, we are concerned with use of a formal language defined in terms of some symbols, their grammar, some axioms and a set of inference rules. Any formal system is self-contained and must be related where necessary to the real world by establishing correspondences between its symbols and real-world entities.

The important thing here is that, being formal, their use involves manipulating a language with a clear grammar, and this is what automated tools are good at. If a problem can be stated in formal terms, then tools can check consistency and, depending on the nature of the language, verify interesting properties like termination and liveness.

In building a model it is vitally important that we have a clear idea of what we are trying to cover; what is our target, what boundaries does it have and what properties are we trying to capture? In the rest of this chapter, we will look at some of the issues involved.

14.2 What Is a System?

If we are going to be talking about the modelling of systems, we had better know what a system is. A system can be anything that is of interest to us both as a whole and as a composition of smaller interacting parts. Where appropriate, a system may be composed hierarchically from some collection of subsystems (see figure 14.1). When we design something, we generally think of it as a system because we are interested both in how it will perform as a whole and how it is to be constructed from parts. The parts concerned are not necessarily fabricated things; a system may involve humans or natural resources.

However, an ODP specification is always concerned with the creation or understanding of an ODP system. It is generally reasonably clear, at an intuitive level, what this system is, which is why we have been able to leave consideration of the question until so late in the book. The understanding of the system is the aim when writing the specification. This does not mean that the system is central to every element of the specification; some views may be concerned only with the environment in which the system is to operate, or may express the business requirements at such an abstract level that the target system is not itself visible.

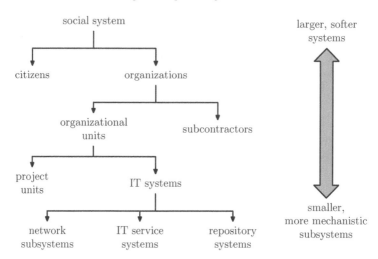

FIGURE 14.1: A hierarchy of systems.

In the PhoneMob specification, for example, the top-level community in the enterprise viewpoint reflects the concerns of the PhoneMob management in terms of the parties involved in their activities, without even mentioning the target system. The target system then appears when the phone repair provider role is refined to a level where the way the system supports individual activities becomes visible. The initial emphasis of the ODP enterprise viewpoint is on establishing the purpose, scope and policies governing the activities of the system to be implemented, and on positioning it within the enterprise of which it forms a part. Depending on the context in question, the term *enterprise* can refer to a single organization or multiple organizations linked, for example, in a supply chain arrangement or by a piece of legislation. The ODP system can describe an existing system and its environment, an anticipated future structure, some new behaviour extending an existing system or a completely new system to be created within some environment.

14.3   Modelling Open or Closed Worlds?

One key question to ask when considering a model is whether or not the model has an external boundary. There are two possible approaches (see figure 14.2). In modelling a component, for example, the model expresses how that component interacts with the rest of the world, but the world outside its boundaries is not modelled. Instead, the component has interfaces where it interacts with its environment. The interfaces and their types form a boundary

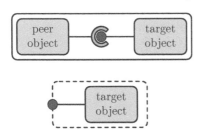

A closed-world model has no free variables and no external environment.

An open-world model has free variables that are bound by its external environment.

FIGURE 14.2: Defining open- and closed-world models.

to the model, but no further information about the world outside is given. This is called an **open-world** model because there is an unknown environment outside.

The alternative is to model the whole of some universe of discourse at a suitable level of abstraction. The model represents a complete system, although the detail becomes increasingly sketchy as we go further from the focus of interest. The resulting model is a bit like the reflection of some scene in a silver sphere; the whole world is in there, but only the major features of distant objects can be made out; this is called **closed-world** modelling. In a closed-world model, there is no boundary or external interface; remote parts of the world are described, but only where this is necessary to account for the interactions and internal state of the objects that are the primary focus of the specification.

One of the main distinguishing features in enterprise modelling is that a community expresses constraints and obligations on the things filling its roles, rather than concentrating on the external interactions of some black box. In other words, it focuses on the contract it embodies, not the interfaces of some component providing a service. Thus, communities are normally expressed in a closed-world style, where the specification covers the complete universe of interest; however, parts of it may be represented in quite an abstract form.

In some situations, however, we want to produce a partial specification, in which case we need to make the fact that some object provides a channel to arbitrary remote parts explicit. This is done by introducing a so-called **interface role**, fulfilled by any object of the appropriate type, whose identity is not of concern in the community. The model is then of an open-world form.

This is not a very common requirement, but the final choice of style will be influenced by the problem being solved. One situation where the open-world style might be appropriate is where a community offers a business service to the general public, without being concerned with the nature of its customers.

Chapter 11 deals with an intermediate situation — that of enterprise federation. In this case, two enterprises cooperate based on a loose coupling; each takes a simplified, abstract view of the objectives, rules and processes of the other. The key to successful federation is to ensure that there is sufficient mutual understanding to see that the objectives will be met without applying unacceptably rigid constraints on the independence and evolutionary potential of the federation members. Note that the federation itself can be considered as a community at a higher level of abstraction, and thus can be reused in higher-level specifications, like any other individual community.

14.4   Capturing Requirements

The formal approach taken in the enterprise language is aimed at improving communication between business stakeholders and designers of the system, but, at the same time, bringing a level of rigour needed to link it to the detailed design of the system. This is of particular importance when using tools to support model-based development; these tools need to provide traceability linking requirements, features in the design and elements of the subsequent implementation. Rigour is achieved by the adoption of a precise set of modelling concepts, carefully selected to reflect the typical business language and jargon, such as the concepts of process, policy, party, accountability, delegation and so on. These modelling concepts allow the expression of the expected structures and behaviour of a projected enterprise or system, either a completely new one or an intended extension of an existing system.

There are various techniques that can be used to facilitate the development of business structures and processes based on the elicitation of business requirements and business rules, making use of interviews with stakeholders. For example, standard use cases or business scenarios provide a way of expressing business and system requirements using structured natural language, reflecting a specific fragment of a system. Typically, several use cases can be combined to arrive at a broader and more generic business model expressed using the enterprise language concepts. These models are more amenable to automated checking than loose collections of use cases. Ideally, a software development tool should provide traceability between requirements and the resulting elements of the enterprise model, to ensure that when requirements change, the elements of the enterprise model that may be affected can be highlighted; increasingly, tools are providing support for such features.

From a modelling point of view, requirements capture has two interesting features. The first is that the relation between a requirements model and a design is a particularly extreme form of refinement, in which the assertions made in the requirements must remain true when an initially underspecified system element is completely replaced by a design compliant with some architecture chosen by the designer. The second feature of requirements modelling is that it will often bring into play some roles and responsibilities not appearing at all in the eventual design, covering things like ownership of the system, its associated runtime and implementation costs, and so on.

14.5 Expressing Obligations

As we have shown, the description of an enterprise involves more conflicting constraints and trades-off than are found in the design of a software process. This leads to emphasis not just on what happens next in a particular situation (as is the case in traditional software design), but also to consideration of what might happen, what can happen and what should or should not happen. We are concerned not just with the rules of a deterministic automaton, but a web of permissions, obligations and prohibitions. The result is a need for a much more powerful set of modelling tools. Technically speaking, it takes us from the world of predicate logic to the world of modal and deontic logics [74,89,99] — giving the ability to reason about possibilities and conformance to accepted norms.

This is a more fundamental change than many people realize. It involves not just extensions to the notations we use, but changes to the way we interpret existing notations. Instead of basing our assessment of a system on whether what it just did is consistent with the specification, we need to ask whether it did the right thing, given all the possible things it could have done in the circumstances. This involves our tools in checking for optimal decisions (or, more often, least bad solutions), rather than just checking for correctness, and few tool builders have yet risen to this challenge.

A simple example can be seen in the treatment of obligations. If I have an obligation, it is reasonable to assume that I should do the action needed to discharge it; but it is not obvious, unless explicitly stated, how urgently I should treat the requirement, or how hard I should strive to overcome other factors that might currently be preventing the action. However, this is just the beginning; it is much more difficult, for example, to see what I am expected to do if I am one of a number of equal members of a community and an obligation is placed on the community. If the thing is not getting done, what personal costs should I accept so that the whole group meets its obligation? Why not leave it to one of the others to do it?

One consequence of these complications is that the statements of expected actions in our contracts are frequently accompanied by exception handling, saying what should be done if an obligation is not discharged, or a prohibition is violated. These may cover what corrective actions are needed or what compensation becomesdue. For example, community contracts often detail penalties for late delivery or processes for replacing faulty goods.

One particular set of concepts that must be treated in this way is concerned with delegation. If an enterprise is to be robust, it must be clear what is to happen when an object fails or when the demands on a role exceed the capabilities of any single object. One solution is to introduce a special kind of community, describing a delegation pattern, in which responsibility can be passed down to exploit a broader range of resources, or an authorized replacement can be located for a failed actor.

These are areas where the current models are just the first steps towards progressively higher-level descriptions of business practices, social norms, or even aspects of the legal system. It is not inconceivable that, in the future, legislation may be supported by suitable formal models of the community concerned. There are already a number of examples of the formal modelling of quite complex laws and regulations in the scientific literature [57,77,87,91].

14.6   Expressing Semantics

So far we have concentrated on issues about expressing behaviour, but there are also many equally important issues in the field of information modelling. Here again, the main issue is how to establish a robust link between a formal model of knowledge and the real world with all its complexity and ambiguity. The models used are generally based on the construction of a large collection of terms, labelled with attributes and linked by relations. These knowledge networks are often called ontologies. There is a great deal of judgement and skill involved in constructing a good ontology because of the need to balance coverage and precision.

As usual, there is a need to limit the resulting complexity, and this is normally done by defining ontologies to cover specific subject domains. These then need to be related, usually via an overarching upper ontology (sometimes called a foundation ontology). This involves the specifier in facing problems very similar to those occurring when creating a federation (see chapter 11). The problem here is, again, that combining different domains can easily lead to inconsistency and ambiguity.

Consider, for example, the interaction between a technical ontology for the mobile phone industry and a general commercial ontology covering sale of products. The mobile phone ontology might cover terms like *handset* and *SIM*, and express the whole-part relationship between them. The commercial ontology might describe *spare-part, ownership* and *warranty*, indicating that ownership of a product implies ownership of its parts. However, when we sell a mobile phone it often involves a preinstalled SIM, perhaps on a pay-as-you-go basis. The simple composition of these ontologies as separate fields of knowledge would conceal a whole range of issues around the more complex relationship between phone supplier, carrier and customer.

Solving these problems requires a detailed analysis of what it means to say a term applies to a real-world entity, and needs much of the same modal machinery outlined previously for the handling of obligations.

Chapter 15

Sharp Tools

"Hello," said Claire, "what are you doing? It looks grim." Nigel was sitting at a long table with two monitors and a laptop, surrounded by printed lists and diagrams. "I'm rebuilding the firewall rules for the federation links with Factotum. It all works OK on the test systems, but when we move to production it is going to need a whole new set of permissions, and I'm going to have to prove to internal audit that there are no loopholes." "That doesn't sound too bad; why is there so much paper involved?"

"Because the configuration data comes from the network management system, but the actual communication patterns are application sequence diagrams, and they are scattered about the different functional designs. To make things worse, the actual data flows are not exactly as the designs say because there are transparent caches in front of the interceptors, so the network flows are broken up by that. The control rules are all in different formats and come from different systems, too."

Claire was getting interested. They worked through the different data sources, and before lunch they had identified five different report types that together held all the key information. After that, some simple shell scripts had extracted a series of relationships and massaged the names into a more manageable form. Claire had got Ira involved because she remembered an open source ontology visualization tool he had been so pleased with earlier in the week. It was now mid-afternoon, and they were gathered round a laptop looking at a display dense with coloured lines.

"What a mess," Nigel said. "It's worse than all the paper." "Yes, but wait," said Ira, pulling down a menu, "here's the really clever bit. The tool does cluster analysis and looks for relational closures that fit with the resulting structure." He clicked a couple of items and the picture writhed and settled down to show a coarse mesh with a small number of lines cutting across the main bundles. "Now then, we want to know about the authorized paths that cross organizational boundaries." After some more option selection, a few bundles were highlighted in red.

Nigel took over and hovered the mouse over these groups, noting the network routes involved. "Yes, that's the structure I was working on, but what about that group of flows up there? Oh, they all go through a thing called the echo responder; what does that do?" Claire thought for a moment. "That's part of the fault tolerance mechanisms; it lets objects check to see if their references are operational." Nigel's eyes gleamed. "But don't you see," he whispered, "it's a backdoor. Anyone can use it and get at or modify any of our data."

There was a moment of stunned silence before Ira spoke. "That all goes to show what happens when you have tools that bring your data together and let you see it as a whole. It's a good job we found it before we went live, but what are we going to do about it?"

15.1   What Should a Tool Do?

We have repeatedly stressed the importance of having effective tools available when designing and implementing any reasonably large system. Without them, it is very difficult to ensure that structured designs are internally consistent because, when compared to computers, humans are just not that good at correlating information on paper. This is particularly true of systems designed using a framework that supports separation of concerns. The separation makes it easier for different parts of the design to be progressed in parallel, but also means that fewer people will have a complete view of how all the parts interrelate.

In a viewpoint-based design, therefore, it is particularly important that there should be continuously available checking mechanisms to ensure that no inconsistencies are introduced when modifications are made. This should cover at least the consistency of the viewpoints and correspondences, but will usually also need to police additional user defined rules, such as global uniqueness constraints.

Powerful tools let us automate the weaving together of information from the various viewpoints, so that there is little need for manual processes to be involved in combining information from the different views when constructing the target system. Here we are talking about a toolchain involving various types of tool, all working in a collaborative way to support system design and specification. This includes traditional tools like editors and compilers, specialized design tools, transformational tools, and tools that check consistency and correctness, like model checkers.

As we shall see, these tools need to come together in order to provide an integrated design and development environment, including support for versioning, repository management and controlled collaboration and sharing of information. This implies the introduction of what some authors have called a tool bus [53, 79] allowing exchange of information, signalling of events and provision of services. Just having a transfer format for models, like XMI, is certainly a start but is not generally enough to provide the level of integration and interaction that is needed.

15.2 Model Editors and Analysis Tools

The first level of tool support required for the development of large systems specification should be provided by model editors. The RM-ODP was originally defined to be independent from any particular notation for expressing its concepts, so as to increase its use and flexibility. In other words, the ODP viewpoint languages are *abstract languages* in the sense that they define what concepts should be used, not how they should be represented. This lack of notations for expressing precisely the different models involved in a multi-viewpoint specification is a common feature for most enterprise architectural approaches, including the Zachman framework, the 4+1 model and the RM-ODP.

The problem with defining only the abstract syntax of a language is that it makes the development of tools for writing the viewpoint specifications more difficult. More information is needed to allow the formal analysis of what is produced, and the possible derivation of implementations from the system specifications, and to manage the myriad other details needed to complete the specification.

There have been many different notations proposed as ODP specification languages. The earlier ones came from academia, based primarily on formal languages such as Z [95], Object-Z [67], LOTOS [1, 18], Alloy [76] and Maude [61]. These notations provide precise system specifications and, more importantly, they allow the rigorous analysis of the systems, with tools for reasoning about the specifications including consistency checking, simulation for prototyping or model checking. However, the precision inherent in formal description techniques and the lack of industrial tool support has hampered their wide adoption.

As we mentioned before, the acceptance of UML, the number of available UML tools, the increasing interest in model-driven development and the model-driven architecture (MDA) initiative, all contributed to motivating ISO/IEC and ITU-T to launch the UML4ODP joint project in 2004. This aimed to promote the use of UML for ODP system specifications. We have already described the UML4ODP project and its notation in section 1.7.2. The goal of this joint project was that ODP modellers should use the UML notation for expressing their ODP specifications in a standard graphical way, and that UML modellers should be able to use the RM-ODP concepts and mechanisms to structure their large UML system specifications.

The fact that the UML4ODP notation is defined as an extension to UML by means of a set of UML profiles makes its adoption easier. UML profiles are available for all the major UML modelling tools, which enables the use of the UML4ODP notation within them. Furthermore, specialized model editors for UML4ODP have been created making use of these profiles and these are also available as plug-ins for some of the widely used UML modelling tools.

One example is the UML4ODP plug-in for MagicDraw. These domain-specific tools allow users to work with the ODP concepts and mechanisms as first class entities in their editors, and provide common skeletons and templates for the specifications.

However, editing with a set of UML profiles may not be enough when building large system specifications. There is also the need to check that the structure and architecture of these specifications is correct. One of the benefits of using a reference model such as the RM-ODP is that it allows structuring the specifications according to a fully tested standard architecture. The fact that the structuring rules of ODP viewpoint languages are explicitly defined in the standard has enabled the development of tools that allow validation of the models, checking that they comply with the ODP reference architecture. This is already possible with some of the plug-ins mentioned previously, which are able to detect missing parts of the specification, architectural problems, conflicting elements or violation of the structuring rules.

Another key role for tools in this context can be seen in the validation of the individual viewpoint specifications. We have mentioned that there are notations for the viewpoints that allow their formal analysis and even simulation. The question is how to connect the UML4ODP specifications with these notations so as to be able to make use of their toolkits. This is where model-driven techniques really come into play.

15.3   Model-Driven Approaches

There has been a great deal of emphasis in recent years on the development of model-driven techniques for system design and development. This movement is marked by a change of emphasis from a situation where models were used primarily to capture requirements and set the scene for a creative coding process to a situation where the models are the prime focus of the design and the source representation for design information, from which a largely mechanical implementation process derives its steering information. The assumption is then that the models are the place to go to answer any questions about the system. Any modifications are carried out as changes to the models followed by an incremental reworking of the implementation process. With strong enough tools, this reworking can be cheap and quick to carry out.

We are all familiar with such almost total reliance on tools in the support of high-level languages. The overwhelming proportion of program development is now carried out in languages like Java, and hardly anyone gives a second thought to the processes of compilation from high-level language to object code, or JIT compilation of object code to machine code, that underlie the execution of such code. Promoting this to start at the model level is not entirely straightforward because the models are more abstract and one single refinement route is not always appropriate, but the rewards of doing so are considerable; this is what the model-driven approach is trying to do.

Work to raise the abstraction level at which designs are formulated has been a major research thread for a long time and, as should now be clear, was an important influence on the development of the ODP viewpoints. However, the ideas gained prominence in 2001 when the OMG brought much of the earlier thinking together in their MDA white paper [92]. This focused initially on one particular problem, the decoupling of application designs from the details of the growing number of middleware platforms available. The answer proposed was to capture the application detail in a quite abstract model and then provide tools that could specialize this single design for each of the platforms available.

One of the main contributions was to recast thinking that had previously been in terms of translation between languages with different grammars so that the ideas were expressed as models whose form was governed by corresponding metamodels (although a metamodel is still, basically, just a grammar). If the transformation that was needed from abstract and concrete models could be defined in terms of metamodels, a single tool generated from them could be used for transforming the whole family of models that shared the same metamodel (see figure 15.1). In practice, transformations need to be parameterized to make them more widely applicable, so the process is steered by a combination of the material embedded in the transformation and some additional information supplied when a particular transformation activity is performed.

Later, the OMG extended their architecture to support more than one refinement step, and identified three major modelling levels, yielding

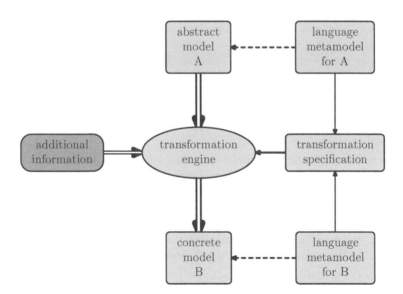

FIGURE 15.1: A framework for model transformations.

computation-independent models (CIM), platform-independent models (PIM) and platform-specific models (PSM) [84]. Note that the terms PIM and PSM are defined relative to some chosen concept of a platform, and may be applied recursively as the system design is refined. Researchers have suggested that one approach to integration of, for example, non-functional aspects such as security is to extend the chain to involve a whole series of transformation steps [63, 80], leading to a convergence with aspect-oriented programming.

It is tempting to try to draw parallels between this family of models and the viewpoints, but there is an important difference that makes such connection inappropriate. This is the fact that the viewpoints are characterized by stakeholder interest, while the ideas of CIM, PIM and PSM are relative to technological detail. Thus, as technologies evolve and the design focus drifts up to higher levels of abstraction, there will be a gradual relative drift between the two systems.

15.4   Model Transformations

Models and transformations are the key ingredients of the model-driven architecture approach. A model transformation is basically an algorithmic specification (either declarative or operational) of the relationship between models, more specifically the *mapping* of information from one model to another. A model transformation involves at least two models (the source and the target), which may conform to the same or to different metamodels. The relationship defined by a model transformation determines the valid mappings between models conforming to these metamodels, and can be of different types depending on the nature of the relation: unidirectional or bidirectional, refining or abstracting, endogenous or exogenous (depending on whether the source and target metamodel are the same or not), and so on. The transformation specification is normally given by a set of model transformation rules, which describe how a model in the source language can be transformed into a model in the target language.

In addition to model-to-model transformations, it is also possible to define text-to-model and model-to-text transformations, in which the language of the source or target model is expressed using a textual notation. The former are called injectors, and are very useful for converting programs or documents into models that can be manipulated using model-driven techniques and tools. Extractors are useful for producing structured documents (text, Word, Excel, HTML, XML or program source code) from models.

A model transformation can also be considered a model in its own right, which presents opportunities for higher-order transformations, that is, transformations that manipulate models representing other model transformations [97]. The metamodel of a transformation corresponds to the language in which the transformation is written.

The initial discussions of model-driven transformations focused on transformations that are one-to-one, with each transformation linking precisely one source to one target. In general, however, the development of structured specifications leads to more intricate patterns, where the transformations are typically many-to-many. One common pattern involves weaving multiple pieces of specification together to yield a single target. Another is the derivation of a number of implementation elements from a single design, yielding, for example, both executable code and deployment control files, such as tailored sets of firewall rules.

Another important use of model transformations is to define bridges between technical spaces or even semantic domains. For example, model transformations can be used to translate specifications written in UML4ODP into their corresponding specifications in Maude or in Alloy, in order to make use of the analysis facilities and tools available in these target domains. Furthermore, model transformations are extensively used nowadays to build two-way bridges between systems or applications that use disparate technologies or live in different technical spaces (such as EMF [55], CORBA, Java or RDBMS, to name but a few).

Finally, it is important to mention that model transformations are not normally defined in isolation, but as part of a set of transformations that are composed together into a model transformation chain that provides a more powerful piece of functionality. This follows the typical pipelined approach used, for instance, by the Unix shells, in which several commands are chained together using pipes to form a specialized application.

15.5 Languages for Transformations

Having an architecture for transformations is not much good without a corresponding language for defining them. The OMG has therefore defined a recommendation known as QVT, or *Meta Object Facility (MOF) 2.0 Query/View/Transformation Specification* in full [41]. This provides a specification toolkit with a range of features for transformation specifiers with differing requirements.

One of the ongoing debates about the use of transformations has been whether they should be defined in a declarative or imperative style. Some claim that a declarative style is more suited to the expression of architectural relationships because it is more abstract, while others prefer an imperative approach as being easier to write and debug. QVT supports both styles by providing two different languages, called QVT Relations and QVT Operational. Both of them are implemented on top of a low-level, imperative language called QVT Core.

Just like programming languages, there are many other model transformation languages currently available, among which ATL (the *ATLAS Transformation Language*) [78] is probably the more widely used. ATL is a hybrid model transformation language containing a mixture of declarative and imperative constructs. ATL transformations are unidirectional, operating on read-only source models and producing write-only target models.

In general, the model transformation language to use depends on the specific characteristics of the relationship we want to establish between the source and target model, and the selection of the best way to express it.

There are also several languages for writing model-to-text transformations, such as MOFscript, JET, TCS or Acceleo. The last of these is an implementation of the OMG MOF model-to-text (MOFM2T) language [32]. TCS (Textual Concrete Syntax) can be used for specifying both injector and extractors. It enables the specification of textual concrete syntaxes for domain-specific languages (DSL) by attaching syntactic information to metamodels. With TCS, it is possible to parse (text-to-model) and pretty print (model-to-text) DSL sentences. Again, the language to use in each case depends on our specific requirements and preferences.

15.6   Viewpoints and Transformations

So, how does this transformation approach relate to the ODP viewpoints? Firstly, it must be made clear that these techniques can be used to support refinement or other automated design steps within a single viewpoint. They could, for example, support the community refinement described in chapter 2. However, the approach is particularly important for integrating and bringing together information from different viewpoints. The transformational approach can be used to support the various steps needed to combine and refine the different viewpoint models to yield a working system, but the nature of the steps to be taken depends on the viewpoints concerned, and there is more than one way of putting the pieces together. However, we can see a number of styles depending on the viewpoints concerned.

In the current context, we can distinguish three kinds of transformation pattern (although there are many more), which differ in terms of the roles the viewpoint specifications play and the nature of the information flows (see figure 15.2). These are:

1. Merging transformations, in which two specifications are combined to generate a composition. This can be performed by following a set of *defined by* correspondences. One example of this is the import of defini-

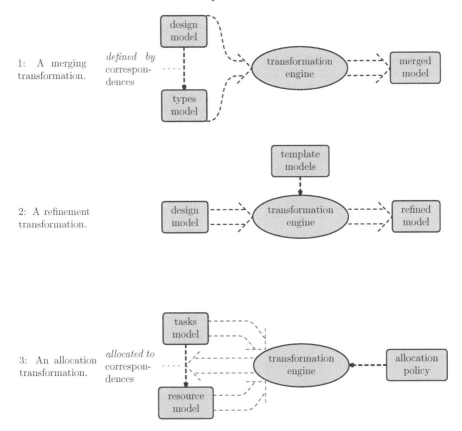

FIGURE 15.2: A schematic view of different transformation types.

tions from one specification to complete another specification that uses the definitions; it includes the well-known process of importing type libraries. Another example is the weaving of different aspects.

2. Refinement transformations, in which one specification provides a set of templates for replacing terms in another specification with specific pieces of supporting mechanism. This includes the classic model-driven transformation in which a platform specification is applied to a platform-independent design to yield a platform-specific one.

3. Allocating transformations, in which some tactic is applied to two specifications in order to construct an optimal relationship between them. This might involve resource allocation in which tasks defined in one specification are associated with resources defined in another. The result could then be expressed by the creation of a set of *allocated to* correspondences. Examples might be the deployment of tasks in an application on available processors, or the building of execution schedules.

Looking at the relationship between specific viewpoints, some follow a single pattern, while others are composite in nature. The relationship between the computational and engineering viewpoints is perhaps the simplest, being a straightforward refinement relation, in which the engineering viewpoint provides a set of templates for refining the computational specification. This results in an ephemeral specification that is not one of the ODP viewpoints, but represents an abstract implementation. Since it will be regenerated afresh whenever necessary, it will track changes in the computational and engineering viewpoints as they occur.

The relationship between the information and computational viewpoints involves a merge, in which information types are imported into the computational specification, where they will generally be used as a starting point for further refinement as part of the computational design process.

The relationship between the enterprise specification and the others is again primarily a refinement, but the rules to be applied depend on the organization and the methodology in use, so that many approaches to unification are possible.

The involvement of the technology viewpoint is more complex because it deals with several different kinds of information. The viewpoint covers the available resources and their configuration, as well as catalogues of implementable standards and conformance requirements. One of the main activities is the performance of an allocation step that associates tasks in the abstract implementation to specific resources; the results of this allocating transformation is added to the technology viewpoint configuration information. There is then an *instance of* relationship between technology viewpoint elements produced and the engineering elements being supported.

These examples give an idea of how transformational tools can manipulate viewpoint information and support the realization of the system that has been designed. There are, of course, other information flows as part of the system generation process, drawn from the patterns given previously, or otherwise, but it should be clear that the tools will each need to act on and combine information from different viewpoints to do their job.

Model transformations can also be very useful for keeping different models synchronized. These models can be either two representations of the same viewpoint specification, or two viewpoint specifications related by a set of correspondences. The first case happens when the user applies two concrete syntaxes to express one viewpoint language, for example a textual and a graphical one. In the second case, changes in one of the viewpoint specifications may need to be reflected in the rest of the related viewpoints. As indicated in chapter 7, the correspondences can be used to propagate these changes, and model transformations provide a natural mechanism for keeping these specifications in step. For instance, think of two elements living in different viewpoints, but related by a correspondence that establishes that their names should coincide. Model transformations can be responsible for changing the name of an element whenever the related one is modified.

Finally, correspondences can also be very useful in multi-viewpoint specifications for checking consistency between the different views. Part 3 of the reference model discusses this problem and explains that, if two viewpoint specifications S_1 and S_2 are related by a set of correspondences that can be specified in terms of a model transformation T, the transformation can be applied to S_1 resulting in a new specification $T(S_1)$. This can then be compared directly to S_2 in order to perform different kinds of checks. Examples of such consistency checks include, for instance, behavioural compatibility [60] between allegedly equivalent sets of objects, or the detection of contradictory constraints in one or another of the viewpoint specifications.

15.7   More Integration

We are a long way from a situation where a system can be deployed from a set of viewpoint specifications at the press of a button. In fact, it is unlikely that we will ever achieve this Utopian objective. Indeed, there are both positive and negative aspects of the move towards greater integration.

On the positive side, there is the possibility of making more information available about the way the organization actually works, and feeding this information back into the system management and control processes. If some information is available about actual patterns of usage, it can be fed back to assist autonomous management mechanisms. We can optimize and balance the use of resources by establishing new paths within the toolchain.

On the other hand, we need to retain a certain looseness of coupling and compartmentalization to allow proper management. We do not actually want changes in the enterprise models to feed through immediately into the running system. We need to observe review processes before changes are accepted, and to allow designers to experiment with, and assess the impact of, possible changes before they are put into effect. One of the requirements that goes hand-in-hand with the progressive increase in the level of integration is the need for more powerful management tools for the whole process, allowing for the exploration of options and the circumscription of activities a designer can carry out, so that they do not exceed their authority.

Chapter 16

A Broader View

Marcus turned back at the door. "One final piece of news," he said, "I've just been told that the PhoneMob system has been nominated for an IT Guild award. Well done everybody." Eleanor looked up. "Have you told Alex yet? And are you going to get him to advise on the new project?"

Marcus looked round the faces of the team, and thought how well they were working together now.

"I'll add a note to his Christmas card, and get my PA to send him a case of his favourite Pinot Noir. But I don't think we need trouble him again. I think you all know how to do it yourselves, now." He smiled briefly at them and closed the door after him.

16.1   Where to Look Next

Having read this far, you probably want to know more; so what next? One answer is to go to the standards themselves. The best place to start is probably with the introduction to UML4ODP, which was the most recently published, but before long you will want to read Parts 2 [3] and 3 [4] of the reference model, as being the source of most of the ideas. These are publicly available online from ISO or ITU-T, as are a number of the other supporting standards. Part 2 explains the basic concepts and vocabulary used across all the viewpoints, while Part 3 introduces the five viewpoint languages, the transparencies and the supporting functions.

More detail of the business-facing aspects can then be found in the enterprise language standard [17]. Some additional detail of the key techniques for supporting the building of configurations in the computational and engineering viewpoints can be found in the *Interface References and Binding* standard [14], while important general material on the manipulation of names in situations where there are many federated domains is provided in the *Naming Framework* [16].

The reference model can be obtained free of charge from the ISO publicly available standards pages at http://standards.iso.org/ittf/ PubliclyAvailableStandards/index.html. The ITU-T makes its versions of all the ODP standards freely available as part of the X series of recommendations from `http://www.itu.int/itu-t/recommendations/index.html`.

A good source of news and general information is the ODP website at `http://www.rm-odp.net/`, which provides links to current activities. You can also download the model for our running example from the authors' website at `http://theodpbook.lcc.uma.es/`. This goes into more detail of the model than is outlined throughout the book and brought together in appendix A.

There are not enough other books on ODP, but two notable ones are Blair and Stefani [52], which deals with ODP largely from a computational perspective, with emphasis on its use with real-time and multimedia systems, and Putman [88], which works through the detailed concepts, following the structure of the reference model closely.

16.2   Integration of Other Standards

The ODP reference model provides a conceptual framework, but concrete notations are needed to express viewpoint specifications. In this book, we have given pride of place to UML, but there are many other notations that can be positioned and used within the framework. Some well-known standards from the OMG that could be used are:

- The *Business Process Model and Notation, BPMN* [40], which provides a graphical notation for expressing business processes, and so is a candidate notation for representing enterprise community behaviour.

- The *Business Motivation Model, BMM* [37], which provides a set of concepts for expressing goals and objectives and so could be used to express enterprise community objectives.

- The *Semantics of Business Vocabulary and Business Rules, SBVR* [33], which says how business vocabularies, facts and rules can be expressed and could be used to express business-oriented types, in either the enterprise or information viewpoints.

16.3   Uses of ODP

This section sketches a number of representative examples of areas in which the ODP framework has been used. There are many more such examples, and pointers to some of these can be found on the ODP website or in the academic literature, particularly in the EDOC series of conferences or the associated series of WODPEC workshops.

16.3.1 NASA RASDS

International collaboration on space exploration and the deployment of space-based data collection platforms has led to a need to share facilities and resources. As always, this has focused attention on the need for a framework to promote interoperability, and the Consultative Committee for Space Data Systems has, as a result, proposed the *Reference Architecture for Space Data Systems* [62]. This has subsequently been published by the ISO as ISO 13537 [11].

This architecture is based on the RM-ODP, but with an expanded set of viewpoints to take into account the special concerns with details of communication and spacecraft system engineering that arise from the special challenges of the space environment.

16.3.2 Service-Aware Interoperability Framework

The RM-ODP has recently been used as input to the Health Level 7 (HL7) standardization efforts. HL7 International is a not-for-profit, ANSI-accredited standards development organization with members from over 55 countries, dedicated to providing a comprehensive framework and related standards for the exchange, integration, sharing and retrieval of electronic health information. It aims to support clinical practice and the management, delivery and evaluation of health services.

RM-ODP has been used to provide architectural underpinning to a broad range of e-health interoperability problems. This part of the HL7 effort is referred to as the Service-Aware Interoperability Framework (SAIF) [73].

SAIF provides a framework for ensuring interoperability when exchanging documents, messages and services between health organizations. This consists of four core subframeworks:

- The Information Framework (IF), which defines how the static information of importance to a given domain is captured and refined through a traceable process to yield an implementable or implemented information artefact.

- The Behavioural Framework (BF), which provides a technology-independent way of describing behaviour in e-health systems. Many of the concepts from the enterprise and computational languages and some of the foundational concepts have been adopted within the SAIF behavioural framework.

- The Governance Framework (GF), which provides an abstract governance model. This can be applied within an interoperability community, within a standards development community, across standard development communities or within a specific enterprise architecture. A subset of the ODP enterprise language is used.

- The Enterprise Conformance and Compliance Framework (ECCF), which provides an organizational framework in which interrelated e-health architectural artefacts are categorized by content. It is used to define conformance and compliance statements, and is based on the treatment of conformance in the RM-ODP.

16.3.3   Use in Other Standards

In previous chapters, we described the main members that make up the ODP family of standards. However, the influence of the ODP work is not limited to this and, in addition, the ODP framework has also been used by a number of other ISO projects.

The most prolific field of application has been in the ITU-T work in support of management of their transport networks. The recommendation *G.851, Management of the Transport Network* [25] and a family of twenty-five associated recommendations dealing with different facets of management information are all built using the ODP framework. Related work is continuing within *ITU-T Study Group 17*, concerned with *Question 13/17 on Formal Languages and Telecommunications Software*.

An example of use in a quite different area is the standard *ISO/TS 17573: Systems Architecture for Vehicle-Related Tolling* [20], which is currently being revised after seven years of use. It uses the ODP reference model to provide an architecture, a standard vocabulary and a modelling approach that allows the system to be seen from different viewpoints, covering a wide range of requirements, from hardware components and network protocols or interfaces to enterprise roles and general policies of the system as a whole. This is accomplished by applying different sets of concepts and terminologies that make up the viewpoint languages. A complete description of a real system is only achieved when all the viewpoint models are present. This allows the experts in vehicle automation to achieve a clear separation of concerns and gives an easier way to define conformant systems.

Another example can be found in the standard *ISO 19119: Geographic Information Services* [21], which provides a framework for interoperability of products involved in the access to and processing of data in geographic information systems. This uses the ODP viewpoints to structure the framework, and has chapters explaining the domain-specific detail associated with each of the ODP viewpoints. Service composition is based on the computational specification, and semantic interoperability on the information viewpoint. The result is a modular, service-oriented toolkit for the construction of workflows involving data repositories for geographic information associated and analysis systems.

The trend is continued in a recent multi-part standard *ISO 12967: Health Informatics — Service Architecture (HISA)* that provides an architectural framework for healthcare informatics, which gives a set of ODP viewpoint specifications for service definition and integration [6–8]. Its aim is to provide a single approach that unifies the integration of new developments and commercial off-the-shelf products with existing legacy systems, so there is a strong emphasis of federation. Each part of the standard addresses one of the ODP viewpoints.

Turning to other architectural standards, the reference model for ODP is called out in IEEE 1471 (and in its successor, ISO 42010) as a prime example of a framework complying with the viewpoint-based architectural descriptions it prescribes. In fact, the RM-ODP and these two standards for architectural description have had a significant influence on each other, and the groups concerned have maintained strong, active liaison to achieve consistency between them.

The use of the RM-ODP continues in new work; a notable piece of work in progress within ISO is concerned with the standardization of a metamodel framework for interoperability, which is underway in *ISO/IEC JTC1 SC32*. This work is basing its description of services on the ODP metamodels, and is likely to be exploited in further work on service equivalence in service-oriented and cloud computing.

These are just a few of the ways the RM-ODP continues to influence and support a broad range of standardization activities.

16.4 Tools

There are several UML tools that offer UML4ODP capabilities. For instance, No Magic's MagicDraw is a popular commercial UML tool, which we used to develop the UML4ODP standard and which has also been used to draw the various UML diagrams in this book. The Spanish team involved in RM-ODP standardization developed a plug-in for this product, information about which can be found at `http://www.magicdraw.com/uml4odp_plugin`. The plug-in adds a custom menu item called *RM-ODP*, which provides access to the basic ODP diagram templates and to some model checking tools. It presents a custom ODP palette for each of the ODP diagram types, allowing easy drag-and-drop diagram creation. The plug-in is easily installed with the UML tool's resource and plug-in manager, which is accessed from the tool's help menu.

Sparx System's Enterprise Architect is another UML tool with which you can add ODP functionality. After installing the ODP capability, users can draw UML4ODP-based diagrams. Further information can be found at `http://www.sparxsystems.com.au/products/3rdparty/odp/index.html`. There are many more UML tools, such as PatternWeaver, with which readers can work on ODP modelling. However, readers are advised to consult with their tool vendors to see what plug-ins are available.

Many of the groups producing standards or other specifications maintain lists of known products using them, and these lists are a fruitful source of information about potential tool vendors and relevant groups in the open source community. Tool vendors usually implement standards enhanced with their own capabilities, look and feel and other special features to appeal to their customers.

The open source community is a place where interested people get together to implement something of common interest to them. In the case of UML and the UML profile, OMG's UML page (`http://www.uml.org/`) and MDA page (`http://www.omg.org/mda/`) are good starting places to find such tool vendors. As a good example of an open source community, you can look at the Eclipse foundation (`http://www.eclipse.org/`). Within the Eclipse community, there is specific support for the creation of modelling tools in the form of the Eclipse Modelling Framework [55]. There are various implementations in the Eclipse modelling projects (`http://www.eclipse.org/modeling/`), including a UML 2 tooling project. You can also find implementations of different modelling styles.

16.5   Comparing Enterprise Architectures

A number of proposals for architectural frameworks have been made in recent years; they all target the design and evolution of enterprise systems. However, they are not easy to compare because they differ in their individual scope and emphasis. This implies that each has its own areas of strength and weakness.

We can divide the proposals into two groups. First, we have those frameworks that aim to classify all the different artefacts, processes and people involved in the specification of the enterprise system and its contents. The earliest example of this style is the Zachman framework [94]. This was produced in the late 1980s and introduced the idea of an architectural framework, which soon became popular.

The Zachman framework provides systematic guidance for organizing the contents of an enterprise architecture and is often used to represent a portfolio of the existing architecture artefacts within an organization. It has evolved through several different revisions, which all use a two-dimensional matrix to offer a taxonomy of architectural elements and processes; depending on the version, this requires choices to be made between as many as 36 matrix cells. However, it focuses on the categorization of the enterprise architecture elements and does not cover other important aspects, such as conformance testing and quality assurance, enterprise planning and federation.

The other group of frameworks focuses more on the processes and methodologies used to build the enterprise architecture. The most prominent example here is The Open Group Architectural Framework (TOGAF) [98]. It divides an enterprise information architecture by using four categories (the business, application, data and technical architectures). However in TOGAF, the emphasis is placed on the ADM (architecture development method), which is the process and methodology that creates the architecture. This methodology-based view of an enterprise architecture is one of the major strengths of TOGAF, which can be seen as complementary to more organizational-based approaches such as the Zachman framework.

TOGAF first made use of a formalized architecture description language in its latest version, TOGAF9, which also adds a certain level of formalism for the relationships between various concepts, including links between IT and business concerns.

There are also more specialized frameworks that concentrate on particular domains, such as defence or government. The Department of Defense Architecture Framework (DoDAF) [66] and the Ministry of Defence Architecture Framework (MoDAF) [85] are examples developed by the US and UK governments, respectively. The Federal Enterprise Architecture Framework (FEAF) [70] is an attempt by the US federal government to integrate all the architectural activities in its multiple agencies under a single common framework.

Unlike Zachman or TOGAF, this group of frameworks has a strong emphasis on high-level management because of the particular requirements and concerns of the organizations being served. This results in reduced coverage of the more technical aspects. In addition, the frameworks reflect the organizational thinking of the domain in which they were developed, making them difficult to reuse in a broader industrial context.

A common problem with all these frameworks comes from their complexity. Although initially relatively compact, they have evolved over the years to accommodate too many aspects and functions, making them hard to manage or to use in an effective way. In general, specifying an enterprise system requires the balancing of many aspects that could be considered, and also of the interests of a variety of different stakeholders. It is important that any framework should allow each stakeholder to express their requirements and solutions in a way that is familiar to them, by using their normal tools and techniques. This means that the framework must allow the integration of the specifications expressed in different ways. At the same time, it provides mechanisms for maintaining and ensuring the consistency of potentially conflicting requirements or different views of the system. Thus, a key requirement for an effective framework is that its components should be cohesive, with clearly expressed correspondences between the elements seen by the different stakeholders. In this respect, many of the proposed frameworks identify their component specifications without ever stating clearly how these should interrelate.

The authors of the RM-ODP took great care to select a small set of viewpoints that deals with the stakeholders commonly found when creating and managing large distributed systems. They avoided the temptation to add complexity by defining further viewpoints covering other less general concerns. They also excluded unnecessary constraints on the way viewpoint specifications were to be structured.

The origins of the reference model as a framework for standardization helped its developers draw on expertise from the different stakeholder areas to ensure that each of the different viewpoint languages used the concepts familiar to the teams producing that kind of standard. However, the writers left flexibility within the viewpoint languages for users to select any appropriate notation and methodology, without imposing unnecessary taxonomic constraints (such as mandatory use of a single set of dimensions) across all the viewpoints.

The reference model is unique in having a well-developed and coherent explanation of viewpoint correspondences, ensuring a consistent set of specifications and laying the foundation for an integrated tool chain. It also provides a clear framework for the expression and assessment of compliance and conformance, which is critical in a world where enterprise systems and applications are not developed and maintained by isolated teams, but composed of multiple models, applications and systems sourced from other companies.

Each of the viewpoint languages contains a precise set of modelling concepts developed based on sound theoretical and engineering foundations, drawn from both the organizational and distributed systems fields. It is the combination of such organizational and technical concepts, and the correspondence between these, that makes the ODP framework an excellent choice to support the expression of various interoperability requirements from separate perspectives, and at different levels of abstraction.

Supporting concepts and mechanisms such as transparencies, federation and contracts also becomes essential for achieving smooth interoperability between enterprise systems. This is particularly important where it involves the crossing of boundaries between organizations or jurisdictions, needing the exchange of information, provision of services and linking of processes in order to do business with other enterprises.

Finally, the fact that the RM-ODP is an international standard ensures vendor independence and long-lived specifications. These aspects are especially important for protecting the investment required for the adoption of any enterprise framework. When augmented with strong links to the widely used UML notation and tools based on it, they are precisely the strengths offered by a mature framework such as the RM-ODP. In addition, the reference model itself can be exploited and tailored for new standardization developments, such as the establishment of architecture frameworks and foundations for new domains; this can be seen from its use in the telecommunications, government and health sectors.

16.6 Coda

Since the RM-ODP was first published, many people have experimented with the approach, and there are now many competing frameworks aiming to satisfy the requirements of different communities and industrial sectors. Indeed, there are now enough of them for interoperability between frameworks to become an issue, so that, more than ever, users need to understand the underlying concepts.

We hope that this description of the ODP architecture and the way it can be used will help readers to understand the benefits of using such a framework, and the importance of maintaining a clear awareness of the need to serve the various stakeholders in the design process. The growing power of the tools we use is opening the way to a much more clearly articulated separation of concerns while, at the same time, ensuring coherence and consistency.

The use of a robust and consistent framework is essential when positioning new technologies and planning their deployment to serve existing enterprises. The ODP reference model can be used to analyse the implications of new ideas, such as cloud computing, social computing and mobile computing. It can help to distinguish what is genuinely new from what is simply differently packaged, and help the understanding of new claims, as it has done for service orientation, leading to a clearer comprehension of the significance of new initiatives.

This is the way forward to the generation of flexible and evolving information infrastructures that stand the test of time and do what their users really need.

Appendices

About the Appendices

These two appendices contain some supplementary material that complements the information provided in the main text of the book.

The first offers a global view of the PhoneMob system specification, focusing on its overall structure. Space limitations do not permit us to show the complete set of models that make up the full system specification, but these are available from the authors' website at `http://theodpbook.lcc.uma.es/`.

The second appendix presents some questions and scenarios that can be used to support teachers and trainers in introducing the concepts and design principles of ODP and for encouraging students to develop their own designs and specifications.

Appendix A

The PhoneMob Specifications

This appendix summarizes the specifications that make up the PhoneMob example, focusing on their structure and organization. While the main text of the book is primarily focused on the individual elements of the ODP specifications, this appendix gives the reader a more global view of its organization.

Overall structure. Figure A.1 shows the overall structure of the PhoneMob specifications, expressed in the UML4ODP notation. It provides a complete view of the UML model shown earlier in figure 1.4, but this time with all of its constituent packages. There are five for the individual viewpoints, and six for the correspondences between them (since, in this case, not all correspondences are required).

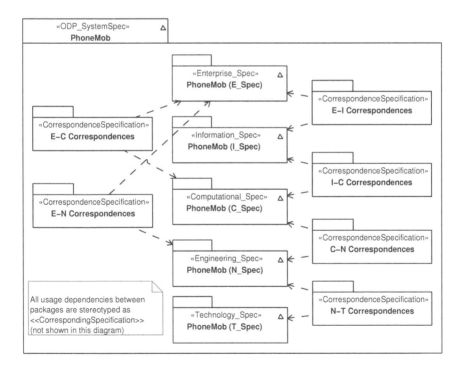

FIGURE A.1: The overall structure of the PhoneMob system specification.

A.1   Enterprise Viewpoint Specifications

The enterprise language defines four key concepts: *enterprise specification*, *system*, *scope* and *field of application*.

In our example, the *system* to be specified is a computerized system that supports the operations of the PhoneMob company. The *scope* of this system describes its expected behaviour, stating the way it is supposed to work and interact with its environment in the business context. The scope of the system is modelled in terms of the set of roles it fulfils (see section A.1.2).

The *enterprise specification* of the PhoneMob system is expressed by one model, stereotyped «Enterprise_Spec», which contains the contracts of all the communities that make up the specification, as shown in figure A.2. This also shows the *field of application* of the specification, which describes the properties that the environment of the ODP system must have for the specification to be used. It is expressed by means of a tagged value of the «Enterprise_Spec» model, giving the enterprise specification of the system.

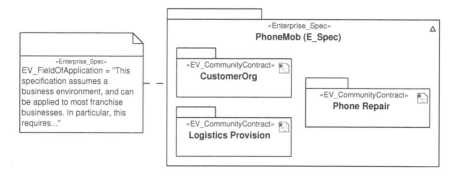

FIGURE A.2: The structure of the PhoneMob enterprise specification.

A.1.1   Communities and Their Contracts

Figure A.2 shows that the enterprise specification of the PhoneMob system is composed of the specifications of three communities: Phone Repair (shown in figure A.3), CustomerOrg (shown in figure A.4) and Logistics Provision (shown in figure A.5).

In general, all community contracts have the same structure: one *objective* (which in a real contract would be more specific and detailed) and four main packages with the specification of the community *roles*, *object types*, *processes* and *policies*.

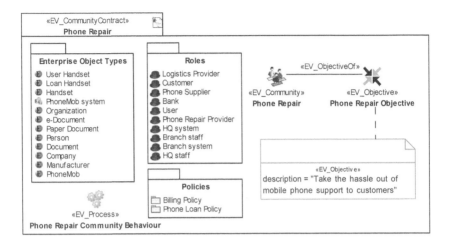

FIGURE A.3: Community contract for the Phone Repair community.

A.1.2 Community Roles and Object Types

The roles of the communities have already been described in detail in the chapter 2. For example, figure 2.2 showed the roles of the Phone Repair community, which are summarized here within figure A.3. The roles for the other communities are named in the Roles package included in the community contracts (shown in figures A.4 and A.5).

Enterprise object types are described in their corresponding packages. For example, figure A.6 shows the object types defined in the Phone Repair community. Assignment policies constraining which enterprise objects can fill which roles in the communities were shown in figures 2.5 and 2.6.

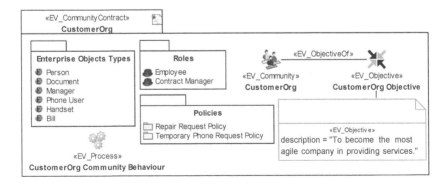

FIGURE A.4: Community contract for the CustomerOrg community.

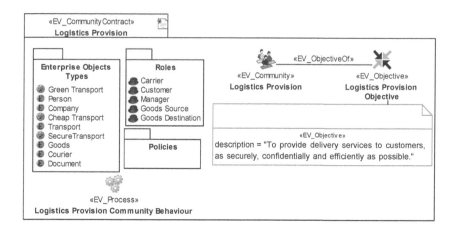

FIGURE A.5: Community contract for the Logistics Provision community.

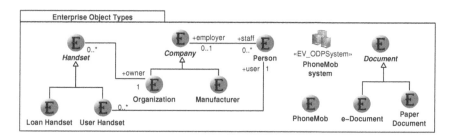

FIGURE A.6: The enterprise objects in the Phone Repair community.

A.1.3 Behaviour

Behaviour can be modelled in the enterprise language in terms of processes or, in a more fine-grained way, in terms of interactions. Processes are expressed in UML4ODP as UML activities. Some of the processes for the Phone Repair community were shown in figure 2.7, and one of them (Repair Process) was further elaborated in figure 2.8, which showed the activity diagram that expresses the steps of the process, and identified the roles involved in each of these steps.

More detailed modelling of behaviour in terms of interactions between roles in a community is appropriate when the modelling focus is placed primarily on the roles and artefacts involved in the behaviour, and on the relationships between them. Figure A.7 shows such an interaction in the CustomerOrg community, in which the Employee and the Contract Manager agree to a repair request.

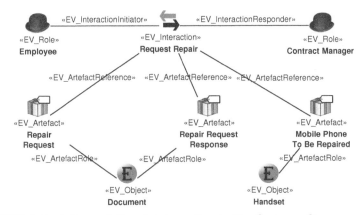

FIGURE A.7: A Request Repair interaction in the CustomerOrg community.

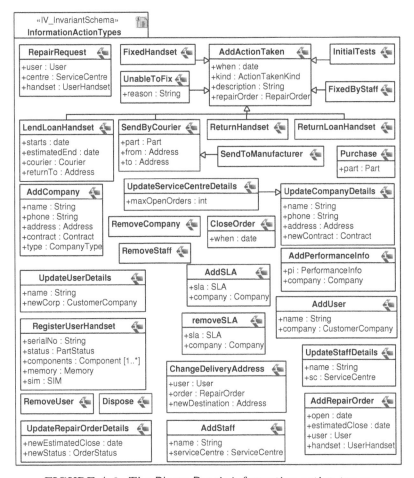

FIGURE A.8: The Phone Repair information action types.

A.2   Information Viewpoint Specifications

The overall structure and contents of the information viewpoint specification of the system was shown in figure 3.5. This comprised a package with the information object types (figure 3.1) and their associated attributes, associations and state machines (figure 3.3); other packages gave a selection of the information action types (figure 3.2), and the specification of one of the static schemata relevant to the system (figure 3.4).

Figure A.8 shows the complete set of information action types used in the specification.

Another example of a static schema is shown in figure A.9. In contrast to figure 3.4, which gave a snapshot of a particular repair order, we show here the initial state of the system, when it has, for simplicity, been defined to have just one service centre, one staff member and only two loan handsets.

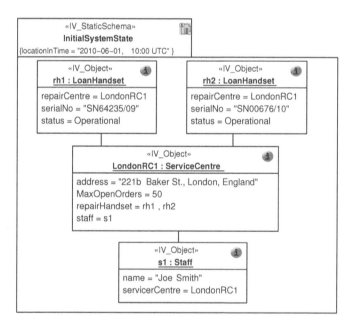

FIGURE A.9: A static schema stating the initial state of the system.

Finally, chapter 3 also showed a UML state machine that represented the dynamic schema of one of the objects. A different style of dynamic schema is shown in figure A.10, which represents the state machine of the RepairOrder information object. The possible triggers for the transitions are information actions, whose types are defined in figure A.8.

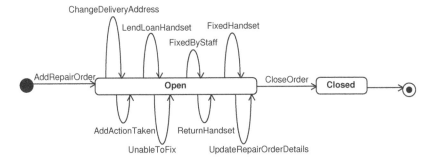

FIGURE A.10: A dynamic schema for the RepairOrder information object.

A.3 Computational Viewpoint Specifications

The overall structure of the computational viewpoint specification of the PhoneMob system is shown in figure A.11. It contains three high-level packages. One describes the software architecture of the application. The second deals with the behavioural aspects of the system. The last one contains the basic data types used in the specification (which were shown in figure 4.8). In addition, the model for the complete computational specification has some associated tag values that determine which transparencies are required for the system. In this case, the transaction and replication transparencies are needed (see the engineering specification in section A.4) together with the ac-

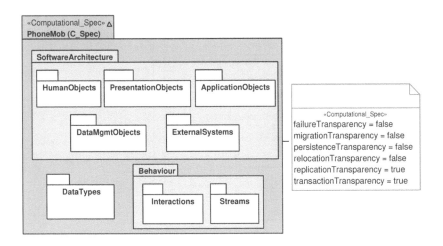

FIGURE A.11: The overall structure of the computational specification.

cess and location transparencies, which are mandatory for any computational specification — and thus there is no need to specify them explicitly.

The internal packages of the computational specification were described in chapter 4; figure 4.5 showed the structure of the SoftwareArchitecture package, which was organized in four layers, and was later refined in figure 4.7. The signatures of the services provided and required by each computational interface were shown in figure 4.6. Finally, some examples of behavioural specifications of the system were shown, using sequences of interactions (figure 4.9) and flows (figure 4.10).

The rest of the computational specification of the PhoneMob system follows a very similar pattern, and hence is not included here.

A.4   Engineering Viewpoint Specifications

The ODP engineering specifications of a system describe how the engineering objects (that correspond to the computational objects that implement the

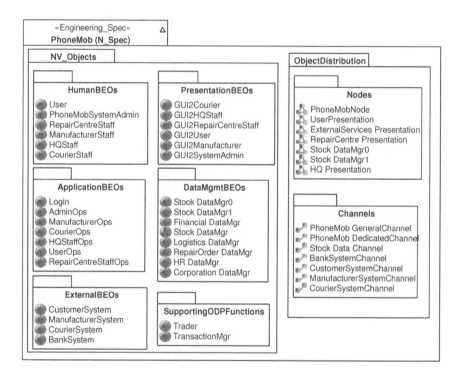

FIGURE A.12: The overall structure of the engineering specification.

functionality of the system) are distributed to processing nodes and how they interact through channels. Both the internal structural organization of nodes (into capsules and clusters) and channels (into stubs, binders, protocol objects and interceptors) are expressed in this viewpoint.

The overall organization of the engineering specification of the PhoneMob system is shown in figure A.12. This contains two main packages, one with the basic engineering object types and the other with the distribution structure.

Package NV_Objects describes the basic engineering objects. They correspond to the computational objects described in the computational specification. The same grouping structure is used again here, although just for packaging purposes, since it does not imply any constraints on the distribution. One package contains the ODP objects that implement either common functions (such as the Trader) or services that provide the required transparencies

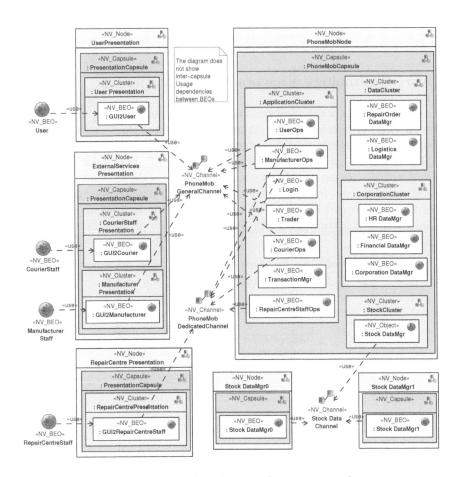

FIGURE A.13: The distribution of engineering objects.

(such as the TransactionMgr; remember that the computational specification stated that transaction transparency was required).

The distribution of the engineering objects is described by the elements of the ObjectDistribution package, which defines seven nodes and seven channels. Some of these elements are represented in figure A.13, which provides an overview of the distribution of the main system processing elements. Nodes contain capsules and clusters that represent groupings of elements for protection and migration management purposes, according to the policies and strategies defined for the system.

Finally, the engineering specification also provides the elements needed to represent the internal elements of channels, as was discussed in chapter 5, where figure 5.3 showed the architecture of one of the channels of the application. The rest of the channels follow a similar pattern.

A.5 Technology Viewpoint Specifications

The technology specifications focus on four main issues: (1) identifying the main types of technology objects used to implement the system; (2) describing the requirements on these objects in terms of implementable standards; (3) stating the extra information for testing (IXIT) that needs to be associated with the technology objects; and (4) describing the relevant processes and activities involved in the provision, deployment, maintenance and evolution of the systems and its parts. In our example, the technology specifications are structured accordingly, with packages for each of these descriptions (see figure A.14).

The contents of these packages have already been described in chapter 6, in figures 6.1, 6.2, 6.3 and 6.4, respectively.

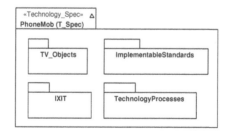

FIGURE A.14: The overall structure of the technology specification.

A.6   Correspondences

We need to specify not only the viewpoints, but also how the elements in the individual viewpoints relate to each other. The PhoneMob system specification defines six pairwise correspondences between the viewpoints (see figure A.1). There is not room here to describe the detailed contents of all these packages; instead, we will focus on how correspondences are identified and expressed.

Chapter 7 explained that the UML4ODP standard provides checklists for identifying the correspondences that should be specified for a system. Some of them are mandatory for any ODP system specification, such as the ones that link the computational and engineering objects. Others depend on the system being specified. Examples of these optional correspondences are the ones that link enterprise and computational objects, or enterprise interactions with computational interfaces. Not every enterprise object or interaction has a corresponding element in the computational viewpoint. The Paper Document enterprise object type, for example, has no corresponding computational element.

In general, we can identify two kinds of correspondences between viewpoint elements, according to the type of relationship between them. In the first place, we have the correspondences between viewpoint elements that represent the same entity, such as a handset, from different perspectives.

Figure A.15 shows the representation of Handset objects in the enterprise, information and computational viewpoints, each one focusing on different aspects, giving rise to slight variations. It also shows the correspondences between them. Note that a handset is an object in the enterprise and information viewpoints, and a data type in the computational viewpoint. As a result, there is no representation for it in the engineering and technology viewpoints.

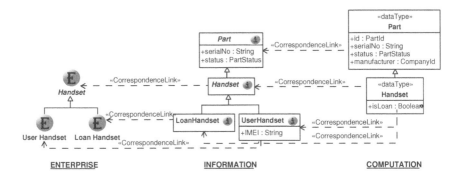

FIGURE A.15: Correspondences between different views of the same entity.

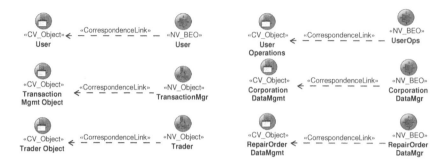

FIGURE A.16: Correspondences from computational to engineering objects.

Another example of this kind of correspondence is the set of relationships between engineering and computational objects. This is shown in figure A.16. Note that object names do not always coincide.

The second kind of correspondence happens when the related objects do not represent the same entity but there is still a relationship between them. A typical example is an enterprise policy that affects several information or computational elements. In this case, the purpose is twofold. Firstly, the correspondences specify how the policy constrains the related elements and, secondly, the correspondences provide the traceability mechanisms required to identify the elements that are affected by the policy and, conversely, the policies that affect an individual viewpoint element.

This kind of correspondence is also used to specify the choice of technology required to implement and deploy the engineering nodes and channels. This is illustrated in figures A.17 and A.18, where the correspondences represent

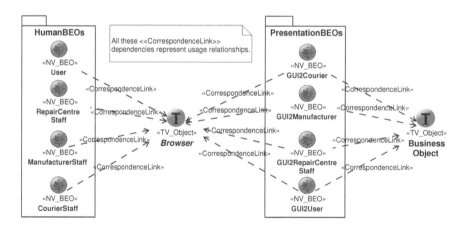

FIGURE A.17: Correspondences from engineering to technology objects.

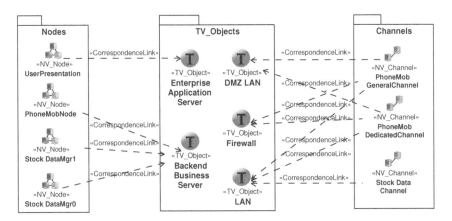

FIGURE A.18: Nodes and channels correspond to technology objects.

usage relationships between the related elements. In a real application, there would be many more styles of access than those shown here, such as access using SMS interactions, or access from programs running in smart phones.

Note that the correspondences shown in this appendix have been drawn using the shortcut notation mentioned in chapter 7, which uses stereotyped dependencies instead of the correspondence classes from the UML4ODP standard. A tool would be responsible for generating these classes from the shorthand form and vice versa, which considerably simplifies the modeller's job.

Appendix B

Selected Exercises

This appendix contains a set of exercises to allow the readers to check that they are able to use the concepts, mechanisms and notations from the book to develop their own designs and specifications. For this we suggest two kinds of activity. First, we consider various situations where the RM-ODP concepts and mechanisms can be used for structuring the specifications of open distributed systems. After this, there is a small set of additional questions to check the understanding of some specific ODP concepts.

B.1 Selected Scenarios

Imagine that you are part of a design team that is faced with the following scenarios. You should consider what form the viewpoint specifications might take and make suitable proposals for an outline design. You should also examine the requirements and determine which viewpoints each of the statements in a scenario have impact on.

The RM-ODP does not prescribe any particular method for building the individual viewpoint specifications of a system. However, we suggest you follow the indications given at the end of the chapters that dealt with the individual viewpoints (chapters 2 to 6), which provided some guidelines on how to proceed.

B.1.1 Twitter

Suppose that you have done a great job at PhoneMob, and other companies are after you to develop enterprise architecture descriptions for their businesses. In particular, Twitter^{TM} requires documentation of its systems before embarking on a major IT reorganization.

For this reason, you are asked to write the ODP *enterprise* and *information* viewpoint specifications of Twitter.

B.1.2   A Web-Based Supermarket

A supermarket wants to start a subsidiary that offers web-based order entry and delivery services to its customers. The way in which the system for such a subsidiary should operate is as follows. The orders are picked from stock in the existing stores, but the subsequent deliveries are carried out by local subcontractors; these are engaged as necessary to meet demand. The orders are transferred from the order entry website to mobile devices in the stores, where staff assemble the order ready for delivery. Confirmation of the order list is printed with the delivery instructions and passed to the delivery drivers. Scheduling information about forthcoming deliveries is provided to the delivery company while the orders are being assembled.

You are asked to develop the ODP *enterprise, information* and *computational* specifications for the system that will support this business.

B.1.3   Skype

Imagine that Skype™ plans to improve its teleconferencing services by allowing large groups to divide and recombine during a session.

To support this, you are asked to write the ODP *information, computational* and *engineering* viewpoint specifications of Skype as it is now, and how the specifications should be changed.

B.1.4   A Loyalty-Points System

A third-party company offers loyalty bonuses for a variety of existing services. The aim of the scheme is to make the services of organizations that participate more attractive. The loyalty-points company offers a package of support to primary service providers, including software components that the primary providers can incorporate into their designs. There is a requirement for uniform rules for bonus collection to be applied in all affiliated services, based on the distribution of common code. However, it must be easy to integrate the support for bonus points into existing provider applications.

Write the *enterprise* specifications of the system, with particular emphasis on its interactions with the communities that represent the rest of the affiliated companies. Once the enterprise specification is written, you are asked to develop the *information* and *computational* specifications, focusing on how the system will interact with the IT systems of the affiliated companies.

B.1.5   Adding Share Trading to Automatic Teller Services

The provider of an existing instant share dealing service, currently operating via a web interface, is undertaking a joint venture with a building society that runs a network of ATM cash dispensers. In this scheme, shares can be bought and sold by interacting with additional menus in the existing cash dispensers. A strategy is needed that causes as little disruption to the established three-tier architectures of the two organizations as possible.

You are asked first to provide a simple ODP specification of the two systems, and then to identify the minimum set of changes that will be required to implement the modifications in both systems.

B.1.6 Google Search Engine

Imagine that you are hired by Google™ as Chief Architect for one of its core products, the Google Search Engine, and that they want you to provide an architectural description of that application, with the goals of:

- Relying on high-level models to understand this application, in a platform- and technology-independent manner.

- Having a conceptual model of the data the application manages.

- Defining the software architecture of the application, for guiding subsequent developments and changes.

- Specifying the deployment architecture and communications infrastructure, expressed in terms of distributed servers, processes and channels, to be able to have a global picture of the system workload, to perform load-balancing improvements or to conduct end-to-end performance analysis of the system.

- Describing the technology adoption, acquisition, provisioning and maintenance procedures for the hardware, software and communications infrastructure that should support the application.

Write the ODP specification of the Google Search Engine, including all five viewpoints and the correspondences between them.

B.2 Some Additional Questions

Answer these questions based on the concepts presented in this book.

1. A designer says, "Now that we have decided to allow persistent data to be stored on mobile devices in our system, the enterprise policy on required availability levels means we will need to add engineering mechanisms supporting replication transparency for all the computational objects, not just those that are currently tagged as having critical requirements in the computational design." Explain, to someone ignorant of the ODP architecture, what the designer is saying, and what the concepts they have used mean.

2. A legacy system consists of a database and a set of data entry, update and query applications. It is necessary to upgrade it without interrupting operation, moving to a new system with an object-based design and a richer set of applications. The applications require transactional operation. Outline the steps that might be taken to perform this transition in a phased way.

3. Two organizations need to interoperate but have commitments to different kinds of middleware and different data formats. Indicate an approach that they might take to establish interoperability, stating what agreements would need to be established initially and how support for necessary protocol and format transformations might be provided. Illustrate how this process might be assisted if each of the partners used import and export naming domains and they established suitable interceptors to provide the translation of structured documents.

4. Avoiding unnecessary detail, but stating clearly the objects, interfaces, operations and actions involved, outline how a design might use the idea of a suitable binding to describe each of the following cases. Your answer should cover both the initialization and the use of the configuration.

  (a) A computational design in which errors in a client-server interaction are signalled to a separate management object.

  (b) A computational design in which a video multicast from a camera to a number of displays is configured dynamically to vary the number of displays and the quality of service provided.

  (c) A computational and an engineering design in which a video binding is created between a source and a sink in domains using different frame rates for representing video.

5. What is a conformance point? Explain the main roles and activities in the ODP conformance model, and describe how they can be used in the following example.

A new computer games console is designed to have open interfaces and to accept games produced by a wide variety of vendors. The console can be connected to the Internet, or can load games from standard prerecorded cartridges. Internally, its system provides a rich set of high-level graphics methods that the game modules can use.

Discuss, with the aid of a functional block diagram of the system, the different classes of conformance point that are likely to be involved in the testing of the console and of the games that vendors supply to run on it.

Bibliography

[1] *ISO IS 8807, Information Processing Systems — Open Systems Interconnection. LOTOS: A Formal Description Technique Based on the Temporal Ordering of Observational Behavior*, 1989.

[2] *ISO/IEC IS 10746-1, Information Technology — Open Distributed Processing — Reference Model: Overview*, 1998. Also published as ITU-T Recommendation X.901.

[3] *ISO/IEC IS 10746-2, Information Technology — Open Distributed Processing — Reference Model: Foundations*, 2009. Also published as ITU-T Recommendation X.902.

[4] *ISO/IEC IS 10746-3, Information Technology — Open Distributed Processing — Reference Model: Architecture*, 2009. Also published as ITU-T Recommendation X.903.

[5] *ISO/IEC IS 10746-4, Information Technology — Open Distributed Processing — Reference Model: Architectural Semantics*, 1998. Also published as ITU-T Recommendation X.904.

[6] *ISO IS 12967-1, Health Informatics — Service Architecture — Part 1: Enterprise Viewpoint*, 2009.

[7] *ISO IS 12967-2, Health Informatics — Service Architecture — Part 2: Information Viewpoint*, 2009.

[8] *ISO IS 12967-3, Health Informatics — Service Architecture — Part 3: Computational Viewpoint*, 2009.

[9] *ISO/IEC IS 13235-1, Information Technology — Open Distributed Processing — Trading Function: Specification*, 1998. Also published as ITU-T Recommendation X.950.

[10] *ISO/IEC IS 13235-3, Information Technology — Open Distributed Processing — Trading Function: Provision of Trading Function using OSI Directory Service*, 1998. Also published as ITU-T Recommendation X.952.

[11] *ISO IS 13537, Space Data and Information Transfer Systems — Reference Architecture for Space Data Systems*, September 2010.

[12] *ISO/IEC IS 14750, Information Technology — Open Distributed Processing — Interface Definition Language,* 1999. Also published as ITU-T Recommendation X.920.

[13] *ISO/IEC IS 14752, Information Technology — Open Distributed Processing — Protocol Support for Computational Interactions,* 2000. Also published as ITU-T Recommendation X.931.

[14] *ISO/IEC IS 14753, Information Technology — Open Distributed Processing — Interface References and Binding,* 1999. Also published as ITU-T Recommendation X.930.

[15] *ISO/IEC IS 14769, Information Technology — Open Distributed Processing — Type Repository Function,* 2000. Also published as ITU-T Recommendation X.960.

[16] *ISO/IEC IS 14771, Information Technology — Open Distributed Processing — Naming Framework,* 1999. Also published as ITU-T Recommendation X.910.

[17] *ISO/IEC IS 15414, Information Technology — Open Distributed Processing — Enterprise Language,* 2006. Also published as ITU-T Recommendation X.911.

[18] *ISO/IEC IS 15437, Information Technology — Enhancements to LOTOS (E-LOTOS),* 2001.

[19] *ISO/IEC IS 17000, Conformity Assessment — Vocabulary and General Principles,* 2004.

[20] *ISO/TS 17573, Road Transport and Traffic Telematics — Electronic Fee Collection — Systems Architecture for Vehicle-related Tolling,* 2003.

[21] *ISO 19119, Geographic Information — Services,* 2005.

[22] *ISO/IEC IS 19793, Information Technology — Open Distributed Processing — Use of UML for ODP System Specifications,* 2008. Also published as ITU-T Recommendation X.906.

[23] *ISO/IEC IS 19793 Cor 1:2010, Corrigendum 1 — Information Technology — Open Distributed Processing — Use of UML for ODP System Specifications,* 2010.

[24] *ISO/IEC/IEEE FDIS 42010, Systems and Software Engineering — Architectural Description,* 2010.

[25] *ITU-T Recommendation G.851, Management of the Transport Network — Application of the RM-ODP Framework.* ITU-T, November 1996.

[26] *ITU-T Recommendation Z.130, ITU Object Definition Language.* ITU-T, 1999.

[27] *OMG Trading Object Service, Version 1.0.* Object Management Group, June 2000. Document formal/2000-06-27.

[28] *OMG Meta-Object Facility (MOF). Version 2.0.* Object Management Group, January 2006. Document formal/2006-01-01.

[29] *OMG CORBA Component Model Specification (CCM). Version 4.0.* Object Management Group, April 2006. Document formal/2006-04-01.

[30] *OMG Unified Modeling Language 2.1.1 Superstructure Specification.* Object Management Group, February 2007. Document formal/2007-02-05.

[31] *OMG Common Object Request Broker Architecture (CORBA): Core Specification. Version 3.1.* Object Management Group, January 2008. Document formal/2008-01-04.

[32] *OMG MOF Model To Text Transformation Language (MOFM2T). Version 1.0.* Object Management Group, January 2008. Document formal/08-01-16.

[33] *OMG Semantics of Business Vocabulary and Business Rules (SBVR), Version 1.0.* Object Management Group, January 2008. Document formal/08-01-02.

[34] *OMG CORBA To WSDL/SOAP Interworking (C2WSDL). Version 1.2.1.* Object Management Group, August 2008. Document formal/2008-08-03.

[35] *OMG UML Profile for MARTE: Modeling and Analysis of Real-time Embedded Systems, Version 1.0.* Object Management Group, November 2009. Document formal/2009-11-02.

[36] *OMG Object Constraint Language (OCL) Specification. Version 2.2.* Object Management Group, February 2010. Document formal/2010-02-01.

[37] *OMG Business Motivation Model Version 1.1.* Object Management Group, May 2010. Document formal/2010-05-01.

[38] *The Architecture of Choice for a Changing World.* Object Management Group, 2010. http://www.omg.org/mda/products_success.htm.

[39] *OMG Additional Structuring Mechanisms for the OTS. Version 1.0.* Object Management Group, January 2011. Document formal/2011-01-05.

[40] *OMG Business Process Model and Notation (BPMN) Version 2.0.* Object Management Group, March 2011. Document formal/2011-01-03.

[41] *OMG Meta Object Facility (MOF) 2.0 Query/View/Transformation (QVT). Version 1.1.* Object Management Group, January 2011. Document formal/2011-01-01.

[42] *Business Transaction Protocol. Committee Draft Version 1.1.* OASIS, November 2004.

[43] *Web Service Coordination Framework (WS-CF). Committee Draft Version 0.2.* OASIS, December 2004.

[44] *eXtensible Access Control Markup Language (XACML) Version 2.0.* OASIS, February 2005.

[45] *Web Services Federation Language (WS-Federation). Version 1.2.* OASIS, May 2009.

[46] *Reference Architecture Foundation for Service Oriented Architecture. Version 1.0, Committee Draft 02.* OASIS, October 2009.

[47] *WS-Trust. Version 1.4.* OASIS, February 2009.

[48] John Langshaw Austin. *How to Do Things With Words.* Harvard University Press, 1962. Second edition, 1975.

[49] L. Bass, P. Clements, and R. Kazman. *Software Architecture in Practice.* Addison-Wesley, 1997.

[50] Gérard Berry and Georges Gonthier. The Esterel synchronous programming language: Design, semantics, implementation. *Sci. Computer Programming*, 9(2):87–152, 1992.

[51] Stefano Bistarelli and Francesco Santini. C-semiring frameworks for minimum spanning tree problems. In *Recent Trends in Algebraic Development Techniques (WADT 2008)*, volume 5486 of *LNCS*, pages 56–70. Springer, June 2008.

[52] Gordon S. Blair and Jean-Bernard Stefani. *Open Distributed Processing and Multimedia.* Addison-Wesley, 1998.

[53] Xavier Blanc, Marie-Pierre Gervais, and Prawee Sriplakich. Model Bus: Towards the Interoperability of Modeling Tools. In *Proceedings of the European Model Driven Architecture Workshop: Foundations and Applications (MDA-FA 2004)*, volume 3599 of *LNCS*, pages 17–32. Springer, 2005.

[54] M.L. Brodie and M. Stonebraker. *Migrating Legacy Systems: Gateways, Interfaces and the Incremental Approach.* Morgan Kaufmann, 1995.

[55] Frank Budinsky, David Steinberg, Ed Merks, Raymond Ellersick, and Timothy J. Grose. *Eclipse Modeling Framework.* Addison-Wesley, 2008.

[56] Stefano Ceri, Piero Fraternali, Aldo Bongio, Marco Brambilla, Sara Comai, and Maristella Matera. *Designing Data-Intensive Web Applications.* Morgan Kaufmann, December 2002. http://www.webml.org.

[57] J. Chomicki, J. Lobo, and S. Naqvi. Conflict Resolution Using Logic Programming. *IEEE TKDE*, 15(1):244–149, January 2003.

[58] Noam Chomsky. *Topics in the Theory of Generative Grammar*. Mouton, The Hague, 1966.

[59] CISCO. Directory-Enabled Networking. In *Internetworking Technologies Handbook*. Cisco Press, 2009. Content also available as http://docwiki.cisco.com/wiki/Internetworking_Technology_Handbook.

[60] Edmund Clarke, Natasha Sharygina, and Nishant Sinha. Program Compatibility Approaches. In *Proceedings of the 4th International Symposium on Formal Methods for Components and Objects*, volume 4111 of *LNCS*, pages 243–258. Springer, 2006.

[61] Manuel Clavel, Francisco Durán, Steven Eker, Patrick Lincoln, Narciso Martí-Oliet, José Meseguer, and Carolyn Talcott. *All About Maude — A High-Performance Logical Framework*, volume 4350 of *LNCS*. Springer, 2007.

[62] Consultative Committee for Space Data Systems. *Recommendation for Space Data System Practices — Reference Architecture for Space Data Systems*, September 2008. CCSDS 311.0-M-1.

[63] Vittorio Cortellessa, Antinisca Di Marco, and Paola Inverardi. Non-Functional Modeling and Validation in Model-Driven Architecture. In *Proceedings of the 6th Working IEEE/IFIP Conference on Software Architecture (WICSA 2007)*, pages 25–28. IEEE Computer Society, 2007.

[64] Nicodemos Damianou, Naranker Dulay, Emil Lupu, and Morris Sloman. *Ponder: A Language for Specifying Security and Management Policies for Distributed Systems. The Language Specification — Version 2.3*. Imperial College, October 2000. Research Report DoC 2000/1.

[65] Jim D'Anjou, Scott Fairbrother, Dan Kehn, John Kellerman, and Pat McCarthy. *The Java Developer's Guide to Eclipse*. Addison-Wesley, 2005.

[66] *The Department of Defense Architecture Framework*, 2009. http://cio-nii.defense.gov/sites/dodaf20/.

[67] Roger Duke, Gordon Rose, and Graeme Smith. Object-Z: A Specification Language Advocated for the Description of Standards. *Computer Standards & Interfaces*, 17:511–533, September 1995.

[68] Hector A. Duran-Limon and Gordon S. Blair. QoS Management specification support for multimedia middleware. *J. System Software*, 72(1):1–23, June 2004.

[69] Huascar Espinoza, Daniela Cancila, Bran Selic, and Sébastien Gérard. Challenges in combining SysML and MARTE for model-based design of embedded systems. In *Proceedings of the European Model Driven Architecture Workshop: Foundations and Applications (MDA-FA 2009)*, volume 5562 of *LNCS*, pages 98–113. Springer, 2009.

[70] *Federal Enterprise Architecture (FEA)*, 2005. http://www. whitehouse.gov/omb/e-gov/fea/.

[71] D. Garlan and D.E. Perry. Introduction to the Special Issue on Software Architecture. *IEEE Trans. Software Engineering*, 21(4):269–274, 1995.

[72] A.J. Herbert. An ANSA Overview. *IEEE Network*, 8(1):18–23, 1994.

[73] HL7 International. *The Service-Aware Interoperability Framework (SAIF)*, 2010. The SAIF report is currently under development, but the latest version can be found via the HL7 website, http://www.hl7.org/.

[74] G.E. Hughes and M.J. Cresswell. *A Companion to Modal Logic*. Methuen, 1984.

[75] IEEE Computer Society. *IEEE Standard 1471-2000: IEEE Recommended Practice for Architectural Description of Software-Intensive Systems*, October 2000.

[76] Daniel Jackson. Alloy: A Lightweight Object Modelling Notation. *ACM Trans. Software Engineering and Methodology*, 11(2):256–290, April 2002.

[77] Andrew J.I. Jones and Marek J. Sergot. A Formal Characterisation of Institutionalised Power. *J. IGPL*, 4(3):427–443, 1996.

[78] Frédéric Jouault, Freddy Allilaire, Jean Bézivin, and Ivan Kurtev. ATL: A Model Transformation Tool. *Sci. Computer Programming*, 72(3):31–39, 2008.

[79] Paul Klint. The ToolBus: A service-Oriented Architecture for Language Processing Tools. *ERCIM News*, 70, July 2007.

[80] Carsten Köllmann, Lea Kutvonen, Peter F. Linington, and Arnor Solberg. An Aspect-oriented Approach to Manage QoS Dependability Dimensions in Model Driven Development. In *Proceedings of the 3rd International Workshop on Model-Driven Enterprise Information Systems (MDEIS 2007)*, pages 85–94, June 2007.

[81] Philippe Kruchten. Architectural Blueprints — The "4+1" View Model of Software Architecture. *IEEE Software*, 12(6):42–50, 1995.

[82] Philippe Kruchten, Henk Obbink, and Judith Stafford. The Past, Present, and Future for Software Architecture. *IEEE Software*, 23(2):22–30, 2006.

[83] Susumu Kuno and Anthony G. Oettinger. Syntactic Structure and Ambiguity of English. In *Proceedings of the Fall Joint Computer Conference*, AFIPS, pages 397–418, Las Vegas, Nevada, 1963. ACM.

[84] Joaquin Miller and Jishnu Mukerji. *MDA Guide*. Object Management Group, January 2003. Document ab/2003-06-01.

[85] *MOD Architecture Framework (MoDAF), version 1.2*, 2008. http://www.mod.uk/DefenceInternet/AboutDefence/WhatWeDo/InformationManagement/MODAF/.

[86] R.M. Needham and A.J. Herbert. *The Cambridge Distributed System*. Addison-Wesley, 1982.

[87] S. Olbrich and C. Simon. Process Modelling towards e-Government — Visualisation and Semantic Modelling of Legal Regulations as Executable Process Sets. *Electronic J. e-Government*, 6(1):43–54, 2008.

[88] Janis R. Putman. *Architecting with RM-ODP*. Prentice Hall, 2000.

[89] Daniel Rönnedal. *An Introduction to Deontic Logic*. CreateSpace, 2010.

[90] John Searle. *Speech Acts*. Cambridge University Press, 1969.

[91] M.J. Sergot, F. Sadri, R.A. Kowalski, F. Kriwaczek, P. Hammond, and H.T. Cory. The British Nationality Act as a Logic Program. *CACM*, 29(5):370–386, May 1986.

[92] R.M. Soley, D.S. Frankel, J. Mukerji, and E.H. Castain. *Model Driven Architecture — The Architecture of Choice for a Changing World*. Object Management Group, 2001. OMG White Paper, http://www.omg.org/mda/.

[93] J.F. Sowa. *Conceptual Structures: Information Processing in Mind and Machine*. Addison-Wesley, 1984.

[94] J.F. Sowa and J.A. Zachman. Extending and formalizing the framework for information systems architecture. *IBM Systems Journal*, 31(3):590–616, 1992.

[95] J.M. Spivey. *The Z Notation. A Reference Manual.*. Prentice Hall, 2nd edition, 1992.

[96] John Strassner. *Directory Enabled Networks*. MacMillan Technical Publishing, 1999.

[97] Massimo Tisi, Frédéric Jouault, Piero Fraternali, Stefano Ceri, and Jean Bézivin. On the Use of Higher-Order Model Transformations. In *Proceedings of the European Model Driven Architecture Workshop: Foundations and Applications (MDA-FA 2009)*, volume 5562 of *LNCS*, pages 18–33. Springer, 2009.

[98] *The Open Group Architecture Framework, version 9.0*, 2009. `http://www.opengroup.org/togaf/`.

[99] G.H. von Wright. Deontic Logic. *Mind*, 60:1–15, 1951.

[100] W3C. *Web Services Description Language (WSDL) Version 2.0, Part 0: Primer*, June 2007.

Index

abstract data types, 57
abstraction, 16, 17
access transparency, 143
accessibility, 52
accountability, 49–50, 53
ACID transactions, 99
actions, 17
  assigned to roles, 40
  atomic, 15
  binding, 71, 72
  business, 116
  information, 58
  internal, 17
  roles in, 17, 35
  type of, 58
activation, 95
activation policy, 97
actors, 44
address spaces, 95
agents, 49
allocation transformations, 203
Alloy language, 197, 201
announcements, 73
architectures
  channel, 96
  deployment, 108
  nodes, 93
  service-oriented, 22
  software, 69, 78, 86
  style of, 77
artefacts, 44, 224
  information objects and, 65
  physical transfer of, 47
  state of, 47
aspect-oriented programming, 200
ATLAS transformation language (ATL),
    202

atomic actions, 15
attributes, 115
authorizations, 21
autonomy, 165, 205

basic engineering objects, 91, *93*, 94,
    102–103
behaviour, 17
  communities of, 35, 44–49
  dynamic modification of, 35
BEO, *see* basic engineering objects
bidirectional transformations, 200
binders (as engineering objects), 97
binding actions, 71, 72
binding objects, 72
  architectural connectors, 72
  correspondence to channels, 103
  encapsulating communication, 72
bindings, 71–73
  complementarity in, 84
  compound, 71, *85*
  concatenation of, 74
  contracts as, 72
  control interfaces to, 72, 81, 84
  modelling of, 22, 78
  multi-party, 85
  primitive, 71, *84*
BMM, *see* business motivation model
BPMN, *see* business process model
    and notation
budgetary constraints, 106
business
  actions, 116
  contexts, 34
  environment of, 36
  evolution, 176
  franchised, 36

247